Why Read This Book?

The Division between us is at an all-time high:

- Liberals vs Conservatives
- Neighbor vs Neighbor
- Lawfulness vs Lawlessness
- Christian vs Non-Christian
- Christian Denomination vs Christian Denomination
- Children vs Parents
- The approval ratings for politicians are at an all-time low.

In Jesus' day, the clear responsibility of the rabbi was to teach them "how to fulfill the Torah". That is to say, "how to live a life pleasing to God". In fact, our entire Bible emphasizes it. Our church leaders carry this responsibility today, as do each who call themselves one of his disciples.

Jesus came to live it out as an example for us.
He taught and showed us how to live in community.

We have lost our way in this. We have isolated ourselves from one another. Judgement and condemnation abound. It's time to once again return to living lives pleasing to God.

Proverbs 16:7
When a man's ways please the Lord,
he makes even his enemies to be at peace with him.

2 Corinthians 5:9
So whether we are at home or away, we make it our aim to please him.

Ephesians 5:6
Let no one deceive you with empty words, for because of these things the wrath of God comes upon the sons of disobedience.

We need to relearn what God says about living in community. Please read this book. *That our children not continue to pay the price for our foolishness.*

Introduction

As our Father does his works in our lives, he graciously intersects our path with the many he has prepared in advance to help us. While Life, Love and Leading has been a work in process for nearly 20 years, its preparation has spanned my lifetime and required the faithful input of hundreds.

What follows is the Life section. "Life" illuminates the foundational aspects of who God is and what he requires of us such that we might better live lives of loving wholly and loving only. That our children know him, our families be strong, and the division and degradation of our nation be reversed.

The God-led life is directed by the power of the Holy Spirit, consistent with the teachings of Jesus, as the Father in us does his works. It does not make of us robots, rather we become *willing participants* in *creative collaboration,* growing hearts after God as the Family of God.

Acts 13:22

And when he had removed him (Saul), he raised up David to be their king, of whom he testified and said, 'I have found in David the son of Jesse a man <u>after my heart, who will do all my will.'</u>

The world is continually telling us that we must think and logic and work our way through to each decision. The equivalent of leaning on our own understanding:

Proverbs 3:3-8

5 <u>Trust in the Lord with all your heart, and do not lean on your own understanding (mind)</u>. 6 In all your ways acknowledge him, and he will make straight your paths. 7 <u>Be not wise in your own eyes (mind)</u>; fear the Lord, and turn away from evil. 8 It will be healing to your flesh and refreshment to your bones.

The wisdom that follows does not so much come from me, but from a lifetime of collaborating with God and the many wise counselors he has put in my path. Proverbs 11:14 tells us that where there is no guidance the people fall, but in an abundance of counselors there is victory. May it be so for you.

If you are not yet a believer in Jesus Christ, may the love God has for you and the good life he is offering you become clear to you as you read. Historically, atheists who read what Jesus had to say about living a good life agree with him on how to do so. Whether or not you believe Jesus is the Son of God, if you will make every effort to live according to the ways he outlined on the pages that follow, you will enjoy a life far better than you could ever dream, hope or imagine yourself.

If you are a Christ Follower, as you read "Life" please think in terms of being a disciple gaining additional language and concepts for disciple-ing. Therefore, also then in terms of being a disciple-er using the language and concepts with doubters and immature believers for their personal disciple-ship. These might also help us in our conversations together, that we grow more mature, balanced and united in heart, soul and mind.
Overcoming the ways of this world.
Living by his.

To receive additional free copies please contact:
Ricky Kroeger
One Kingdom Worldwide
OneKingdomWorldwide.org

PDF files of this book may be legally shared. Revised March 2026

LIFE

Living The Good Life God Offers Us

(Revealing The Deception As Old As Time Itself)

From the book

Life, Love & Leading

Life

All scripture is English Standard Version (ESV) unless otherwise indicated.

LIFE

Living The Good Life God Offers Us

(Revealing The Deception As Old As Time Itself)

All scripture is English Standard Version (ESV) unless otherwise indicated.

Chapter One

Before The Beginning: A Fresh Look At The Decision To Give Life

As I write this our daughter is giving birth to our 7th grandchild, their son. What hope they have for him! What hope both of our children have for all seven of them!

But why did they do it? Why have they risked bringing children into this mess of a world of division and war and theft and tension and brutality and abuse? How could a good person do such a thing? Our first grandchild has brain damage caused by a reckless anesthesiologist. Others they know of have had unspeakable things done to them. The possibility, no, the likelihood of trauma – or worse yet tragedy – for each of their children is quite high. No one escapes this world without enduring some form of great physical or emotional or financial hardship. Why have they purposely brought these children into the world? Certainly they do not wish them harm!

Of course, it is for the same reason that most of us do – to love them, be loved by them and to live their lives knowing and caring for each other.

We find great joy in the lives of children, especially when they are ours. We find great joy as they participate with us in the family experience. We find great joy in watching them learn and love and share their lives with us. How could we *not* give them life? What a shame it would be to not have them with us! How could we withhold life from them when it is within our power to give it? Though we know that life will be hard, it is better than the alternative of no life at all!

My wife and I were determined to raise our children in safety and security. We were vigilant in teaching them how to identify risk, danger and those who would use or abuse them in some way. We taught them about right and wrong. We taught them about God. We warned them of the evil among us. We worked to give them financial security and a university education if they wanted one. We shared with them as you probably shared with your children – or would if you will have any.

Nonetheless, we failed. Not entirely, they are wonderful people, but we have certainly built some things into them that we regret. Over the years they have identified some of these failings for us and have sworn not to make the same mistakes with their children. And so they won't. They'll make different mistakes.

****

How are things between you and God?

Many see God as having failed us in ways which they believe must surely be correct, and upon that judgement determine that they will not believe in any such being. It's like saying you don't believe in your parents because they brought you into a cruel world. The obvious difference being that it's impossible to dismiss parents who are physically visible.

I have heard many renditions on the reasons to doubt the existence of a holy and loving God. Some simply claim that there is no God, but the most basic premise of science is that something cannot be made from nothing. *Something* created all of this, *and* is allowing the good and the bad to occur. Even so, many who believe in God wonder why it is true that he allows such evil to take place against his people, or against any person for that matter. The evidence is clear, however. This Intelligent Designer we call God created it all and *is* allowing it. This much is true.

Are you unable to give doubters this simple satisfactory defense for the creation of the universe? It is important that you can. Not that God needs defending, but that they have missed the point and are at risk of living for the brief here and now while squandering eternity. One answer for those who blame God for the problems in this world comes in the form of a question: How can we blame God for doing what *we* do? …a portion of *our* children are the ones doing evil today…

He is simply doing what parents have always done: Create life where there once was none - to love and be loved, to participate together in making our world a better place, to live lives of knowing and caring for each other - as a family. We are following along after what he has done and is still doing ...and a portion of our children will be the ones doing the evil in the future.

Still, the fact remains that this world is a harsh and dangerous place fraught with people who choose to do the unthinkable and unspeakable! At the same time, we all know amazingly good and giving people who are a great encouragement to us. The evidence worldwide identifies great numbers of people who are willing to go through tremendous suffering to benefit those they do not even know. Yet, as we have seen, bad things happen to good people, don't they?

Could that be why it's all over in the blink of an eye? Could our fast-fleeting lives be one of the mercies of a holy and loving God? Is this not just a brief period of time whereby we are given the opportunity to freely choose life in the Family of God – or not? I believe the brevity is intended to be merciful to those of us who Accept him. Though our lives seem to be long, the old among us relate that life is really quite short. And so does scripture:

1 Peter 5:10
And after you have suffered a little while, the God of all grace, who has called you to his eternal glory in Christ, will himself restore, confirm, strengthen, and establish you.

Romans 8:18
For I consider that the sufferings of this present time are not worth comparing with the glory that is to be revealed to us.

2 Thessalonians 1:5
This is evidence of the righteous judgment of God, that you may be considered worthy of the kingdom of God, for which you are also suffering

James 1:9-10
9 Let the lowly brother boast in his exaltation, 10 and the rich in his humiliation, because like a flower of the grass he will (soon) pass away.

1 Peter 1:24
for "All flesh is like grass and all its glory like the flower of grass. The grass withers, and the flower falls,

James 4:14

yet you do not know what tomorrow will bring. What is your life? For you are a mist that appears for a little time and then vanishes.

Psalm 90:10

The years of our life ... they are soon gone, and we fly away.

Psalm 39:4-5

4 "O Lord, make me know my end and what is the measure of my days; let me know how fleeting I am! 5 Behold, you have made my days a few handbreadths, and my lifetime is as nothing before you. Surely all mankind stands as a mere breath! Selah

Psalm 102:11

My days are like an evening shadow; I wither away like grass.

When I was in my late twenties with a thriving business, many employees, and a wife and two children, we celebrated the 80th birthday of my wife's grandmother. As the evening wound down, I noted that she sure seemed to have been able to slow life down, to live with balance and to really enjoy her days. While she agreed partially, the portion she could not agree with was that she had been able to slow life down. In fact, she related, it is going faster and faster all the time. Forty came faster than thirty. Fifty faster than forty. Sixty faster than fifty. Seventy faster than sixty and eighty faster than seventy. I remember her counseling me that it is truly over in the blink of an eye, and that it felt like she had just been in her forties a few years prior. Now in my sixties, I agree! I warmly remembered her and was thankful for that conversation the day we buried her body a few years later.

This is one of the cases where the wisdom of the aged is helpful to the young. At fifteen, it seemed as though I would NEVER turn sixteen and be able to get my driver's license. When Debbie and I were engaged, we spoke frequently about the interminable wait for our wedding day and in our impatience discussed eloping.

We have decisions to make every day of our lives. With most, we will be deciding along the scale opposites of patience and impatience, and love of self and love of others. Like me, you may regret some of those choices, especially because impetuous self-focused choices have consequences, often long-term consequences.

The possibility of the joy of an eternal life with God requires an earthly decision on our part, too, and actions that follow that are consistent with that decision. The one we call Satan also had a choice to make and actions to take. His choice was for rejection and actions in defiance. Whether we are an Acceptor of God or a Rejector of God, our actions will be consistent with that choice. Satan's mind worked out a decision, and he acted on it. God allowed that, and, as a Rejector, Satan has thereby determined his own personal eternity.

Before giving him life, God knew that Satan would soon become enamored with himself, reject his benevolence, never ever repent of it and, by the finality of that choice would eventually be separated from him forever. He also knew that Satan would corrupt Adam and Eve and take them down with him. He knew that.

Before giving the universe its start, he knew that if he followed through with it Acceptor men, women and children everywhere would suffer at the hands of Rejector men, women and children. He knew that. Just as human parents know it now - never thinking that any of the children that *they* will raise will be the cause of such suffering to others.

But some will and many have been. He knew that they would. He knew that Hitler would be deceived, corrupt others, take them along with him on his horrible mission and incinerate millions. God knew that. Just as we are aware of evil dictators on the earth now.

He knew that pedophiles would stalk innocent children. He knew that the lust of men would find pleasure in the violent rape of women. He knew that some would choose murder, making women widows and children fatherless. He knew that those who desired much would enslave others to attain it. He knew that. Just as human parents know it today.

He knew that, at any given moment in the world, millions would be starving in Third World countries and be drinking polluted water, though the means to end it have become available. He knew that, and now we do, too.

He knew that drunken drivers would kill our parents, friends, sons and daughters. He knew that doctors would carelessly and recklessly commit malpractice and forever change the lives of those they swore an oath to never harm. He knew that politicians would be corrupted by their power and do great harm to others rather than serve people with integrity. He knew that. Just as we do now.

... and a portion of our children will be the ones doing the evil in the future.

So why do we do it? Why did he do it? Why has he allowed so much evil and destruction to have a place to wreak its havoc? How could this good and gracious and loving God allow such a thing?

Before the beginning God had the choice of either giving us life or never giving us life. And if he never gave us life, those of us that would have chosen him for eternity would have never been given the chance. The opportunity for an abundant life and a loving relationship with him for all eternity would never have been more than a possibility that God himself chose not to allow. A better question, or maybe observation, would be: Would a good and gracious and loving God choose to never give us the chance?

All need to have the chance *to choose*. Acceptors and Rejectors are both described in the following parable. God birthed good people, but the Enemy corrupts a portion:

Matthew 13:24-30
24 He put another parable before them, saying, "The kingdom of heaven may be compared to a man who sowed good seed in his field,
25 but while his men were sleeping, his enemy came and sowed weeds among the wheat and went away. 26 So when the plants came up and bore grain, then the weeds appeared also. 27 And the servants of the master of the house came and said to him, 'Master, did you not sow good seed in your field? How then does it have weeds?' 28 He said to them, 'An enemy has done this.' So the servants said to him, 'Then do you want us to go and gather them?' 29 But he said, 'No, lest in gathering the weeds you root up the wheat along with them. 30 Let both grow together until the harvest, and at harvest time I will tell the reapers, "Gather the weeds first and bind them in bundles to be burned, but gather the wheat into my barn."'"

Maybe that is why it's all over in the blink of an eye. Why his offer to Accept him or Reject him is for such a mercifully brief period of earthly time - our lifetime. Soon, Rejectors will die and be separated from God and his Acceptors forever. Acceptors will always be safe, secure and joy-filled participating in the Family of God eternally. It's simply a matter of our choice for self or a relationship with him that is guided by him, and the actions we will take to reflect that choice.

Thank you, God, that you decided to give us the opportunity to choose. Because you did there will be millions, maybe billions of Acceptors in heaven with you eternally, who otherwise would have never had the chance.

Chapter Two

The Half-Told Truth

In this chapter you will begin to see my use of capital letters in the personification of various characteristics and behaviors so as to identify them with God or his Enemies.

Over the last two thousand plus years the followers of Jesus have been relating how Jesus came to inform us of God's love for us, our opportunity to choose a relationship with him that will survive our earthly death, and an afterlife of eternal joy in his presence - absent the Rejectors who chose otherwise.

They share that Jesus warned that a portion of the religious leaders of their day had been borne of a Corrupt lineage, intent upon using their positions for personal advancement and the Control and Direction of people.

He shared that another portion of the religious leaders of their day were simply well-intentioned Fools, unaware of the harm they were bringing upon themselves and others by their ignorance.

He went on to explain a third portion of the people who he called Wise, their Wisdom coming from their understanding of the ways of God. He advised that the Wise could be counted upon to become Wise and effective leaders in the service of the people.

For all of our benefit, he further explained how we might tell the difference between the Corrupt, the Fool and the Wise: through the behaviors which set them apart. People of these three types had been identified in detail throughout the Hebrew scripture, and are now throughout the entire Bible.

Even now leaders still come from portions of all three; whether they be church leaders, business leaders, family leaders or the leaders of government: the Wise, the Fool and the Corrupt.

According to surveys and polling regarding churches, a great many of the people of our day are claiming insight into the ways of their church leaders and have chosen to stop attending. Another portion have tried other churches in vain and decided to give up their search, thinking that all are the same. Nonetheless, speaking from experience, I have found that Wise church leaders *do* still exist in a portion.

We will be able to identify which are which if we will learn what <u>*are*</u> *the ways of God and what* <u>*are not*</u> *the ways of God.*

Still, we must take great care with what we will do with our assessments. Many of the Foolish desire to be Wise, though some just want to defend their positions. The ways of God inform us on how to handle these situations and these will be discussed as we proceed.

Great theological debates are occurring in the world over the finer points of what is in the Bible. Unfortunately, not all of these are respectful or even helpful. This book will not delve into the finer points that may raise conflict, but rather focus upon what is broadly foundational and common in understanding the ways of God – ways which inform the behavior of the Wise.

Recognize, too, however, that some seemingly harmless statements have been passed down through the ages. Statements that may sound right to us, but might confuse the less knowledgeable still trying to understand who God is.

These are a bit like what some call *The Telephone Game*. In it, the first person whispers something into the ear of the second person, who then whispers it to the third and them to the fourth until as many as are present have heard. Then, finally, the last person speaks out loud what was whispered into their ear for all to hear. As any who have played the game will attest, what the first and the last said typically bear little resemblance!

If we will consider statements that come out of our mouths so easily, we may see that some have become shortened versions of the original statement. These half-told-truths, short-hand for us if you will, become obstacles for the "beginners" trying to make sense of it all. As we proceed, I will raise examples of some of these points for your consideration, that you might consider who is in your hearing before speaking. Here is one: God is in control.

People tell us that we have been given free will to make our own choices, so choose Wisely! Then, on another day when something bad is happening, they tell us not to worry because God is in control.

Well, which is it?

God *has control* of the universe, but he has *given us control* over ourselves. We *do* have free will and we *do* have the right to decide for ourselves. While it is true that he *has control*, it is only a portion of the story - a half-truth. The half-told-truths we tell may easily cause confusion for others, and may later be used to blame God for what has happened (or is happening).

A popular worship song says that "he tells every lightning bolt where it should go". If a lightning bolt has hit a tree in your yard, or your house, or worse yet a person you know and killed them – did God do it? According to the song he did, but that is simply not true. Could he have stopped it? Yes, of course, but there is no scripture that supports the claim that he directs all lightning to where it will strike.

A distraught person asked why a good God would kill their family member in a car accident. When asked what happened, it was told that a drunk driver had crossed the median and hit them head-on. Having been told that God is in control, they wanted to know why he would do such a thing. This half-told-truth was causing them to doubt God, though he did not kill their family member - the person who made the decision to drive drunk did.

God has control of the universe,
but he has given us control over ourselves.

Decades ago, I told God that I wanted him to have control of my life. I told him that I do not trust me to do his will, though I try, and so wanted him to *take control* any time I was going off on my own. What I have found, and learned from others as well, is that he will not do that. What he *will* do is gently speak a warning in these moments, identify that we are entering into the temptation of something we would regret and identify a way out - a different choice that may be made that will end better.

God does not want robots, so he helps us see our options and lets us decide for ourselves. Being human, I still manage to make some bad choices along the way. Still, afterwards, he gently helps me to learn from them. A work in process, and with his help, I have been making fewer bad choices as the years have gone by.

God is not trying to control our decisions; he is informing us - that we might choose Wisely.

He *could* control us, but he will not. He has instead set a *finite period of time* during which he will allow Acceptors to accept and Rejectors to reject - and so during it the damage of Rejectors will continue to be possible. And then Jesus will come back with a shout to put a stop to it.

1 Thessalonians 4:16 (NKJV)
For the Lord Himself will descend from heaven with a shout, with the voice of an archangel, and with the trumpet of God. And the dead in Christ will rise first.

What will he shout? I don't know, but I'm guessing it will be something like, "Enough! Time's up! No more!". When Jesus comes back, the infinite will follow the ending of the finite. Acceptors with him forever in eternity. Rejectors separated from us and him always. Acceptors safe eternally. Rejectors lost forever.

****

What we miss is that the Enemy has been able to plant the seeds of various seemingly harmless half-told-truths into previous generations who then repeated them to us over many generations. Some of these have been passed along through well-meaning teachers and worship music. As these have continued to be restated, tiny deceptions have grown and grown and grown into giant broadly accepted misunderstandings about God.

Some have found their way into our seminaries and Bible colleges where they continue to be perpetuated – and are then passed on to our congregations where parents pass them on to their children.

Some teach that you must speak in tongues to prove the indwelling of the Holy Spirit – so they "teach" God's spiritual *gift* of Speaking in Tongues. There is scripture to make one wonder about their claim, but other scripture seems to contradict it. The point is that many are being told that they "are not really saved" if they can't do it. We must be careful here, the scriptures are clear. Jesus will judge them, not us. Not being God we cannot say who is really (being) saved and who is not. Quite simply:

Romans 9:15
God can have compassion and mercy on whomever he chooses

Others claim that miracles no longer occur, but the incontrovertible evidence of miraculous healings worldwide abound otherwise. The proof for thousands are there in the reading and are referenced in a book by Lee Strobel called <u>The Case for Miracles</u>. We must take great care, lest we cause conflict, confusion and division among us.

Perhaps the reason they claim that miracles have ceased is in response to another segment who believe that they are "able to heal at will" because they believe we have been given the Power and Authority to do so. As we will see, no matter where the truth lies, the greater issue is the division being caused between us as we claim a superior knowledge, and the confusion it causes those around us.

Well-meaning but mistaken teachings that continue to be shared do not represent God and are not honoring to him. They serve to confuse us and divide us against ourselves into the various denominations. Our house, divided against itself, is wobbling. Jesus asked of the Father that we all be One together - with Christ as the Head – but the Enemy has deceived us ever-so-slowly over such a very long time that we hardly recognize the damage of the authoritarian based hierarchical divisions we have been taking part in. This will be addressed in the coming chapters as we discuss how God would have us relate with each other.

But God can utilize all of these differences for good if we will but submit to him as the only authority and come together in his Spirit of Unity across denominational lines. The Lausanne Covenant, signed in 1974 by the Christ Followers of over 150 nations, espouses such Unity and the synergy it will bring. The Leading section of this book describes a workable approach for the uniting of God's people to more productive service in any community. Now, fifty years later, its time has come!

****

Still, God is not unwilling to hear our concerns. In fact, he is the one who said to pray unceasingly, in other words ask, inquire, petition and request of him unceasingly. When we do not understand, a level of doubt or curiosity exists. Doubt can either diminish our faith or lead us to inquire of him in that curiosity for greater understanding - a faith building exercise. So ask. He told us that he will teach us what we need to know:

Isaiah 11:10
In that day the root of Jesse, who shall stand as a signal for the peoples - of him shall the nations inquire, and his resting place shall be glorious.

Luke 12:32
"Fear not, little flock, for it is your Father's good pleasure to give you the kingdom.

1 Thessalonians 5:17-18
17 pray (inquire, ask, petition, request) without ceasing, 18 give thanks in all circumstances; for this is the will of God in Christ Jesus for you.

John 6:45
It is written in the Prophets, 'And they will all be taught by God.' Everyone who has heard and learned from the Father comes to me.

John 14:2
In my Father's house are many rooms. If it were not so, would I have told you that I go to prepare a place for you?

John 17:24
Father, I desire that they also, whom you have given me, may be with me where I am, to see my glory that you have given me because you loved me before the foundation of the world.

Isaiah 56:7a
these I will bring to my holy mountain,
and make them joyful in my house of prayer;

Jeremiah 29:11-13
11 For I know the plans I have for you, declares the LORD, plans for welfare (peace) and not for evil, to give you a future and a hope. 12

Then you will call upon me and come and pray to me (inquire of me), and I will hear you. 13 You will seek me and find me, when you seek me with all your heart.

Matthew 22:27
Jesus replied: "Love the Lord your God with all your heart and with all your soul and with all your mind."

John 6:44a
... And I will raise him up on the last day.

2 Peter 1:3-4
3 His divine power has granted to us all things that pertain to life and godliness, through the knowledge of him who called us to his own glory and excellence, 4 by which he has granted to us his precious and very great promises, so that through them you may become partakers of the divine nature (loving with all of your heart, soul and mind), having escaped from the corruption that is in the world because of sinful desire.

1 Timothy 2:3-4
3 This is good, and it is pleasing in the sight of God our Savior, 4 who desires all people to be saved and to come to the knowledge of the truth.

Philippians 1:6
And I am sure of this, that he who began a good work in you will bring it to completion at the day of Jesus Christ.

Are you thinking clearly about who you are, what you believe and how you choose what you will do? We tend to look at our life and see it someday ending, but that is not what God is doing. You were made for eternity with him. He is giving us a chance to choose it with him or reject him, among and around others who are in the process of doing the same thing.

There is a cosmic battle going on for your soul. Understand it, comprehend the depth of how it works – and you will no doubt find your way home. To eternal life and joy in the presence of the one true God!

Satan Deceived the tyrannical like Stalin, Mussolini, Mao and Hitler - Rejectors who caused pain and suffering on purpose. Satan tells us that this is the world God made for us, but it is not. It is the one Satan tricked us into. We risked Paradise for the lie he told us to believe, that God is a liar and that we can be Gods if we will just believe him (trust him). And so, we did not trust what God said but what Satan said, and by that choice we left the perfect safety of Eden and entered the Enemy's world of disease and destruction. From living in his paradise and perfection, to the Enemy's world of disease, destruction and death. Where he would eventually use the tyrannical like Stalin, Mussolini, Mao and Hitler to tell our children that God is not good to have caused this. But we are the ones who threw it all away. We are responsible for leaving the paradise and perfection of Eden for the suffering of Satan's version.

We of the modern day continue to do what was done in the beginning. We make gods of ourselves as we Reject God and trust the Enemy's lies. Living by codes of our own making, we cause relational strife to grow such that we battle others and war against nations. All because we are self-focused and desirous of more. More for ourselves and our families, though we will neglect the great need of our neighbors.

Trust God and live! Love your neighbor as yourself! In Eden, we had it all and still wanted more. In death we will gain eternal life in his presence, but not unless we first trust God! Live in his ways! Trust him and he will help you to know him more day by day. He is the more you are looking for.

James 4:7
Submit yourselves therefore to God. Resist the devil,
and he will flee from you.

Nehemiah 8:10b
...And do not be grieved, for the joy of the Lord is your strength."

This sense we have that our life will soon be ending is a mistake. It keeps us short-sighted, focused upon our self and life in the here and now. More importantly, we must keep in mind that what *will* soon be ending is this brief *period of time* during which we may choose him or reject him. Is this why some have a sense of urgency about their life? Is this why those of us who are self-focused have a realization, a sort of recognition potentially of impending doom hiding out in some corner of our lives? Interestingly, those of us who have come to know him, trust him, understand him and follow his leading instead have peace that surpasses all understanding. Which is you?

It is a testimony that the difficulty of living among and around the self-focused doesn't really matter. That, because our time with them is so brief in comparison to the reward of eternity with God - if we will only keep it in view.

In our hearts and souls and minds Acceptors really do know that he cares for us, that he really does love us and has eternity with us in mind. Armed with that eternal view and Acceptance of his love, he teaches *us* persevering love and care. First, how to love him as he loves us. Then, how to love others as ourselves. He teaches and trains us so that we become capable of caring for even the most difficult among and around us. For, in fact, the difficulty, the struggle and the perseverance required to love them like he loves them - is so brief that it is bearable.

These big picture thoughts are very helpful for our daily attitude and in helping us remain joyful in our interactions. This is what it means to en-joy life. We have an optimism for our personal end times while the world among us and around us are choosing theirs. More importantly, we have the daily opportunity to help them with that choice. We may at once be *sorrow-filled* for the lost and *joy-filled* that the Father will never stop drawing them back to himself. Part of the joy of living in the Family of God is that he leads us to participate *with* him for the benefit of others. That is why we are here. His desire is to give us joy through our participation *with* him. He will lead us and allow us to participate in the leading of others *by* that leading.

Thank you, O God, for giving me a chance to choose life with you on earth surrounded by this mixture of Acceptors and Rejectors for this short finite time, in exchange for infinite time with you!

Thank you for giving me the opportunity to share your unfathomable love with others, to help them overcome their pain and sorrow and to find what I have found in you, the all-loving merciful gracious giver of life eternal. You have always been, and will always be, for us! Precious are you, life giver, peace giver, purpose giver, our deliverer! In your goodness you inspire your people to serve others to reflect your love for them, that they might also come to know you and love you and trust in your abiding love and care.

How precious it is to be loved by you! Give us hearts, souls and minds of abiding love and care like yours! Thank you for the opportunities to learn the differences between our ways and your ways. Thank you for what you did in our lives yesterday. Thank you for what we were able to do with *you, together. Instruct us in our thoughts today that our words and actions accomplish your great and precious will for us.*

I hope my prayer of thankfulness has been your experience, too. If not, it can be.

Chapter Three

Do Not Eat From That Tree

I believe in Christianity as I believe the sun has risen,
not just because I see it, but because by it, I see everything else.
C. S. Lewis

God told Adam and Eve that all things were theirs except one. But why not the one thing? Much has been written on that with many good points made, but I believe that one of the reasons was so that Adam and Eve would have a way to respond to God with a loving action of their own. If he had not withheld something from them, what could they have given him? What can the made provide the Maker?

God did not guilt, shame, threaten, coerce or subtly manipulate Adam and Eve into loving him. Instead, he gave them a way to love him and told them that it was all that was required. He gave them a way in which they could prove their choice *for* him. He gave them something to *not* do, and then also shared the information that they would need to understand him if they disobeyed. To paraphrase:

> *Everything is yours to enjoy except one thing, the Tree of the Knowledge of Good and Evil. In your freedom to choose, choose to not touch it, and if you go so far as to eat of its fruit you will surely die, for by choosing it for yourself you will have Rejected me. By this you will demonstrate your love for me: If you do not eat of it, we will live together in peace and joy. If you do eat of it, you will cause our separation forever.*

God is not a tempter. He is a choice giver. He gave us our very lives, it is not unfair and it is frankly very gracious, that he ask us to choose to love him by *not doing* something. But again, it is a request even while it is a command. No coercion. No manipulation. He gives us information and lets us choose freely. He even gives the answer to the dilemma. He is the teacher in class who gives the test and walks around to tell each person the answers. He is the one who gave us dominion to enjoy the earth. We are the ones who choose to eat the modern-day forbidden fruit anyway when the Tempter arrives.

He has also given us ways to love him by *not doing*. We have choices for doing and not doing, and the related joy or sorrow-filled consequences that will come should be of no surprise. We too have been forewarned; he's made it clear throughout scripture. Let's take a look at just one of them here:

"I warn you, as I warned you before, that those who "do" such things will not inherit the kingdom of God."

This was originally written in Greek. The Greek have a verb tense that we do not. Often, when we read a verse with the word "do", the actual tense in the Greek will mean "continue to do". Similarly, we are to "keep on knocking" that the door be opened to us, "keep on asking" God for the replenishing supply of the Holy Spirit, and so forth. There are lots of other important implications here, but we need to stay focused on this one:

Galatians 5:19-21
19 Now the works of the flesh are evident: sexual immorality, impurity, sensuality, 20 idolatry, sorcery, enmity, strife, jealousy, fits of anger, rivalries, dissensions, divisions, 21 envy, drunkenness, orgies, and things like these. I warn you, as I warned you before, that those who (continue to) do such things will not inherit the kingdom of God.

There are many places in scripture similarly so. Similar to Adam and Eve, he has warned us of eternal separation from himself if we "continue to do" the things listed, *"and things like these*".

Understanding this verb tense issue is very helpful to those who have done these things. The above list is quite broad. We have *all* been one of these people! From time to time I will have someone show me this verse and say that they believe they cannot be allowed into heaven. But that is not what it means. We must not "continue to do" them if we are to join him in his kingdom.

Translation allows for interpretation, and we have so many English translations trying to be helpful that many of them are saying slightly different things than what was meant in the original Hebrew, Aramaic or Greek context. What a burden it can be to the reader! In this case, it is possible for us to see the word "do" and have a sense of "continue to do", or "keep on doing", but it is not always clear for everyone. Especially if they are one of the people having doubts about their salvation anyway.

But continuing onward, there are other trees that he is telling us not to eat from in our day. These trees are eaten from quite commonly these days, and we have come to believe that it is right, or at least okay, to do so. However, the fruit of these trees serve to weaken relationships, not grow them.

Eating from the tree of Judgement leads us to Condemnation that leads us to Anger that causes us to act in Division. Eating off of that tree will lead us in one of at least two directions: Isolation or Attack. When we perceive an injustice, we rationalize that "They started it, so I can retaliate!", and the relationship is weakened if not severed.

Our Adversary is so deceptive. Do you see how the last sentence above makes sense to those of the natural world? The response Satan is leading us toward is one of Vengeance, Retribution, Judgement and Condemnation so that we may then use Shaming or some other method to make happen what *we* want to have happen.

That is not God's way. One with him, we instead share information in fruit of the Spirit language to produce fruit of the Spirit – to strengthen relationships.

Galatians 5:22-24

22 But the fruit of the Spirit is love, joy, peace, patience, kindness, goodness, faithfulness (perseverance), 23 gentleness, self-control; against such things there is no law. 24 And those who belong to Christ Jesus have crucified the flesh with its passions and desires.

Sharing information as God does, we are Gentle, Patient, Kind and Persevering in Goodness so that the information we share is void of manipulation or coercion. The Holy Spirit helps in Self-Control so that the end result offers a desired outcome that will grow Peace, Joy and Love. Then, like God, we remain available for dialogue (avoiding *fight* or *flight*) and let them choose for themselves.

There is a difference between unconditional love and enablement. Like God, we are to provide the information. Like God, we are to allow others to make their own choice, no matter how Foolish – and continue to love them unconditionally. One of the expressions of that love is to allow them to go out and learn on their own what they have chosen not to learn from the Wisdom of God and others. When we love unconditionally, we bathe them in prayer when they go their own way, asking God to intervene that they may learn quickly. Enablement *saves them quickly* such that they learn little and so "continue to" repeat their folly. As we Gently inform with Patience and Kindness, we are not telling them how to behave - we are telling them how God says to behave.

Nowhere in the creation story do we find God behaving in any way that would elicit fear. No, God was generous. He was a gentleman. He is the original gentleman. Unlike some of us who only give to be able to later get something in return, God simply gave, providing the associated information needed. Nowhere does it show that he wagged his finger in their faces and threatened them, instilling fear into them. That they were so easily made willing to eat of the forbidden fruit attests to the fear that they did not have. No, what he gave them was his love and the whole world, plainly withholding just one tree. I want to learn to love like that!

People do what people do because we are free to Accept him or Reject him - *during the finite period of time he offers us to decide.* To Accept him and his ways - or not. Eternity lies in the balance.

Isn't it time we let God off the hook for the evil around us? There is a cosmic battle going on for our souls. If we will understand it and comprehend the ways of our Enemy's deceptions - we and our children may no doubt find our way to our eternal home. The blessing of abundant life in the here and now and ongoing joy in the presence of the one true God will result as we humble ourselves, orient ourselves in God's ways and therefore operate in fruit of the Spirit language and actions.

Wonderful Counselor, gracious God:
Give us insight into the ways in which we fail you. Help us to realize the impact our ways are having on the lives of others today, and how

our ways are affecting future lives in big picture ways. Teach us that we perceive how our ways are blocking the coming of your kingdom today and are rebellion against your will for us. Train us up in your ways, O God! El Shaddai (the All Sufficient One): You are our greatest need. All we need may be found in you. All we need to accomplish your will for us today is being provided by you; Jehovah Shalom (the LORD is our peace - even under great pressure), thank you for your peace as we remember that.

You have given me and so many others abundant life, O God! It brings me great sorrow to see those who have not chosen you wasting the precious little time they have on this earth; chasing after the fleeting pleasure of everything but you. Show me what to do and give me what to say as I participate with you in drawing them to yourself.

Still, now in my 60's, knowing what I know now, living in the joy of relationship with you, I would go back and live this brief challenging life all over again! I have come to understand how it feels to be rejected, how it is that you give peace in the midst of it and how your yoke is truly easy and your burden truly light. Continue raising me up in your ways, growing me up into a reflection of you, making me one with you and my joy complete. You have made known to me the path of life; here in your Presence there is fullness of joy; at your right hand are pleasures forevermore. I look forward to life everlasting with you!

Chapter Four

What Is Your Orientation?

The biggest business of the hour is to draw near to God that He may draw near to us. His presence with us is too often an assumption in our heads, instead of an awareness in our hearts.
Havner, Day by Day, August 14

What is your orientation? In over 30 years of consulting in 20 countries, I have found that your answer to that question informs every decision you will make. How will you respond to criticism? How will you respond to conflict? How will you respond to success? How will you respond to… you name it. Your orientation will determine it.

An orientation to personal holiness will take you far. Very simply, a commitment to personal holiness will cause you to focus upon who God is and what God asks of us. And you will orient yourself to do just that.

But what I know about you and what I know about me is that we started out focused upon self and the need to coerce for what we wanted from the time we were born. When we wanted our mother's milk we could get it by crying, or screaming if need be. Our earliest learning was that crying and screaming are useful in making others give us what we want.

We didn't care what our mother was doing when we felt the need to eat either, we just knew that we wanted our milk and we wanted it now! We were *necessarily* self-focused at birth, and screaming and crying were the only words we knew to communicate that we were hungry.

By the time we hit the Terrible Twos, screaming, crying, temper tantrums and shouting "No!" had become our favorite methods of trying to force people to do as we wanted. We were born with minds that were necessarily selfish and coercive to survive, but many of us have carried our manipulative ways into adulthood!

As children, most of us learn that shouting our disapproval is often effective in changing the mind, or at least adjusting the position, of the person we are shouting at. When we were very young, the shout could include throwing something to emphasize the point – and some of us still use this strategy as adults.

We also learned that our facial expression and body posture may speak louder than words to intimidate people and get them out of our way. Some still use these face to face today, and anonymously as drivers who tailgate us - pressuring us to drive faster or get out of their way.

When children realize that they can sweet-talk their parents, they find a new tool for manipulation: being nice! Pouting and withdrawing can be effective, too. Sweet-talk people or make people feel sorry for you and many will cave in to your desires – and many of us still use these methods as adults.

In school we learned that bullies go to the principal's office for detention, so many of us watched and learned that we do better when we use quiet voices to get our way. Quiet voices can be more effective when making a threat, keep you out of the principal's office and get you what you want without anybody else knowing about it. Some still use it to control members of their families, people in the workplace and beyond.

Others showed us that we could promise something, get what was wanted from them, and then not deliver on our end of the bargain! Yes, there are lots of adults still using this version.

When a behavior works in our favor, we tend to do more of it.

Unbeknownst to our young selves, self-focus becomes more subtle and more sophisticated in usage with each passing year as we learn new methods from those around us. Whether in raised voice or quiet tones and imposing body language, we are quite capable of utilizing *manipulate to control* behavior in most any setting.

As the years go by, our manipulative strategies collide with those around us trying to use theirs. As this happens, it reinforces our value for strength and the use of leverage in getting what we want. At some point most come to believe that initiating conflict is simply a necessary part of living in this world. As we look around and see so many others operating in similar orientations, it reinforces the belief that this is just the way it is.

"That's just the way it is.
Some things will never change!
That's just the way it is...
Awwww, but don't you believe them!"
Bruce Hornsby, The Way It Is, 1986

Why is there conflict between people? Because from the time we were born what has been driving us is getting what <u>we</u> want. Our Father said so after the flood:

Genesis 8:20-21
20 Then Noah built an altar to the Lord and took some of every clean animal and some of every clean bird and offered burnt offerings on the altar. 21 And when the Lord smelled the pleasing aroma, the Lord said in his heart, "I will never again curse the ground because of man, <u>for the intention of man's heart is evil from his youth</u>. Neither will I ever again strike down every living creature as I have done.

****

By the time we arrive in adulthood, our list of options for *manipulate to control* behaviors will have become quite long. Colossians 3, Galatians 5 and Romans 1 record some of them:

...fits of anger, wrath, lies, enmity, strife, rivalries, dissensions, divisions, obscene talk and things like these. ...gossips, slanderers, haters of God, insolent, haughty, boastful, inventors of evil, disobedient to parents, foolish, faithless, heartless, ruthless, covetous, malicious, envious, murderous, deceitful.

It is interesting to note that, in the Romans 1 portion above, gossips make the same list as the ruthless, the murderous and the haters of God!

The coercive manipulate to control behaviors that have been so deeply engrained in us since childhood are hard habits to break, but this is exactly what God asks us to do when we ask his help in becoming *mature Acceptors*:

1 Corinthians 13:11

When I was a child, I spoke like a child, I thought like a child, I reasoned like a child. When I became a man, I gave up childish ways.

The manipulative style collides, too, with those who have given up these childish ways. The manipulate to control strategy can be very effective, but it frequently comes with a relational cost as the mature recognize what the childish are doing. Hopefully, manipulators come to realize that they are the cause of their rejection by others for friendship, career advancement and group acceptance – and reform their childish ways.

Galatians 5:22-24

22 But the fruit of the Spirit is love, joy, peace, patience, kindness, goodness, faithfulness (perseverance), 23 gentleness, self-control; against such things there is no law. 24 And those who belong to Christ Jesus have crucified the flesh with its passions and desires.

If our parents failed in training us up in the fruitful behaviors, we will probably be one of the many selfish who make it into adulthood. I have also seen many cases in which appropriate parenting was overcome by the wiles of the selfish upon their children as they were befriended by them in school, sports and other activities. However it occurs, by the time we begin working most of us will have become masterful in our ability to subtly threaten, manipulate and coerce – as well as rationalize these actions - and most of the problems and conflicts in our lives will come from not understanding that.

Colossians 3:5a, 7-9

5 Put to death therefore what is earthly in you... 7 In these you too once walked, when you were living in them. 8 But now you must put them all away: anger, wrath, malice, slander, and obscene talk from your mouth. 9 Do not lie to one another, seeing that you have put off the old self with its practices

Galatians 5:17-21

17 For the desires of the flesh are against the Spirit, and the desires of the Spirit are against the flesh, for these are opposed to each other, to *keep you from doing the things you want to do. 18 But if you are led by the Spirit, you are not under the law. 19 Now <u>the works of the flesh are evident</u>: sexual immorality, impurity, sensuality, 20 idolatry, sorcery, enmity, strife, jealousy, fits of anger, rivalries, dissensions, divisions, 21 envy, drunkenness, orgies, and things like these. <u>I warn you, as I warned you before, that those who (continue to) do such things will not inherit the kingdom of God.</u>*

Proverbs 6:16-19

16 <u>There are six things that the Lord hates, seven that are an abomination to him</u>: 17 haughty eyes, a lying tongue, and hands that shed innocent blood, 18 a heart that devises wicked plans, feet that make haste to run to evil, 19 a false witness who breathes out lies, and one who sows discord among brothers.

Romans 1:28-32

28 And since they did not see fit to acknowledge God, God gave them up to a debased mind to do what ought not to be done. 29 They were filled with all manner of unrighteousness, evil, covetousness, malice. They are full of envy, murder, strife, deceit, maliciousness. They are gossips, 30 slanderers, haters of God, insolent, haughty, boastful, inventors of evil, disobedient to parents, 31 foolish, faithless, heartless, ruthless. 32 Though they know God's righteous decree that those who practice such things deserve to die, they not only do them but give approval to those who practice them.

Ephesians 4:29-32

29 Let no corrupting talk come out of your mouths, but only such as is good for building up, as fits the occasion, that it may give grace to those who hear. 30 And do not grieve the Holy Spirit of God, by whom you were sealed for the day of redemption. 31 <u>Let all bitterness and wrath and anger and clamor and slander be put away from you, along with all malice</u>. 32 Be kind to one another, tenderhearted, forgiving one another, as God in Christ forgave you.

Colossians 3:12-15

12 <u>Put on then</u>, as God's chosen ones, holy and beloved, compassionate hearts, kindness, humility, meekness, and patience, 13 bearing with one another and, if one has a complaint against another, forgiving each other; as the Lord has forgiven you, so you *also must forgive. 14 And above all these put on love, which binds everything together in perfect harmony. 15 And let the peace of Christ rule in your hearts, to which indeed you were called in one body. And be thankful.*

****

One of the difficulties in raising a child is in counseling them to use their mind such that you do not diminish the heart that must be used to bring it balance. It is possible to slowly and surely drive youngsters into their brains and away from their hearts with continual admonishments like, "Think!" and "What are you doing? Use your head!". This trains them to trust in their thinking as they go through life, and their hearts easily become hardened.

Romans 1:21

For although they knew God (with their mind), they neither glorified him as God nor gave thanks to him, but their thinking became futile <u>and their foolish hearts were darkened</u>.

Jeremiah 17:9-10

9 The heart is deceitful above all things, and desperately sick; who can understand it? 10 "<u>I the Lord search the heart</u> and test the mind, to give every man according to his ways, according to the fruit of his deeds."

Matthew 6:21

For where your treasure is, <u>there your heart will be also</u>.

Exodus 7:14

<u>Pharaoh's heart is unyielding</u>; he refuses to let the people go.

But God promises us a new heart if we will only seek him:

Deuteronomy 4:29

If from there you seek the Lord your God, <u>you will find him if you seek him with all your heart</u> and with all your soul.

Ezekiel 36:26

And I will give you a new heart, and a new spirit I will put within you. And I will remove the heart of stone from your flesh and give you a heart of flesh.

Proverbs 3:3-8

3 My son, do not forget my teaching (mind work), but let your heart keep my commandments, 2 for length of days and years of life and peace they will add to you. 3 Let not steadfast love and faithfulness forsake you; bind them around your neck; write them on the tablet of your heart. 4 So you will find favor and good success in the sight of God and man. 5 Trust in the Lord with all your heart, and do not lean on your own understanding (mind). 6 In all your ways acknowledge him, and he will make straight your paths. 7 Be not wise in your own eyes (mind); fear the Lord, and turn away from evil. 8 It will be healing to your flesh and refreshment to your bones.

Mark 12:28-34a

28 And one of the scribes came up and heard them disputing with one another, and seeing that he answered them well, asked him, "Which commandment is the most important of all?" 29 Jesus answered, "The most important is, 'Hear, O Israel: The Lord our God, the Lord is one. 30 And you shall love the Lord your God with all your heart and with all your soul and with all your mind and with all your strength.' 31 The second is this: 'You shall love (heart, not head) your neighbor as yourself.' There is no other commandment greater than these." 32 And the scribe said to him, "You are right, Teacher. You have truly said that he is one, and there is no other besides him. 33 And to love him with all the heart and with all the understanding and with all the strength, and to love one's neighbor as oneself, is much more than all whole burnt offerings and sacrifices." 34 And when Jesus saw that he answered wisely, he said to him, "You are not far from the kingdom of God."

And he will strengthen us:

2 Chronicles 16:9

The eyes of the Lord range throughout the earth to strengthen those whose hearts are fully committed to him.

Romans 5:5

And hope does not put us to shame, because God's love has been poured out into our hearts through the Holy Spirit, who has been given to us.

Philippians 4:13 NKJV

I can do all things through Christ who strengthens me.

Nehemiah 8:10b

...And do not be grieved, for the joy of the Lord is your strength."

Chapter Five

The Landscape Of Fear

A portion of our nation has taken to the use of intimidation to instill fear so as to silence us. Our fear having done so, they gain power, take Control and work to assume Authority over us. Our relationships stifled, we have become extremely Divided in our politics, our families and our governments.

These people have learned to apply what zoologists call the Landscape of Fear. In it, the hazards of proximity to roaring lions sends others into hiding. Then, just like in the animal kingdom, the intimidating lions become kings and rule the territory. The Enemy has us on the run. Many *are* quietly in hiding.

It is clear that many, including a portion who call themselves Christian, are finding the Landscape of Fear a very effective tool, and that many respectful Christ Followers have been silenced. We simply must learn how to speak up - in fruit of the Spirit language and actions - lest the disintegration of our relationships, families and nation continue.

If you turn on TV news, watch video clips on the internet or read news of any kind – it would seem that ours is a nation of people living according to their own understanding and own way of thinking. Conflict is everywhere. Acting in judgement and condemnation, we justify our actions on the basis of theirs. The division between us has reached an all-time high. The worst of our political leaders are majoring in manipulation using divisiveness. Divide and conquer - that we might join *them* in *their* purpose. They make people pick sides, threaten them so that they choose theirs, and then shame them if they disagree with them.

In my experience, the name callers are the ones doing what they accuse the others of.

Why are we falling for their destructive manipulative deception? The only evidence we need to withstand them is recognition that their fruit cannot be of God. They are about *enmity, strife, jealousy, fits of anger, rivalries, dissensions, divisions, ... and things like these*. His never is.

Romans 1:28-32

28 And since they did not see fit to acknowledge God, God gave them up to a debased mind to do what ought not to be done. 29 They were filled with all manner of unrighteousness, evil, covetousness, malice. They are full of envy, murder, strife, deceit, maliciousness. They are gossips, 30 slanderers, haters of God, insolent, haughty, boastful, inventors of evil, disobedient to parents, 31 foolish, faithless, heartless, ruthless. 32 Though they know God's righteous decree that those who practice such things deserve to die, they not only do them but give approval to those who practice them.

Isaiah 1:2-5, 15-21a, 23

2 Hear, O heavens, and give ear, O earth; for the Lord has spoken: "Children have I reared and brought up, but they have rebelled against me. 3 The ox knows its owner, and the donkey its master's crib, but Israel does not know, my people do not understand." 4 Ah, sinful nation, a people laden with iniquity, offspring of evildoers, children who deal corruptly! They have forsaken the Lord, they have despised the Holy One of Israel, they are utterly estranged. 5 Why will you still be struck down? Why will you continue to rebel? The whole head is sick, and the whole heart faint. ...15 When you spread out your hands, I will hide my eyes from you; even though you make many prayers, I will not listen; your hands are full of blood. 16 Wash yourselves; make yourselves clean; remove the evil of your deeds from before my eyes; cease to do evil, 17 learn to do good; seek justice, correct oppression; bring justice to the fatherless, plead the widow's cause. 18 "Come now, let us reason together, says the Lord: though your sins are like scarlet, they shall be as white as snow; though they are red like crimson, they shall become like wool. 19 If you are willing and obedient, you shall eat the good of the land; 20 but if you refuse and rebel, you shall be eaten by the sword; for the mouth of the Lord has spoken." 21a How the faithful city has become a whore, [become unchaste] she who was full of justice!... 23 Your princes are rebels and companions of thieves. Everyone loves a bribe and runs after gifts. They do not bring justice to the fatherless, and the widow's cause does not come to them.

Luke 13:34
O Jerusalem, Jerusalem, the city that kills the prophets and stones those who are sent to it! How often would I have gathered your children together as a hen gathers her brood under her wings, and you were not willing!

God will not produce bad fruit. "Not fruit of the Spirit" is "not God". God's purpose brings forward information, facilitates thoughtful discussion and promotes united action.

Proverbs 27:17
Iron sharpens iron, and one man sharpens another.

Still, *how* we say what we say is just as important as our position on it. Iron sharpening iron through fruit of the Spirit language in conversations aimed at discerning the will of God (not ours) brings greater Unity, synergy and therefore productivity. The Fear Mongerer slanders their opponent, shaming them for their position and accuses them of all the things that they themselves are doing. If it is not facilitating Unity, but uses any one of a number of manipulative methods to divide and conquer so as to control outcomes, it is "not God". "Not love" is simply "not God".

"Gossip can do its work with tones of voice or a roll of the eye. While we may think of gossip as a harmless diversion, the New Testament lists it along with envy, murder, strife, and hating God" (Romans 1:8-30). Timothy and Kathy Keller, "The Songs of Jesus," Viking, 2015, p. 86

Leaning on our own understanding, we are a hard-hearted nation in chaos, trusting ourselves to figure out what we should do. We *think* our way through - rationalizing our behavior with hearts as cold as ice. Some will remind us that the scriptures relate that Jesus took a whip into the temple, turned over the tables of the money-changers and ran them off. We would do well to note that Jesus had been going in and out of the temple for twenty years by that time. Don't you think that he had been talking to them about this for many years?

John 2:13-17

13 The Passover of the Jews was at hand, and Jesus went up to Jerusalem. 14 In the temple he found those who were selling oxen and sheep and pigeons, and the money-changers sitting there. 15 And making a whip of cords, he drove them all out of the temple, with the sheep and oxen. And he poured out the coins of the money-changers and overturned their tables. 16 And he told those who sold the pigeons, "Take these things away; do not make my Father's house a house of trade." 17 His disciples remembered that it was written, "Zeal for your house will consume me."

But it is highly unlikely that he used the whip on any person. Neither Luke nor Mark mention the whip in their accounts. Further, those familiar with ancient languages state that the grammar indicates a separation such that the whip was used on the animals, not on any humans. Looking at the totality of his behavior in the Bible, it is more likely that he swung the whip around over his head (if at all) to make the money-changers back away from their tables, enabling him to flip them over without harming anyone. I can imagine him saying, "Get out, and take these tables with you!"

Let's not justify angry behavior by comparing ourselves to Jesus. This story is the only one of its kind in his lifetime, and it is being taken out of context. However, some will still say he used the whip on people so as to rationalize and justify their own use of intimidation and violence to Control others.

Taking notice of the angry and violent rationalizations happening around them, children learn all sorts of these manipulative and coercive tools from their parents, friends, TV, movies, the internet and other media. Domestic violence and the disintegration of the family over the past 60 years should be of no surprise to us. Each generation is following in the footsteps of the last.

Exodus 34:6-8

6 The Lord passed before him and proclaimed, "The Lord, the Lord, a God merciful and gracious, slow to anger, and abounding in steadfast love and faithfulness, 7 keeping steadfast love for thousands, forgiving iniquity and transgression and sin, but who will by no means clear the guilty, visiting the iniquity of the fathers on the children and the children's children, to the third and the fourth generation." 8 And Moses quickly bowed his head toward the earth and worshiped.

Our actions are not unlike dominos that fall one after the other once the first has been tipped over. However, unlike dominos that we line up to fall every which way for our enjoyment, the dominos of our actions may also lead to *unintended* consequences that *hurt* our families for *generations*.

It might correctly be said: he will not clear the guilty *of the consequences of their actions* to the third and the fourth generation. In other words, though forgiveness is available, the dominos we knock down will be allowed to have their associated ongoing impacts. As you look around, our national division at an all-time high, it is clear that the cumulative impact of previous parenting has negatively affected our nation. The peaceful civil disobedience of rallies and picketing for change have become violent. We are reaping what we have sown through our allowance and indulgence of the childishness of our children as they have grown, but it is nothing new. The Old Testament is replete with sad stories of poor parenting and the harm their Foolish children sought in anger.

King David's horrible parenting caused additional horrible things to occur in many, many ways. These then caused still other horrible things to occur, and others followed still. If you are unaware, it would be worthwhile to go back and read through his life. Nonetheless, he had a heart after God. So, as he realized the depth of his failings, he was commensurately deeply repentant. The Psalms are full of his writings praising God for his forgiveness, his faithfulness, his mercy, and his willingness to walk with him and lead him through each day.

If you will read about David in the Samuel, Kings and Chronicles portions of your Old Testament, don't forget to also read through the Psalms. Here, you will come to realize just how deeply he loved our

Father, trusted him and would therefore change his behavior as he learned his ways more and more.

One thing David *never* did was reject the will of the Father as he came to know it. You can find many accounts where the easiest thing for him to do would have been to reject or resist and instead trust himself and his own understanding. But he never did. The life of David proves that forgiveness is always available, that the Father is most interested in the condition of our hearts and that we will evidence that as we turn from our former ways.

When we are guilty of self-focus rather than oneness with *his* will, in our ignorance we risk harming the very people we love - just as David did – and the people suffer. God’s ways are higher than our ways, so he leads us that we would do *them*!

No one really plans to end up with rotten relationships, but that's exactly how bad relationships happen - no planning. Good relationships don't happen that way. Good relationships take planning. If you want a good relationship with your parents or children or husband or wife, you're going to have to <u>want</u> it. You'll have to <u>plan</u> for it, <u>work</u> at it and <u>persevere</u> in it. But it's more than worth it. It will make the difference between what is worthless and what is precious.
Jonathan Kahn, February 5, 2021

Chapter Six

Eyes That See And Ears That Hear

1 John 2:6
whoever says he abides in him
ought to walk in the same way in which he walked.

What do you do when a friend or associate has a better idea? You follow theirs! Jesus said that he only does and says what the Father tells him. So will we as we learn how his ways are better than our ways. Our hearts, souls and minds will respond, "YOUR will be done, O God, not mine!"

John 14:21
Whoever has my commandments and keeps them, he it is who loves me. And he who loves me will be loved by my Father, and I will love him and manifest myself to him."

John 15:9-11
9 As the Father has loved me, so have I loved you. Abide in my love.
10 If you keep my commandments, you will abide in my love, just as I have kept my Father's commandments and abide in his love.
11 These things I have spoken to you, that my joy may be in you, and that your joy may be full.

John 5:19
So Jesus said to them, "Truly, truly, I say to you, the Son can do nothing of his own accord, but only what he sees the Father doing. For whatever the Father does, that the Son does likewise.

John 12:49-50
49 For I have not spoken on my own authority, but the Father who sent me has himself given me a commandment - what to say and what to speak.
50 And I know that his commandment is eternal life. What I say, therefore, I say as the Father has told me."

1 John 2:4-6

4 Whoever says "I know him" but does not keep his commandments is a liar, and the truth is not in him, 5 but whoever keeps his word, in him truly the love of God is perfected. By this we may know that we are in him: 6 whoever says he abides in him ought to walk in the same way in which he walked.

1 John 2:28

And now, little children, abide in him, so that when he appears we may have confidence and not shrink from him in shame at his coming.

Matthew 6:9-10

9 Pray then like this: "Our Father in heaven, hallowed be your name. 10 Your kingdom come, your will be done...

It would not be fair for him to tell us to do his will for the coming of his kingdom and then not give us a way of knowing what it is. We know his will because he tells us! This is not to say that God will be telling us everything to do moment by moment. No, but just as we have nearly automated actions in this natural life, so will we in our God-led life.

Just as we know we need to brush our teeth, comb our hair, get dressed before going out, tie our shoes, turn the doorknob to open the door, use our turn signals before turning and so forth, so will we grow more and more to have similar *God-led actions and responses*. Education and practice are preparation for greater education and practice that become Wisdom and maturity. As we mature in Christ, what we were in the natural will be overcome by the spiritual and bring us more into his likeness. So too will we *become* more aware and automatic in catching ourselves that we *not do*, stepping on the brake *before* doing the bad behavior that we would likely have done formerly. As we grow up in him, our eyes and ears will become more and more attuned to hearing and seeing and accomplishing his will. Otherwise…

Matthew 13:14-15

14 Indeed, in their case the prophecy of Isaiah is fulfilled that says: """You will indeed hear but never understand, and you will indeed see but never perceive." 15 For this people's heart has grown dull, and with their ears they can barely hear, and their eyes they have closed, lest they should see with their eyes and hear with their ears and understand with their heart and turn, and I would heal them.'

Our Adversary, however, uses our natural personality predispositions against us to try to minimize our spiritual growth, and if possible, keep us self-focused *on* the natural.

Our understanding of the predispositions of personality is a well-developed and well documented science that has been refined and re-refined in great depth over the last 60 years. One of the most favored in helping us understand ourselves is Meyers-Briggs. In it, it may be said that there are four basic personality types from which all of the multiplicity of types spring. For two of them, their basic premise in decision-making is that *the ends justify the means*. The most divisive of our politicians see no harm in lying, deceiving, bending the truth and harming a portion of the people so long as the "good" ends they desire are achieved. Leaning on their own understanding, this basic childish behavior is in direct conflict with the teachings of Jesus on so very many fronts. Even those closest to Jesus were willing to go against him. I know I have. I'll bet you have.

Like Judas, we have been guilty of imagining what we think to be right and then making our attempt to force it to happen. Judas was likely a zealot, from a group called The Zealots, a people passionate for throwing out their Roman occupiers. Like Judas, we are all politicians, maneuvering to some degree for what we think would be best. In our zeal, passion and arrogance, we think we know better than others what must be done. Like Judas, we think that if we can initiate the first thing, the thing we want to have happen will then follow. Though Judas believed that the angels would come down from heaven to protect Jesus when they tried to take him away, that the battle for Jerusalem would then be waged against the Romans, and that the Romans would then be defeated and Jerusalem restored - it did not happen:

Matthew 26:47
While he was still speaking, Judas came, one of the twelve, and with him a great crowd with swords and clubs, from the chief priests and the elders of the people.

Luke 22:47
While he was still speaking, there came a crowd, and the man called Judas, one of the twelve, was leading them. He drew near to Jesus to kiss him, but Jesus said to him, "Judas, would you betray the Son of Man with a kiss?"

Luke 22:52-53
52 Then Jesus said to the chief priests and officers of the temple and elders, who had come out against him, "Have you come out as against a robber, with swords and clubs? 53 When I was with you day after day in the temple, you did not lay hands on me. But this is your hour, and the power of darkness."

Matthew 27:1-2
1 When morning came, all the chief priests and the elders of the people took counsel against Jesus to put him to death. 2 And they bound him and led him away and delivered him over to Pilate the governor.

Matthew 27:3-5
3 Then when Judas, his betrayer, saw that Jesus was condemned, he changed his mind and brought back the thirty pieces of silver to the chief priests and the elders, 4 saying, "I have sinned by betraying innocent blood." They said, "What is that to us? See to it yourself."
5 And throwing down the pieces of silver into the temple, he departed, and he went and hanged himself.

Like Peter, we have seen what we believe should not happen and made our attempt to stop it from occurring. Our will our way, not God's will his way.

Matthew 16:21-23
21 From that time Jesus began to show his disciples that he must go to Jerusalem and suffer many things from the elders and chief priests and scribes, and be killed, and on the third day be raised. 22 And Peter

took him aside and began to rebuke him, saying, "Far be it from you, Lord! This shall never happen to you." 23 But he turned and said to Peter, "Get behind me, Satan! You are a hindrance to me. For you are not setting your mind on the things of God, but on the things of man."

Then, seeing he had still not learned his lesson, Jesus warned him that he was at risk - a target of the Enemy…

Luke 22:31-34

31 "Simon, Simon, behold, Satan demanded to have you, that he might sift you like wheat, 32 but I have prayed for you that your faith may not fail. And when you have turned again, strengthen your brothers."
33 Peter said to him, "Lord, I am ready to go with you both to prison and to death." 34 Jesus said, "I tell you, Peter, the rooster will not crow this day, until you deny three times that you know me."

…still trying to stop it, he again tried to interfere with the will of the Father when they came to get him.

Luke 22:49-51

49 And when those who were around him saw what would follow, they said, "Lord, shall we strike with the sword?" 50 And one of them struck the servant of the high priest and cut off his right ear. 51 But Jesus said, "No more of this!" And he touched his ear and healed him.

Matthew 26:50b-54

Then they came up and laid hands on Jesus and seized him. 51 And behold, one of those who were with Jesus stretched out his hand and drew his sword and struck the servant of the high priest and cut off his ear. 52 Then Jesus said to him, "Put your sword back into its place. For all who take the sword will perish by the sword. 53 Do you think that I cannot appeal to my Father, and he will at once send me more than twelve legions of angels? 54 But how then should the Scriptures be fulfilled, that it must be so?"

John 18:10-11

10 Then Simon Peter, having a sword, drew it and struck the high priest's servant and cut off his right ear. (The servant's name was

Malchus.) 11 So Jesus said to Peter, "Put your sword into its sheath; shall I not drink the cup that the Father has given me?"

We interfere like Peter interfered. Thank you for your forgiveness, O God! Consider the forgiveness and comfort Jesus gave Peter after his resurrection, after Peter had failed so miserably. Thank you, God, that you bring peace to the mourning and comfort to the sorrowful:

John 21:15-17, 19b

15 When they had finished breakfast, Jesus said to Simon Peter,
"Simon, son of John, do you love me more than these?" He said to
him, "Yes, Lord; you know that I love you." He said to him, "Feed my
lambs." 16 He said to him a second time, "Simon, son of John, do you
love me?" He said to him, "Yes, Lord; you know that I love you." He
said to him, "Tend my sheep." 17 He said to him the third time,
"Simon, son of John, do you love me?" Peter was grieved because he
said to him the third time, "Do you love me?" and he said to him,
"Lord, you know everything; you know that I love you." Jesus said to
him, "Feed my sheep. ...19b ...And after saying this
he said to him, "Follow me."

When we work to accomplish *our* will, seeing what we think we know for sure, we must keep in mind that we just might be resisting the workings of God our Father. Don't be drawn in by Satan's deceptions! God's fruit of the Spirit ways lead us to actions in humility and with the attitudes of the Beatitudes, Jesus' attitudes (Matthew 5:2-12 below). These lead us to say and to do in ways consistent with his character, that give us a reputation for walking in his will, that bring Peace that surpasses all understanding, and a quiet confidence borne of him. Though in this world we will have trouble (John 16:33), be still and know that he is God (Psalm 46:10). Trust in the Lord with all your heart, and do not lean on your own understanding (Proverbs 3:3).

Matthew 5:2-12

2 And he opened his mouth and taught them, saying: 3 "Blessed are
the poor in spirit, for theirs is the kingdom of heaven. 4 "Blessed are
those who mourn, for they shall be comforted. 5 "Blessed are the meek,
for they shall inherit the earth. 6 "Blessed are those who hunger and

thirst for righteousness, for they shall be satisfied. 7 "Blessed are the merciful, for they shall receive mercy. 8 "Blessed are the pure in heart, for they shall see God. 9 "Blessed are the peacemakers, for they shall be called sons of God. 10 "Blessed are those who are persecuted for righteousness' sake, for theirs is the kingdom of heaven. 11 "Blessed are you when others revile you and persecute you and utter all kinds of evil against you falsely on my account. 12 Rejoice and be glad, for your reward is great in heaven, for so they persecuted the prophets who were before you.

Matthew 11:28-30

28 Come to me, all who labor and are heavy laden, and I will give you rest. 29 Take my yoke upon you, and learn from me, for I am gentle and lowly in heart, and you will find rest for your souls. 30 For my yoke is easy, and my burden is light."

Philippians 4:7

And the peace of God, which surpasses all understanding, will guard your hearts and your minds in Christ Jesus.

Otherwise,

Luke 13:34

O Jerusalem, Jerusalem, the city that kills the prophets and stones those who are sent to it! How often would I have gathered your children together as a hen gathers her brood under her wings, and you were not willing!

Isaiah 30:15 NIV

This is what the Sovereign Lord, the Holy One of Israel, says: "In repentance and rest is your salvation, in quietness and trust is your strength, But you would have none of it.

We need to be aware and attentive in our spirits, one with him, so as to be able to hear his warning and stop ourselves that we not enter into temptation. Though we may have an idea or opinion, he asks us to share these with him before acting *out of our own understanding*. What God would have is that we take what is occurring to him, offer our thoughts and ask for his will and Direction. Made in his image, he very much desires that we would be creative like he is creative. We are not to be robots simply following his commands, but rather *participants* with him in the administration and operation of his kingdom. Consider our first creative participation with him:

Genesis 2:19-20
19 Now out of the ground the Lord God had formed every beast of the field and every bird of the heavens and brought them to the man to see what he would call them. And whatever the man called every living creature, that was its name. 20 The man gave names to all livestock and to the birds of the heavens and to every beast of the field...

Consider also the fall of wicked King Ahab:

1 Kings 16:33
"[King Ahab] did more to provoke the Lord, the God of Israel, to anger than all the kings of Israel who were before him".

God had made a decision to deliver his people from King Ahab's evil, but he brought the *creation of how* to the members of his divine kingdom:

1 Kings 22:19-23
19 And Micaiah said, "Therefore hear the word of the Lord: I saw the Lord sitting on his throne, and <u>all the host of heaven</u> standing beside him on his right hand and on his left; 20 and the Lord said, 'Who will entice Ahab, that he may go up and fall at Ramoth-gilead?' And one said one thing, and another said another. 21 Then a spirit came forward and stood before the Lord, saying, 'I will entice him.' 22 <u>And the Lord said to him, 'By what means?'</u> And he said, 'I will go out, and will be a lying spirit in the mouth of all his prophets.' And he said, 'You are to entice him, and you shall succeed; go out and do so.' 23 Now therefore behold, the Lord has put a lying spirit in the mouth of all these your prophets; the Lord has declared disaster for you."

1 Kings 22:37-38

37 So the king died, and was brought to Samaria. And they buried the king in Samaria. 38 And they washed the chariot by the pool of Samaria, and the dogs licked up his blood, and the prostitutes washed themselves in it, according to the word of the Lord that he had spoken.

They participated with him then, and later the disciples participated with him as well. Jesus didn't do it alone:

Mark 6:34-44

34 When he went ashore he saw a great crowd, and he had compassion on them, because they were like sheep without a shepherd. And he began to teach them many things. 35 And when it grew late, his disciples came to him and said, "This is a desolate place, and the hour is now late. 36 Send them away to go into the surrounding countryside and villages and buy themselves something to eat." 37 But he answered them, "You give them something to eat." And they said to him, "Shall we go and buy two hundred denarii worth of bread and give it to them to eat?" 38 And he said to them, "How many loaves do you have? Go and see." And when they had found out, they said, "Five, and two fish." 39 Then he commanded them all to sit down in groups on the green grass. 40 So they sat down in groups, by hundreds and by fifties. 41 And taking the five loaves and the two fish, he looked up to heaven and said a blessing and broke the loaves and gave them to the disciples to set before the people. And he divided the two fish among them all. 42 And they all ate and were satisfied. 43 And they took up twelve baskets full of broken pieces and of the fish. 44 And those who ate the loaves were five thousand men.

If we will *participate* with him on earth as it is in heaven *now*, we will also participate with him on the *new* earth after he comes again:

Matthew 19:28-29

28 Jesus said to them, "Truly, I say to you, in the new world, when the Son of Man will sit on his glorious throne, you who have followed me will also sit on twelve thrones, judging the twelve tribes of Israel. 29 And everyone who has left houses or brothers or sisters or father or mother or children or lands, for my name's sake, will receive a hundredfold and will inherit eternal life.

1 Corinthians 6:2-3a

2 Or do you not know that the saints will judge the world? And if the world is to be judged by you, are you incompetent to try trivial cases? 3 Do you not know that we are to judge angels?

2 Timothy 2:12

if we endure, we will also reign with him; if we deny him, he also will deny us;

Revelation 2:26

The one who conquers and who keeps my works until the end, to him I will give authority over the nations,

Revelation 3:21

The one who conquers, I will grant him to sit with me on my throne, as I also conquered and sat down with my Father on his throne.

Revelation 20:6

6 Blessed and holy is the one who shares in the first resurrection! Over such the second death has no power, but they will be priests of God and of Christ, and they will reign with him for a thousand years.

Revelation 21:1

Then I saw a new heaven and a new earth, for the first heaven and the first earth had passed away, and the sea was no more.

Revelation 22:5

And night will be no more. They will need no light of lamp or sun, for the Lord God will be their light, and they will reign forever and ever.

Thank you, Father, that you made us to participate with you in the growing of your kingdom. Thank you that Jesus is available to teach us, that your Spirit is available to lead us, and that you are doing your works in us – that our Joy may be complete. I have truly found that repentance and rest bring your salvation, and that quietness and trust bring your strength. Thank you that you want us to inquire of you continually that we know you better and learn your ways more and more. Thank you for the Joy we find when we put aside our own desires to control people and events and instead follow your ways, allowing all to choose without coercion, manipulation or veiled threat.

As Acceptors, so many of us formerly thought that what we were doing <u>for</u> you was <u>from</u> you, but it was not. It was us moving in our desire to control people and events, according to our best understanding of what we <u>thought</u> you would want – and many have been hurt by us. Thank you for your forgiveness, your training and your leading - that we do better in the future. May we forgive others as you have forgiven us! Thank you for the Peace and Joy that I have found in learning and following your ways!

Chapter Seven

What Is Your Operating System?

All of the preceding is why leadership development is really, really, really near and dear to my heart. Our only way out of the pervasive disintegration of our families and the resulting national chaos is through leadership in oneness with God - led by God alone - in personal holiness. And it isn't just for large scale leaders. It must penetrate the hearts of parents and be built up in their children. Strong families build strong nations. The children of weak families grow up to tear them apart. Pray for the children!

What I've learned over the years is that everyone is a leader in at least some small way with at least someone. Maybe most important of all is the leadership of parents with their children, the future leaders of our nations. An orientation to personal holiness will not only take you far, it will turbo-charge your trajectory and ability by the power of the Holy Spirit. And personal holiness that leads to corporate holiness is the stuff that greatness is made from.

All of the problems in the world are the result of people living out of something other than personal holiness. In the culture of today, you will hear people say, "That's how I roll." or "That's how she rolls." Organizationally, we would call that their Operating System. What is your operating system?

For many decades, the most widely used computer operating systems were Macintosh (Apple) and Windows (Microsoft). The two are mutually exclusive. The same is true for God's Unity Operating System and the Enemy's World Operating System. They are mutually exclusive. You cannot use apps designed for Windows on a Mac and vice versa. You must choose which operating system you will use based upon the benefits you perceive. The same is true for *your* operating system, how you will roll.

Quite a few years ago it became possible to operate both computer systems on one computer when Parallels came out with a product that will run Windows on a Mac as a type of software. No longer constrained, people may now use whichever operating system they wish at any time. If we think that the Windows app will be easier, we can select it. Vice versa for the Mac app. I have become quite proficient in operating in Parallels. In my life, too.

At any moment I may choose to operate in God's Unity Operating System or in the Enemy's World Operating System. An easy example would be my "at church" behavior compared to my "at work" behavior. Formerly, they were quite different! How about you? Since childhood, we have learned how to chameleon ourselves so as to fit operationally with whomever we are around.

I remember being in the car going to my management job 40 years ago. One day I noticed me saying to myself, "Time to put on the mask." Suddenly I realized that I had been trying to live a double life! I didn't respect the managers above me in my organization and would hide behind my mask of agreement - going along in disagreement. I was stuck in their operating system, behaving so as to fit and not compromise my family's sole source of income.

Is the same true for you? Are you stuck trying to operate so as to fit in both worlds? Are you hoping that God will understand? If so, is this about the God you want? Or the God who is? Jesus did not compromise while he was here, and he promises to help us do the same as we grow up into him:

Hebrews 4:14-16

14 Since then we have a great high priest who has passed through the heavens, Jesus, the Son of God, let us hold fast our confession. 15 For we do not have a high priest who is unable to sympathize with our weaknesses, but one who in every respect has been tempted as we are, yet without sin. 16 Let us then with confidence draw near to the throne of grace, that we may receive mercy and find grace to help in time of need.

It is not God honoring to situationally "continue to" be *both* a Rejector and an Acceptor as we deem it appropriate. God does not allow for a Parallels type of holiness. We are to function in the world using his Unity Operating System and not rationalize other behavior because of it. Fruit of the Spirit language is the key to us uncompromisingly communicating our disagreement while also defending their right to choose as they wish. When it is clear to them that we are without judgement or condemnation of their behavior, they will be more and more likely to consider the benefits of ours.

God's operating system allows everyone to make their own personal choice to Accept that operating system or Reject it. Fruit of the Spirit behavior in Unity with his system uses language that leads to Peace, Love, Joy and therefore abundant life in him. Since Eden, the Enemy has been telling us that God is a liar. Adam and Eve chose to Reject what God said back then and trusted the Enemy instead. We left God's Unity Operating System to live in the Enemy's. Outside of his Edenic protection, we now live in a world that is deteriorating, disintegrating and devolving to include debilitating defects, disease and the pain, suffering and destruction caused by *our* Rejecting.

Though Adam and Eve started it, we are now the ones who suffer under tyrannical Rejectors like Stalin, Mussolini, Mao and Hitler, and we do not have to look very far to find Rejectors like them who are causing pain and suffering on purpose today. Satan tells us that *this* is the world *God* made for us, and that he cannot be good to have created it. Rather, it is the one *Satan tricked us into leaving him for*. We went from God's paradise and perfection out into the Enemy's world of chaos, disease and tyranny. We are the ones who threw it all away. Many still are today.

Introducing a term I will use more as we proceed, we *self-selected* departure from Eden. God did not kick out Adam and Eve. He gave them the information they needed beforehand and allowed them to decide what they wanted to do. They were the ones who decided that the risk of death was worth what the Enemy promised they would gain. And so it was that *they* made the choice to leave God and follow his Enemy – so he let them. And many still choose to do so today.

I self-selected departure from my position 40 years ago, deciding that I could not work the way they wanted me to. Nonetheless, my personal Parallels operating system was not much better. I was judgmental in my heart and critical in my thoughts as I left. It has taken me a very long time to come around to understanding the things I am sharing with you. To my Joy, little by little he has Kindly and Gently been working to transform me into his image – and given me Peace that surpasses all understanding.

2 Corinthians 3:18

And we all, with unveiled face, beholding the glory of the Lord, are being transformed into the same image from one degree of glory to another.

Notice that it says “from one degree of glory to another”. That is to say little by little. Bit by bit. More and more.

We are not under pressure to be perfected all at once. He is Gentle with us along the way. Scripture is clear: Jesus is our Teacher, the Holy Spirit Leads us and the Father dwells in us, doing his Works. That we become more and more like him.

Most of what I have learned came the hard way as I leaned on my own understanding. When I began to inquire unceasingly of the Father as to these difficulties, Jesus took me by the hand to Teach me, the Holy Spirit to Lead me, and the Father did his Works in me to help me grow. Little by little. As I share within these pages, I am for the most part relating learnings from my failings. I pray you will submit yourself quickly to the transformation he offers and avoid the pain I have put myself and others through.

Chapter Eight

One With Him, In His Presence

In John 17, Jesus identifies that he manifested (established, engrained, developed, activated and made real) the *character and attributes of God* in his disciples *(personal holiness)*, that all of us may grow to manifest them (live according to his Unity Operating System) and that these are essential behaviors if we are to accomplish his will for us – that his kingdom come and will be done on (the whole) earth as it is in heaven.

If *we* will manifest the character and attributes of God, Jesus said we will "Love the Lord your God with all of your heart, with all of your soul, with all of your mind and with all of your strength." and "Love your neighbor as your self." The essential content of all that we are to do to grow in personal holiness? Love wholly. Love only. From the totality and depth of who we are: with all of our heart, soul and mind, and with all of our strength.

It wouldn't be fair for God to say love wholly and love only and then not tell us how to do it. The Bible is loaded with clear descriptions of behaviors that we are to do and to avoid. Summarizing again, anything that is "not love" is simply "not God".

"Not love" is most often just us succumbing to a destructive passion, pleasure or desire. If you ask the Father to help you understand the conflicts in your life, you can be sure that he will respond to help you with loving fruit of the Spirit. He is Gentle when offering his correction to us, and we need to behave the same way if we will appropriately correct others. Led *by* the Spirit, our interactions will produce fruit *of* the Spirit for the benefit of all.

1 Thessalonians 5:17-18

17 pray (inquire, ask, petition, request) without ceasing, 18 give thanks in all circumstances; for this is the will of God in Christ Jesus for you.

Philippians 1:6
And I am sure of this, that he who began a good work in you will bring it to completion at the day of Jesus Christ.

So inquire of God! When the disciples asked Jesus to teach them how to pray, what he gave them was the most all-encompassing prayer that could be prayed. I believe that this prayer similarly sums up the essential content of all that *we* might pray, in agreement with him that his kingdom come in us and that his will be done in and through us. For the development of our hearts and souls and minds as he strengthens us. That we love in alignment with him, wholly and only. And in so doing, that he will develop in us a lifelong orientation toward personal holiness.

Just as the enormous depth of the practical application of the two greatest commandments may be found in the scriptures, the enormous depth of the content of the prayer he taught us to pray may also be found there. During the past 25 years I have been asking that I be taught how to pray that he would develop my heart, soul and mind in complete alignment with him. What I have learned is that this prayer, when expanded upon through examination of the scripture, explains personal holiness as his Presence in us producing the character and attributes that we, his disciples, will share as one with him - if we will bring *his* kingdom and do *his* will.

What does it mean to be his disciple? It is probably different than you think because we do not have any word for it in our English language. The Hebrew word translated for us to English is *talmid.* The plural is *talmidim.*

Unlike the words disciple or student or apprentice that suggest a learning and doing process, the word talmid is a Hebrew term that describes a *becoming* process. Talmid desire to *become just like* their rabbi. It is more than the practical application of the knowledge we gain. It is more than taking actions based upon our understanding of his teachings. A talmid of Jesus will be growing to reflect the very *character* of Jesus, have *a heart after the Father,* and be gaining *the mind and attitudes of Christ. Becoming* all he would have us be requires that we trust the teachings of Jesus, the Father in us doing his works and the power of the Holy Spirit in us to will and to do it - for the benefit of all of us.

At Pentecost, those gathered went from having *learned* how to become like their rabbi Jesus (operating in the character and attributes Jesus established in them) to then additionally having the Presence of the living God *in them*. Personal holiness is now more fully available and attainable through what Jesus taught us, by the power of the Holy Spirit and with the Father in us doing his works!

2 Corinthians 3:17-18

17 Now the Lord is the Spirit, and where the Spirit of the Lord is, there is freedom. 18 And we all, with unveiled face, beholding the glory of the Lord, are being transformed into the same image from one degree of glory to another. For this comes from the Lord who is the Spirit.

Romans 8:26-29

26 Likewise the Spirit helps us in our weakness. For we do not know what to pray for as we ought, but the Spirit himself intercedes for us with groanings too deep for words. 27 And he who searches hearts knows what is the mind of the Spirit, because the Spirit intercedes for the saints according to the will of God. 28 And we know that for those who love God all things work together for good, for those who are called according to his purpose. 29 For those whom he foreknew he also predestined to be conformed to the image of his Son, in order that he might be the firstborn among many brothers.

John 6:45

It is written in the Prophets, 'And they will all be taught by God.' Everyone who has heard and learned from the Father comes to me.

John 14:10

Do you not believe that I am in the Father and the Father is in me? The words that I say to you I do not speak on my own authority, but the Father who dwells in me does his works.

1 Corinthians 2: 10, 12, 13, 14, 16

10 these things God has revealed to us through the Spirit. For the Spirit searches everything, even the depths of God. 12 Now we have

received not the spirit of the world, but the Spirit who is from God, that we might understand the things freely given us by God. 13 And we impart this in words not taught by human wisdom but taught by the Spirit, interpreting spiritual truths to those who are spiritual. 14 The natural person does not accept the things of the Spirit of God, for they are folly to him, and he is not able to understand them because they are spiritually discerned. 16 "For who has understood the mind of the Lord so as to instruct him?"
But we have the mind of Christ.

Everyone who has heard and learned from the Father comes to me, Jesus, to be taught my mind: the mind of Christ. I was an example to you. I have made my Spirit available to you. That you be taught *by* God for *oneness with God* in the "name" of the Father, the Son and the Holy Spirit. Our heart after the Father's.

I have never heard it in a sermon before or since, but when I went back and studied the etymology, I found it to be true:

Outside of Eden, they would sometimes feel God's supernatural presence and recognize that a supernatural activity was occurring – though they could not see him. The Hebrew word for presence is panim, so as they felt his "panim" over a period of time, they decided that they should give this presence (panim) a name. They took the ancient Hebrew word shem (meaning name) and added "ha" which formalized it to "The Name". So, presence (panim) evolved to shem (name) and finally Hashem (The Name).

When they felt his presence and "heard" from him, they could talk with him - calling him Hashem (The Presence). Later, even after he told them his name (Yahweh) they still called him Hashem because they were afraid to say that name aloud. The Hebrew people continue to use Hashem in their daily prayers to this day.

Translation to English over time has left us in a place of confusion because our English Bibles use "name" or "the name" everywhere the word Yahweh or YHWH or Hashem shows up in the original language. Very importantly, the point of all of this is that Hashem refers to "The Presence" of God as he expresses his character, reputation and attributes into our lives. So when we talk of asking in his "name", what we are really speaking of is asking while in his Presence, thankful for his reliable reputation - and for the development of his character and attributes in us more and more.

Unfortunately, ending our prayers "in the name of Jesus" has become a sort of incantation that has come about due to the mistranslations in our Bibles.

John 14:14
If you ask me anything in my name, I will do it.

As he lives in us and leads us into the abundant life, we will find Joy and Peace that surpass all understanding. As we learn that his ways are better than our ways, what we will want will more and more become what he wants us to want. In this way, we will begin our prayers acknowledging his Presence, agreeing for his will, learning to ask "in his presence" for what he wants us to be asking for! In the character and attributes of Jesus, consistent with the reputation of the Father, in and for the Father's will.
No more incantations!

****

More and more, God will help us to know what he wants us to want and will bring us the best life we could possibly live. Jesus did this for his *talmidim* over a period of three years. Present with them, he taught them his character, his attributes, his attitudes, how to overcome their destructive passions and desires, how to live by the power of his Presence and do the Father's will. Despite whatever their life circumstances were or would be, they found his promise of Joy in him to be true. He molded and shaped their character day by day and rooted it into them.

In Galatians 5, God tells us what it will look like when we are operating as *talmidim* in the power of his *Presence* and *in his character and attributes*. The "fruit of the Spirit" described there - *love, joy, peace, patience, kindness, goodness, faithfulness (perseverance), gentleness and self-control* - are God's reference points to us for our behavior and the tools with which we are to contend, even as people around us behave otherwise.

In Ephesians 6 we are told that the whole armor of God is our protection when others attack us, absorbing the blows for us. Our ability to brush aside attacks so as to engage and respond always and everywhere with fruit of the Spirit requires our assent and agreement *with* the Holy Spirit that he do so *in* us and *through* us. This is sanctification, a process of refining us for our benefit and the benefit of the world around us. (In the "Love" section we will expand upon how the prayer Jesus taught us to pray Gently leads us through prayer and reflection that facilitate sanctification.)

When you read scripture, it will be far more meaningful if you will watch to see whether the meaning of "name" is "name", or if it would be more appropriate to substitute "Presence", "the presence", "the character and attributes", "in the power of the presence", "in the power of the presence and in the character and attributes" or another contextually appropriate phrase. Occasionally, "reputation" will be most appropriate.

Remembering the mistranslation of The Presence into "name": in the Lord's Prayer, the prayer Jesus taught us to pray, doesn't "Presence" make more sense than "name"? Our Father in heaven, hallowed be your Presence! Your kingdom come, your will be done!
Thank you for your Presence!

After all, it is the power of his presence working in us that strengthens us to overcome the difficulties of living in this world. We are not to take this world on alone. Our Father in heaven, thank you for your presence!

Now consider these portions of the prayer Jesus prayed for them (and for us) to our Father in heaven before knowingly going off to die on the cross on our behalf:

John 17:6-11, 17, 18, 22-26

6 "I have manifested (rooted, established, developed) your name (character & attributes) to (in) the people whom you gave me out of the world. Yours they were, and you gave them to me, and they have kept your word. 7 Now they know that everything that you have given me is from you. 8 For I have given them the words that you gave me, and they have received them and have come to know in truth that I came from you; and they have believed that you sent me. 9 I am praying for them. I am not praying for the world but for those whom you have given me, for they are yours. 10 All mine are yours, and yours are mine, and I am glorified in them. 11 And I am no longer in the world, but they are in the world, and I am coming to you. Holy Father, keep them in your name (the power of your presence, with your character & attributes), which you have given me, that they may be one, even as we are one. 17 Sanctify them in the truth; your word is truth. 18 As you sent me into the world, so I have sent them into the world. 22 The glory that you have given me I have given to them, that they may be one even as we are one, 23 I in them and you in me, that they may become perfectly one, so that the world may know that you sent me and loved them even as you loved me. 26 I made known to them your name (reputation, character & attributes), and I will continue to make it known, that the love with which you have loved me may be in them, and I in them."

This is Jesus' prayer for us. God's desire is to lead us through each day in one-ness with him, taught by him, to grow us to reflect his character and attributes to others more and more, little by little, success by success, glory by glory (2 Corinthians 3:18); conformed to the image of his Son (Romans 8:29), that none should perish (2 Peter 3:9).

Jesus clearly states that, during the three years with his talmidim, he manifested in them (established in them) *the character and attributes of God*. That was before Pentecost and their receiving of the Holy Spirit within them! If they could manifest the character and attributes of God *without* yet having the Holy Spirit, we can surely do so *with* the Holy Spirit. Jesus asked our Father for this during that same prayer:

John 17:20-21

20 "I do not ask for these only, but also for those who will believe in me through their word, 21 that they may all be one, just as you, Father, are in me, and I in you, that they also may be in us, so that the world may believe that you have sent me.

Colossians 3:17

17 And whatever you do, in word or deed, do everything in the name (in the power of the Presence, character & attributes) of the Lord Jesus, giving thanks to God the Father through him.

We are Present *together*, him in us and us in him. Any "not fruit of the Spirit" behavior is "not him", "not love". We are to be always listening for his voice, asking him to help us monitor our behavior in order that, more and more, we will love wholly and love only, doing everything *with* him, in the power of his Presence, consistent with the character & attributes of the Father as seen in the life of our Lord Jesus, giving thanks to God the Father through him. This requires the bending of our will to his - including the aligning of our hearts, souls and minds – that he manifest himself to us, establishing himself *in* us. One with him, he will regenerate our hearts and fill us with his Spirit, speak to our spirit, and lead our minds perfectly. That we have the mind of Christ, his character and attributes, and hearts after the Father's.

He is the One who will be helping always. Sometimes whispering it and sometimes shouting it, he says, "Look how special you are! I made you for a purpose, with passion and giftedness to help you know with great certainty! Be one with me, your heart fully after my heart! Listen to my Spirit in your spirit that your mind may know how to proceed! Love, risk rejection, give selflessly! My Spirit is in you, I am teaching you to give, for my supply will replenish you! Love! Serve! Reconcile! My sheep know my voice and follow me! Learn my ways that you may have a joyful life, and have it abundantly! Listen, look and do as I did, the Father accomplishing his Works within me!"

Chapter Nine

I Only Say And Do As My Father Tells Me

Deuteronomy 18:18
I will raise up for them a prophet like you (Moses) from among their fellow Israelites, and I will put my words into his mouth. He will tell them everything I command him.

John 12:49-50
49 For I have not spoken on my own authority, but the Father who sent me has himself given me a commandment—what to say and what to speak. 50 And I know that his commandment is eternal life. What I say, therefore, I say as the Father has told me."

John 14:10
Do you not believe that I am in the Father and the Father is in me? The words that I say to you I do not speak on my own authority, but the Father who dwells in me does his works.

John 5:19
So Jesus said to them, "Truly, truly, I say to you, the Son can do nothing of his own accord, but only what he sees the Father doing. For whatever the Father does, that the Son does likewise.

John 5:19
30 I will no longer talk much with you, for the ruler of this world is coming. He has no claim on me, 31 but I do as the Father has commanded me, so that the world may know that I love the Father.

One with him, *becoming* like Jesus, we will only want to say and do what the Father makes known to us. While we will certainly err along the way, God is Gentle as he points out the better way, always treating us with fruit of the Spirit: love, joy, peace, patience, kindness, goodness, perseverance, gentleness and self-control. As he models these for us, we learn to model them for others.

1 Corinthians 6:19

Or do you not know that your body is a temple of the Holy Spirit within you, whom you have from God? You are not your own,

When we think of ourselves as mobile temples in which he lives, as houses of prayer committed to knowing him, knowing his ways and knowing his will, we will find ourselves praying unceasingly. Having *become* keenly aware, we will remember that we are offering our thoughts in the *presence* of the Father, and of the Son and of the Holy Spirit.

The Catholics start and end their prayers with the Sign of the Cross saying, "In the name of the Father, and of the Son and of the Holy Spirit." I have adapted this into my formal prayer life, acknowledging and reminding myself that I am in the *Presence* of the Father, and of the Son and of the Holy Spirit. Then, spiritually face-to-face with the One who cares most about me, I am better able to be present myself for dialogue with Adonai, our triune God. Better able to listen, and better able to remember that it is his will, Guidance and Direction that I am asking for.

If you will join me in this, it will therefore more and more be his will that *we* are asking for, to know and agree with and desire to do – for we know that our Joy will be full as *we participate* in his will *with* him - believing and trusting that his way is better than our way, our hearts after his, desiring only *his* will.

Gaining this conversational intimacy, an all-day long attentiveness, an ability to wear an earbud and microphone so to speak as we go through our day, requires a process. Cultivating an ear that hears God requires education, training and discernment to know when it is his Spirit speaking to our spirit and when it is a Rejector spirit attempting to deceive. If we will ask God to train us up to know his voice and follow him, he will be Faithful to do it – another fruit of his Spirit. (The Love section has been designed to help you in this.)

What a marvelous difference it is living in this way versus my former ways of pressing my will upon others through blame, shame, demands, subtle coercion, threats, manipulation, anger, accusation, judgement and/or condemnation. For what my mind thought they should do. For what my mind wanted them to do. Like our Father in heaven, we are to allow people to choose, and then love them unconditionally no matter their choice. This is the heart of God, it is his will that we allow a choice to Accept or Reject as we give information without manipulation or coercion. Always available to point the way home. Our early childhood programming trains us to manipulate. God in and through us deprograms us that we might love unconditionally. The abundant joyful life of Peace that surpasses all understanding awaits!

2 Corinthians 6:16b, 18
"I will make my dwelling among them and walk among them, and I will be their God, and they shall be my people.... 18 and I will be a father to you, and you shall be sons and daughters to me, says the Lord Almighty."

Luke 12:32
"Fear not, little flock, for it is your Father's good pleasure to give you the kingdom.

John 14:23
Jesus answered him, "If anyone loves me, he will keep my word, and my Father will love him, and we will come to him and make our home with him.

Isaiah 56:7a
these I will bring to my holy mountain, and make them joyful in my house of prayer;

Romans 12:2
Do not be conformed to this world, but be transformed by the renewal of your mind, that by testing you may discern what is the will of God, what is good and acceptable and perfect.

Micah 6:8
8 He has told you, O man, what is good; and what does the Lord require of you but to do justice, and to love kindness, and to walk humbly with your God?

Matthew 18:14
So it is not the will of my Father who is in heaven

that one of these little ones should perish.

Proverbs 3:11-12

11 My son, do not despise the Lord's discipline or be weary of his reproof, 12 for the Lord reproves him whom he loves, as a father the son in whom he delights.

Proverbs 16:25

There is a way that seems right to a man,
but its end is the way to death.

Colossians 2:8

See to it that no one takes you captive by philosophy and empty deceit, according to human tradition (use of Authority), according to the elemental spirits of the world (the World OS), and not according to Christ.

James 4:8a

Draw near to God, and he will draw near to you.

James 1:17

Every good gift and every perfect gift is from above, coming down from the Father of lights, with whom there is no variation or shadow due to change.

Luke 11:11-13

11 What father among you, if his son asks for a fish, will instead of a fish give him a serpent; 12 or if he asks for an egg, will give him a scorpion? 13 If you then, who are evil, know how to give good gifts to your children, how much more will the heavenly Father give the Holy Spirit to those who ask him!"

Philippians 1:6

And I am sure of this, that he who began a good work in you will bring it to completion at the day of Jesus Christ.

John 17:8, 13

8 For I have given them the words that you gave me, and they have received them and have come to know in truth that I came from you; and they have believed that you sent me. ...13 But now I am coming to you, and these things I speak in the world, that they may have my joy fulfilled in themselves.

1 John 1:4
And we are writing these things so that our joy may be complete.

John 15:11
These things I have spoken to you, that my joy may be in you, and that your joy may be full.

Ephesians 3:19
and to know the love of Christ that surpasses knowledge, that you may be filled with all the fullness of God.

Ephesians 4:13
until we all attain to the unity of the faith and of the knowledge of the Son of God, to mature manhood, to the measure of the stature of the fullness of Christ,

Psalm 23:6
Surely goodness and mercy shall follow me (characterize me) all the days of my life, and I shall dwell in the house of the Lord forever.

John 10:10
The thief comes only to steal and kill and destroy. I came that they may have life and have it abundantly.

2 Peter 3:9
The Lord is not slow to fulfill his promise as some count slowness, but is patient toward you, not wishing that any should perish, but that all should reach repentance.

1 Timothy 2:3-4
3 This is good, and it is pleasing in the sight of God our Savior, 4 who desires all people to be saved and to come to the knowledge of the truth.

Philippians 4:7
And the peace of God, which surpasses all understanding, will guard your hearts and your minds in Christ Jesus.

John 20:31

but these are written so that you may believe that Jesus is the Christ, the Son of God, and that by believing you may have life in his name (in his Presence).

1 John 5:13

I write these things to you who believe in the name (presence, power, character, attributes and reputation) of the Son of God, that you may know that you have eternal life.

Chapter Ten

Like Caesar?

Unfortunately, so many of us are like the portion of our politicians who want the earthly benefits of being Caesar.

Matthew 22:15-25
15 Then the Pharisees went and plotted how to entangle him in his words. 16 And they sent their disciples to him, along with the Herodians, saying, "Teacher, we know that you are true and teach the way of God truthfully, and you do not care about anyone's opinion, for you are not swayed by appearances. 17 Tell us, then, what you think. Is it lawful to pay taxes to Caesar, or not?" 18 But Jesus, aware of their malice, said, "Why put me to the test, you hypocrites? 19 Show me the coin for the tax." And they brought him a denarius. 20 And Jesus said to them, "Whose likeness and inscription is this?" 21 They said, "Caesar's." Then he said to them, "Therefore render to Caesar the things that are Caesar's, and to God the things that are God's." 22 When they heard it, they marveled. And they left him and went away.

We want the power of Caesar. We want the power to change the world around us. To remake it according to our own understanding. Living in the world and dissatisfied with it, we posture to become Caesar. We use sometimes subtle and sometimes obvious name calling, shaming, judgement and condemnation to bring Division and make others choose a side. Our side or the other side. That by our influence we might gain followers. That we might gain more power. To redesign this fallen world. But if that is us, *we* are the fallen. So many of them. So many of us. Are we arrogant enough to believe that they and we know best?

And before we know it we are too much in this world. Too deep in to save ourselves. At the beck and call of those we have submitted to. With those whom we have aligned ourselves. To share in the power of the worldly.

As stated previously, a portion of our people and politicians have been employing the Landscape of Fear to silence us. Our fear having done so, they have been gaining more and more power to take Control and assume Authority over us. Our relationships stifled, we have become extremely Divided in our politics, our families and our governments. The Enemy has us on the run. Many *are* quietly in hiding.

We simply must learn how to speak up in fruit of the Spirit language and actions lest the disintegration of our families and nation continue.

It might accurately be said that the depth of our trust and understanding will bring us to the depth of our faith in one another - and that the depth of our intimacy and therefore the depth of our love is based upon these. As long as our conversations concede to those utilizing *Landscape of Fear* language, the trust required to develop strong workable relationships will be squelched.

When we are mature, balanced and united with him in our hearts, souls and minds, we may more effectively communicate with the lions of this world. Practice utilizing *fruit of the Spirit* language and actions that you more and more *become* a talmid of Jesus, and therefore a more effective communicator doing the will of the Father. Kindly, Gently, Perseveringly, Peaceably and with Goodness. As we learn to live with hearts after the Father and in the attitudes of the Beatitudes, this posture and humility will prepare us for fruit of the Spirit language and actions in each and every interaction:

Matthew 5:2-12

2 And he opened his mouth and taught them, saying: 3 "Blessed are
the poor in spirit, for theirs is the kingdom of heaven. 4 "Blessed are
those who mourn, for they shall be comforted. 5 "Blessed are the meek,
for they shall inherit the earth. 6 "Blessed are those who hunger and
thirst for righteousness, for they shall be satisfied. 7 "Blessed are the
merciful, for they shall receive mercy. 8 "Blessed are the pure in heart,
for they shall see God. 9 "Blessed are the peacemakers, for they shall
be called sons of God. 10 "Blessed are those who are persecuted for
righteousness' sake, for theirs is the kingdom of heaven. 11 "Blessed
are you when others revile you and persecute you and utter all kinds of

evil against you falsely on my account. 12 Rejoice and be glad, for your reward is great in heaven, for so they persecuted the prophets who were before you.

God gave us all the information we need, that we would not *become like them*, that we would not follow *them – but that we would become like him. Why* we should not follow them and *how* we will know with whom we should *not* unite has been made clear through the stories of man's folly throughout the Bible. Quite simply:

1 Corinthians 15:33
Do not be deceived: "Bad company ruins good morals."

Titus 3:10
As for a person who stirs up division, after warning him once and then twice, have nothing more to do with him,

Galatians 5:19-21 (shortened list)
19 Now the works of the flesh are evident: ... enmity, strife, fits of anger, rivalries, dissensions, divisions, 21 envy, and things like these. I warn you, as I warned you before, that those who (continue to) do such things will not inherit the kingdom of God.

Those who continue to do these things will not inherit the kingdom of God. Are you following them to their *eternal* death? Are you using name calling, judgement, condemnation or shaming to persuade others to follow them? To redesign the world around you according to your own understanding?

Or are you following God according to the teaching of Jesus and the leading of the Holy Spirit as the Father in you does his works?

Proverbs 3:5
Trust in the Lord with all your heart,
and do not lean on your own understanding (mind).

Matthew 4:4
But he answered, "It is written, "'Man shall not live by bread alone, but by every word that comes from the mouth of God.'"

Jesus told us that all of the law and the prophets, the entire Old Testament, may be summed up in these two all-encompassing commandments: "Love the Lord your God with all of your heart, with all of your soul, with all of your mind and with all of your strength." and "Love your neighbor as your self." The essential content of all that we are to do? Love wholly. Love only. Are you willing to be obedient to this direction? If so, it is to your benefit. He will manifest himself to you and lead you into Joy.

Later in John 13:34-35, Jesus gave us one more commandment, *"A new commandment I give to you, that you love one another: just as I have loved you, you also are to love one another. By this all people will know that you are my talmidim, if you have love for one another."* To accomplish these three commandments we need to agree with the Holy Spirit to will and to do in our lives. To conform us, to transform us, to grow us, to change us and to bring to us the abundant life - that our Joy may be full.

Chapter Eleven

There Is Nothing New Under The Sun

Ecclesiastes 1:9
What has been is what will be, and what has been done is what will be done, and there is nothing new under the sun.

During the Greek occupation of Israel from 300BC to 150 BC, the relatively new Sadducee sect adopted the culture of their Greek occupiers, merging with them so as to gain governing support over the Jews.

Then, around 200BC, to counter the Sadducees growing departure from Judaism, the Pharisees birthed a new sect. In it, they initiated a distinct and *opposing* religious movement that did not embrace Greek culture but denounced it.

The Pharisees and Sadducees were much like the Democrats and Republicans of our day, each opposing the other, seeking to gain and hold political power over the people. Each sect pressured the people for *what* they needed to know to decide *which side* they should be on. Like our Christian denominations of today, they were arguing about *who* was *right*; and *who* knew *best* how to live a life pleasing to God according to *them*. *They* debated what *they* thought was necessary to *know*... and therefore what *they* thought the people should be doing.

Debates are about winners and losers,
not Unity and the collective wisdom God provides us together.

Much like the Democrats and Republicans of today, each slandered the other in Israel's governing body (much like our Congress) called the Sanhedrin. The Sanhedrin was composed of Pharisees, Sadducees, scribes and elders. These are the Jewish politicians who later conjured up the accusations against Jesus that he be put to death.

In 150-100BC, God responded by initiating the Rabbinic/Talmidic way in the small area of Bethsaida, Korazin, and Capernaum on the northern end of the Sea of Galilee. The Rabbinic/Talmidic way didn't exist anywhere else in Israel at that time. The role of the rabbi in Jesus' day, was to teach the people *how* to live a life pleasing to God.

It is also at this time that children began to learn to read and write by memorizing and copying the torah. All of this was to prepare the people of these small towns for Jesus' teaching later upon his arrival.

Then came Rabbi Jesus to oppose the politically Religious and the Religiously political. As a rabbi, He taught, trained, *simplified* and lived out *how to live a life pleasing to God... HOW*. Contrary to the *what to know and what to do* of the Pharisees and Sadducees.

If you live a life pleasing to God, your life and the lives of those around you will be better.

Jesus continually pointed to the criticality of a personal relationship with God the Father. In Conversational Learning, he explained how the meaning of all scripture pointed to *how to live in right relationship with God.* He spoke of it in Conversational Learning in all of the synagogues on the sabbath; in Conversational Rabbinic/Talmidic Learning with the twelve; and by piquing the people's interest through his preaching in public - that they might want to know more and more - and be drawn in to Conversational Learning themselves. (We will go into great detail about this in the chapter: The Two-Way Conversation.)

Jesus did not have anything good to say about the Pharisees and Sadducees - and now here *we* are *again* - being pressured by the various religions of our day. Much like the Pharisee and Sadducee sects of that day, our 250 Christian denominations are dividing us into Democrats and Republicans - each telling us that we would all be better off if we would just follow *them*. King Solomon famously said, "What has been is what will be, and what has been done is what will be done, and there is nothing new under the sun." This has been repeated over and over forever since with the words: Those who do not learn from history are condemned to repeat it.

Now, like the Old Testament people of *that* day, most of these Politics and Religions are using our bibles against us to try to influence us for political power - for the ability to Control us, and so Direct our country's future. And unfortunately, so very many of our well-intentioned pastors are pawns in the game. (We will discuss this in great detail in the chapter: Never Talk About Politics Or Religion.)

Come, let us reason together:

Titus 3:10
As for a person who stirs up division, after warning him once and then twice, have nothing more to do with him,

Matthew 18:21-22
21 Then Peter came up and said to him, "Lord, how often will my brother sin against me, and I forgive him? As many as seven times?"
22 Jesus said to him, "I do not say to you seven times, but seventy-seven times.

John 13:34-35
34 Jesus gave us one more commandment, "A new commandment I give to you, that you love one another: just as I have loved you, you also are to love one another. 35 By this all people will know that you are my talmidim, if you have love for one another."

Isaiah 1:18
"Come now, let us reason together, says the Lord: though your sins are like scarlet, they shall be as white as snow; though they are red like crimson, they shall become like wool.

Let me reason with you this way. It would seem:

1. We should have nothing to do with divisive politicians, and we should certainly not vote for them.
2. But if we know them, anyone for that matter, we must continue to forgive them for their behavior, even while we continue to inform them of our disagreement regarding their behavior. Hopefully, that will include sharing the love of the Father and what God has to say about it, but minimally we must allow the relationship to survive so that we might participate over time *with* the Father as he *continues to draw them* back to himself.
3. If they claim to be a Christ Follower, the relationship may be further plumbed to include conversations on all that God has

to say about them *continuing to do* that behavior. Still, our reputation must not tarnish the reputation of God: *just as I have loved you, you also are to love one another. By this all people will know that you are my talmidim, if you have love for one another.* While they may choose to separate themselves from us, we are not to separate ourselves. We are not to quit on them unless God tells us to quit on them.

As we strive to love, I believe that we should resist the urge to take a political side. As Christ Followers, we do not follow in the things of mankind, we follow Christ our Head, our King, the Reconciler. It's not about who's right and who's wrong, but what is "Love" and what is "Not Love".

Democrats and Republicans have opinions that they are entitled to have, but neither can be totally "right" according to their "Party Platform". Without joining a centrist Independent Party, we must remain independent and vote according to the leading of God. If enough of us do it, they just might move in our direction, that is, God's direction for behavior, and the world will be a better place. If we align with a Party, we are part of the Division. Love is not divisive, Not Love is.

If you feel God leading you into politics, you must certainly go. However, the wiles of the party will surely be working to trick you into becoming one of them. We very much need competent capable and mature Christ Followers to change the divisive discourse. Many are they who have entered in hoping to bring Unity, only to find themselves among the Dividers not all that much later. Be not Deceived!

1 Corinthians 15:33
Do not be deceived: "Bad company ruins good morals."

The role of the rabbi in Jesus' day, was to teach the people <u>*how*</u> *to live a life pleasing to God. If you live a life pleasing to God, your life and the lives of those around you will be better.*

Chapter Twelve

Freedom & Independence

2 Corinthians 3:17-18
17 Now the Lord is the Spirit, and where the Spirit of the Lord is, there is freedom. 18 And we all, with unveiled face, beholding the glory of the Lord, are being transformed into the same image from one degree of glory to another. For this comes from the Lord who is the Spirit.

We must not be Republican or Democrat, or Capitalist or Socialist. The entrepreneurial mindset and the socially responsible mindset may easily coexist. Unfortunately, the conversation for the balance has become a battle for the political hacks among us. Corrupt politicians are all about power. They are purposefully Dividing us into factions against ourselves so as to strengthen their power base. Wisdom, my friends. Neither should win and expand their power base at the expense of the weak.

Both the Democratic Socialist and the Republican Capitalist need to find the middle ground where the poor may find jobs, the lazy are encouraged to work, and the country has a business climate that fosters innovation. Divide and conquer is as old as time, let's not fall for it any longer. They use scripture to defend the Division they seek among us. Both are right, both are wrong. Wisdom will be found situationally. Scripture on these subjects does not confuse. Rather, it illuminates the extremes and helps us to recognize where we stand *today*. So that we might see which way the pendulum has swung - too far right, or too far left.

"It is Christ Himself, not the Bible, who is the true word of God. The Bible, read in the right spirit and with the guidance of good teachers, will bring us to Him. We must not use the Bible as a sort of encyclopedia out of which texts can be taken for use as weapons."
C. S. Lewis

President John F. Kennedy famously said,

"Let us not seek the Republican answer or the Democrat answer, but the right answer. Let us not seek to fix the blame for the past. Let us accept our own responsibility for the future."

DEMOCRATS – LIBERALS

(Republicans say: Democrats give you things to *try to buy your vote*!)

* Hebrews 13:16 - Do not neglect to do good and to share what you have, for such sacrifices are pleasing to God.
* Luke 3: 10-11 - 10 And the crowds asked him, "What then shall we do?" 11 And he answered them, "Whoever has two tunics is to share with him who has none, and whoever has food is to do likewise."
* Matthew 5:42 Give to everyone who asks you for something.
* Proverbs 22:9 Whoever has a bountiful eye will be blessed, for he shares his bread with the poor.
* Proverbs 19:17 The one who is gracious to the poor lends to the LORD, and the LORD will repay him for his good deed.
* Luke 6:38 - give, and it will be given to you. Good measure, pressed down, shaken together, running over, will be put into your lap. For with the measure you use it will be measured back to you."
* Psalm 41:1 - Blessed is the one who considers the poor! In the day of trouble the Lord delivers him;
* Proverbs 29:7 - A righteous man knows the rights of the poor; a wicked man does not understand such knowledge.
* 1 Timothy 6:17-18 As for the rich in this present age, charge them not to be haughty, nor to set their hopes on the uncertainty of riches, but on God, who richly provides us with everything to enjoy. They are to do good, to be rich in good works, to be generous and ready to share,
* Psalm 112:9 He has distributed freely; he has given to the poor; his righteousness endures forever; his horn is exalted in honor.
* Proverbs 28:27 Whoever gives to the poor will lack nothing, but those who close their eyes to poverty will be cursed.
* Deuteronomy 15:10 Be sure to give to them without any hesitation.
* Proverbs 25:21 If your enemy is hungry, give him some food to eat, and if he is thirsty, give him some water to drink.
* Deuteronomy 15:7-8 If there should be a poor man among your relatives in one of the cities of the land that the Lord your God is about to give you, don't be hard-hearted or tight-fisted toward your poor relative. Instead, be sure to open your hand to him and lend him enough to lessen his need.

REPUBLICANS – CONSERVATIVES

(Democrats say: Republicans are *heartless, cold* and *cruel*!)

* 2 Thessalonians 3:10-12 For even when we were with you, we would give you this command: If anyone is not willing to work, let him not eat. We hear that some among you are idle and disruptive. They are not busy; they are busybodies. Such people we command and urge in the Lord Jesus Christ to settle down and earn the food they eat.
* Proverbs 18:9 - Whoever is lazy regarding his work is also a brother to the master of destruction.
* Proverbs 21:25 The desire of the sluggard kills him, for his hands refuse to labor.
* Ephesians 4:27-28 and give no opportunity to the devil. Let the thief no longer steal, but rather let him labor, doing honest work with his own hands, so that he may have something to share with anyone in need.
* Proverbs 12:11 - The one who works his field will have plenty of food, but whoever chases daydreams lacks wisdom.
* Proverbs 10:4 - Idle hands bring poverty, but hard-working hands lead to wealth.
* Ecclesiastes 10:18 Because of laziness the roof caves in, and because of idle hands the house leaks.
* Ephesians 5:15-17 Be very careful, then, how you live—not as unwise but as wise, making the most of every opportunity, because the days are evil. Therefore do not be foolish, but understand what the Lord's will is.
* 1 Thessalonians 4:11-12- aspire to lead a quiet life, to attend to your own business, and to work with your own hands, as we commanded you. In this way you will live a decent life before outsiders and not be in need.
* Proverbs 21:25 The craving of a sluggard will be the death of him, because his hands refuse to work.
* 1 Timothy 5:8-9 But if someone does not provide for his own, especially his own family, he has denied the faith and is worse than an unbeliever. No widow should be *put on the list* unless she is at least sixty years old, was the wife of one husband,
* John 4:34 Jesus said to them, "My food is to do the will of him who sent me and to accomplish his work."

At the extremes, both Democrat and Republican are correct about the other. At the extremes, Democrats are out of balance with Hearts that won't Think, and Republicans as Thinkers without Hearts.

But Wisdom may be found by those seeking balance situationally:
We must give gracious and undying support to
those who are unable to care for themselves.

We must not enable the Foolish or lazy person who can work but will not to continue to prey upon the sympathies of others for their income.

Is God a Democrat or a Republican? Neither! Both! Love requires discernment and Wisdom. What is the situation? What is the trend?

Which direction is the government pendulum swinging? Too far right? Too far left? Too much heart? Too much mind?

Where is the Wisdom? What is in the best interest of the people of the future? What is in the best interest of the people of today?

There is a difference between unconditional agape love and enablement. Like God, we are to provide the information. Like God, we are to allow others to make their own choice, no matter how Foolish – and continue to love them unconditionally. One of the expressions of that love is to allow them to go out and learn on their own what they have chosen not to learn from the Wisdom of God and others. Enablement *saves them quickly* such that they learn little and so "continue to" repeat their folly.

The Foolish have a habit of looking for the easy way out, of not truly changing the way they live, and to look for a bailout from those certain people who are confused about the difference between love and enablement. Our love should strengthen, support the maturation of others, and allow them to reap the reward or consequences of their actions. Agape love does not *save them quickly* and enable the continuation of Foolish behavior.

Decades ago, Democrat President Bill Clinton & Republican Speaker of the House Newt Gingerich crafted a reform to balance welfare policy that easily passed through Congress. It included work requirements for certain categories of the people receiving checks so that they not become *dependent* upon that financial support but remain motivated to find work. This, because it had been proven that a significant portion of welfare assisted homes had become satisfied in working the welfare system *rather* than a job. Then, as their children learned how to work the system and did, their children's children utilized it as well.

Exodus 34:7b
The sins (the ways) of the parents are passed down to the third and fourth generation.

The work requirements were effective in motivating people to return to employment while helping children to realize the value of a good education and its importance in attaining financial stability.

Give us situational Wisdom in our welfare policies, O God! Our children are at stake. Our nation is at stake.

For decades now, surveys identify that roughly 7 out of 8 of our people are dissatisfied with those in Congress. Nonetheless, when our elections come around, the Fear Mongerers convince us to keep our existing politician, Slandering that the candidate on the other side is such a huge threat to democracy, fairness and the will of the people. As they utilize the Landscape of Fear and the sowing of Division and Discord to win, isn't it clear that we are more committed to the *party* than we are the *person*? Rather than seeking the truth and selecting the Wise from the middle, *we* are the problem as we fall for their personal propaganda and the media propaganda, biased to manipulate and attempt to Control outcomes.

We very badly need competent capable and mature Christ Followers to change the Divisive discourse to respectful iron-sharpening-iron conversations that represent the will of the people. As it is, the tail (the politicians) is wagging the dog (the people) and their Divisive rhetoric continually results in their retention of power. Though Congressional Term Limits are desired by 70% of the nation, the politicians themselves have to vote to make that happen – and they never do. A movement is underway to bring that vote, but pressure from the voters will be required before they will actually approve it. If approved, politicians will no longer have any ability to amass power, and will hopefully instead be motivated to serve rather than stonewall while they are there – and that will enable the depth of iron- sharpening-iron conversations that we are unable to get now.

Chapter Thirteen

The Wise, The Fool And The Corrupt

Earlier we made mention of Jesus and Old Testament scripture describing that there are really only three types of people in this world: the Wise, the Fool and the Corrupt. Wise people have twin dreams: One for their own financial stability and the other to grow in the ability to share themselves and their possessions with others. If we only look to our financial stability in the success we seek, we will miss the other half of who we are to be. You may have great knowledge and even great wealth, but without Wisdom, you are a Fool and maybe even Corrupt.

The accumulation of knowledge and wealth are for the express purpose of sharing according to his Direction and Leading. It is Wise to give *yourself* away as well, that you therefore find and live in the abundant life of Joy in service. In this way, our individual Republican Conservative Christian work values lead to our ability to give Liberally as Democratic Christians. These are to live side by side scripturally throughout our lives. Not waiting to gain some level of wealth first, we share of ourselves commensurate with our ability and according to his leading every day of our lives. Personally. In addition to the money we send Caesar. Scripture supports the Wisdom found between the political extremes.

Made In His Image, are you a Democrat or a Republican?
Neither! Both!

Financially, Fools say things like: "What's mine is mine and what's yours is yours. Good luck getting yours!", and "My charity is given to the poor through the taxes I pay to the government."

A frequently heard Old Testament teaching says that if you give God 10% of your income (the tithe) the rest is yours to do with as you wish.

Malachi 3:8-10

8 Will man rob God? Yet you are robbing me. But you say, 'How have we robbed you?' In your tithes and contributions. 9 You are cursed with a curse, for you are robbing me, the whole nation of you. 10 Bring the full tithe into the storehouse, that there may be food in my house. And thereby put me to the test, says the Lord of hosts, if I will not open the windows of heaven for you and pour down for you a blessing until there is no more need.

Still, in Luke 12:48 in the New Testament, Jesus does not say, "to whom much is given, only 10% (the tithe) is required." Rather, he says:

Luke 12:48b

Everyone to whom much was given, of him much will be required, and from him to whom they entrusted much, they will demand the more.

Psalm 24:1 and over twenty other scripture references, however, clarify that *none of it* is actually ours. Rather, it is all his – including our very selves.

Psalm 24:1

The earth is the Lord's and the fullness thereof,
the world and those who dwell therein,

Our lives and all we have are his, on loan to us during the *finite period of offering*. His desire is to lead us into financial stability and an intimate relationship with him so that we may be a *flow through* from himself to others. Blessed to be a blessing. Knowledge *and* wealth by the power of the Holy Spirit.

John 7:38-39

38 Whoever believes in me, as the Scripture has said, 'Out of his heart will flow rivers of living water.'" 39 Now this he said about the Spirit, whom those who believed in him were to receive, for as yet the Spirit had not been given, because Jesus was not yet glorified.

Made In His Image, are you a Democrat or a Republican? Neither! Both! Unfortunately, the evidence in more and more lives is their allegiance to Democrat *or* Republican and Socialist *or* Capitalist (or Libertarian or Catholic or Lutheran or Baptist or Buddhist or Pentecostal or Muslim or Assembly of God or Hindu or Jehovah's Witness or Mormon or Presbyterian or Methodist or ...) than Christ Follower and talmid of Jesus Christ.

Attempting to change the world around us according to *our* understanding of it assumes that we are wiser than God. Aligning ourselves to do so with any, other than the Creator himself, makes us a part of the problem as we behave in ways that press our will upon those around us.

As the various religious Divisions of Catholic and Lutheran and Baptist and Buddhist and Pentecostal and Muslim and Assembly of God and Hindu and Jehovah's Witness and Mormon and Presbyterian and Methodist and Republican and Democrat and Libertarian *et al* tell others to follow *them*, they arrogantly state that *they* have the *best* understanding of who God is and what God wants. As they Divide us against ourselves, too frequently there is not respectful Dialogue but rather Divisional desire – that they might increase their Power Base. Relational loss results, as does a growing national disunity.

Until we see that ourselves and all we have are his, and that he Directs each of us to share of ourselves <u>according to his Leading</u>, we will continue to retain a measure of self-focus – and to some degree be deceived – influenced by the powers of Darkness.

In Galatians 5 where it tells us the behaviors we must stop doing, it also states "…and things like these." So let me expand on this list with "things like these" that are more common words for us: anger, judgment, condemnation, pride, blame, resentment, vengeance, coercion, subtle manipulation, deception, shaming, efforts to demand, command & control, retribution, selfishness & refusals to give, accusation, rationalization, lies, retaliation, lust, trickery, excess, covetousness and abuse of power.

I think we know what most of those words mean, but the word enmity found in Galatians 5 bears defining since it is not frequently used by us: animosity, antagonism, antipathy, bitterness, grudge, hostility, rancor.

None of the above are loving actions. None of these draw people together with a sense of love and honor. Whatever is "not love" is "not God". Political Parties are rife with enmity and the rest of the list of behaviors that we are to <u>not</u> *do*.

Is your church led by democratic vote? Are there winners and losers? If so, the politics will bring Division. This is described in detail and with case studies in the Leading book section.

He promises to love us for all eternity, conform us to his image, transform us by the renewing of our mind, bring us to the abundant life, give us Peace that surpasses all understanding and Joy to the full. Are you willing to forego the above lists and trade them in for the previous sentence? Do you want to take part in the solution for this world or, Rejecting, be part of the problem? It is a black and white decision. Either/Or. Accept or Reject.

****

Last week, during a gathering of those talking about *Life* and the gaining of Wisdom, several of us related hearing of fathers who had told their sons to get out there with the girls and sow some wild oats. We were all thankful that *our* fathers had shared with us the Wisdom of abstaining.

Each year over 900,000 abortions are performed. Each year 900,000 women go through an experience that they will not be able to forget for the rest of their lives. Statistics show that 86% of these women are unmarried, that 57% are in their 20's and that 8% are in their teens. We wondered together about the percentage of the boys and young men involved who were never told of the pregnancy and eventual abortion. Certainly, some will have been informed, and the memory of the choice made will forever be theirs as well.

Every year more than a million people will go on living, knowing that they took part in snuffing out the life of an unborn child. Every year another 900,000 aborted. Every year more than a million more storing the lifelong memory that they did it. Though God's forgiveness is available in repentance, regret will remain.

What is your position on sex before marriage? Is it Wise or Foolish? Is it reckless behavior to open the door to a pregnancy that would cause you to consider taking the life of your unborn? Do you tell your sons and daughters and any young person who will listen that sex before marriage can have lifelong consequences, consequences that may forever haunt them?

Jeremiah 1:5a
"Before I formed you in the womb I knew you,
and before you were born I consecrated you;

With 86% of the abortions going to the unmarried, we could reduce the number of abortions annually by more than 700,000 if we would take the responsibility as parents to raise Wise children. Recognizing that some will still give in to their passions and desires, it is at least reasonable to assume that a half million abortions could be avoided each year if Wise parents made a greater attempt to raise Wise children. How Wise are you? How Wise are the children you are raising?

The sins of the parents are passed down to the 3rd and the 4th generation. Will you pass Wisdom down to children instead, and reduce the number of people who *become* statistics?

Following with eyes & ears that see & hear, and hearts after the Father; taught and trained by Jesus in the character and attributes of the mind of Christ; and strengthened and led by the Holy Spirit – one with God – *we and they* will be able to choose Wisely.

Pray for the children – and our parenting! Explain well in advance how selfish Rejectors will advise for indulging in sex before marriage. Help them to avoid the trap that could haunt them the rest of their lives! Don't instill Fear in the hope of gaining their agreement. Rather, in relationship with him, your heart after the Father's, in the attitudes of the Beatitudes (Jesus' attitudes) and with fruit of the Spirit language and actions, share the Wisdom and value of following God's Leading all of the days of their lives!

Chapter Fourteen

Authority Is Out!

An interlinear Bible is a word study tool that lists the original Hebrew or Greek word and the corresponding English word below it. It is not a translation, but a way to see how a Bible was translated into English or any other language.

In a search for the English word authority, what we find in the original language is that it is only ever used as it applies to that of God or government. The only exception in which God's people are described as having authority is in Matthew 10:1.

Matthew 10:1

Jesus called his twelve disciples to him and gave them authority to drive out impure spirits and to heal every disease and sickness.

The word authority has sometimes been added by well-meaning Bible translators but is not in the original text. Here the ESV includes it, but the NIV does not. Though theologians say that the ESV is very reliable (and I agree), this is a case where it is in err. Interlinear Bibles confirm the NIV to be accurate. Try an interlinear search on the internet and see for yourself.

3 John 1:9 ESV

I have written something to the church, but Diotrephes, who likes to put himself first, does not acknowledge our authority.

3 John 1:9 NIV

I wrote to the church, but Diotrephes, who loves to be first, will not welcome us.

****

God's operating system functions in Unity and produces good fruit, fruit of the Spirit. The Enemy's operating system facilitates self-focus, hierarchy, Authority and Division - producing in-fighting, politics, religious denominations, the development of power, and Corruption.

Separated from God outside of Eden, the Enemy Adam and Eve chose to believe had ongoing access. Engraining the Deception as old as time itself, he has forever since been facilitating a foundational deception that we need to *take Authority* over people. His World Operating System has now become so deeply engrained across the world culturally and throughout history that we do not even realize it is from whence chaos grows. (We will discuss this in greater detail in the later chapters.)

Do you want to achieve the same eternal result as Adam and Eve?

Scripture identifies that Christ is the Head, our only authority, and he gives us leadership roles that collectively facilitate Wisdom in choosing – producing good fruit and Unity among his people. As you will see in the *Leading* section, even the international consultants for large Fortune 500 multi-national corporations have come around to abandoning authoritarian models based upon the military chain of command and are instead teaching the use of God's Unity Operating System. They have been proving that God's way works best. It's clear, the use of Authority is out! Relational collective Wisdom is *in*!

"Nobody gets to tell me what to do!" is the wrong way to say it, but it's true! Rather, we should say, "How can we do this best <u>together</u>?"

Most of us would not want to admit that the Parallels operating system that we have personally customized for ourselves is Divisive because we believe that the associated problems are not exclusively our fault. For example: *Others were involved who caused the division when we were the boss*. But that is not what God says. *He* is the boss, *he* knows best. His ways are not our ways. His ways will give us a life better than we could ever hope, dream or imagine. His ways are collaborative so that we may participate in the Joy of *his* results.

Ephesians 3:20-21

20 Now <u>to him who is able to do far more abundantly than all that we ask or think, according to the power at work within us</u>, 21 to him be glory in the church and in Christ Jesus throughout all generations, forever and ever. Amen.

He has clearly identified which kinds of behavior are "in" in his "system of operation" and which aren't. Leaders are to lead in Unity *collaboratively* - discerning the *collective Wisdom* in decision-making. (We will see this in greater detail as we proceed.)

His ways will provide the most abundant life possible. Why do we keep choosing the misery of our own ways? Jesus is available to Teach us, the Spirit is available to Lead us, and the Father is doing his Works in us – let's trust him in all things, that our Joy may be complete.

God has been clear that we have been given the right to choose anything.

We have come to believe that we must think our way through these things and make the decision that seems right to us. That is the same lie believed in Eden.

Believing that lie, the Enemy can more easily convince us that it is sometimes necessary to take Authority over people - and in so doing usurp the authority the Father gave solely to the Son.

The truth is that we have the right to make choices, and whatever we choose to do on this earth will likely be allowed by God - though it may cause us eternal separation from him.

Leaning on our own understanding, we feel compelled to intervene and take control of things. But as Bob Griffin commented in one of his weekly postings:

When Jesus walked among us, Rome dominated the culture with injustice, cruelty, and absolute control. What did Jesus do about it? Basically, He made no mention of these things. Ken Gire says: "Oddly, Jesus addresses none of the pressing issues that plagued the first century. The government was godless, yet He led no revolt to overthrow it. The populace was heavily taxed, yet He led no rally for economic reform. Many of the people were slaves, yet He led no movement to liberate them. Poverty. Class-ism. Racism. The list of social ills was as long as it was ugly. Jesus was content to plant the tiniest of seeds in the unlikeliest soil, to hide a lump of grace in the life of a nobody." (Ken Gire, Moments With the Savior, Zondervan, p. 228-229) Bob Griffin, Musings Along Life's Journey

Politics breed Division. But before you simply don't vote at all, inquire of God. Perhaps he would have you vote for the lesser of two evils – that the greater of two evils not be elected.

****

In addition to Love Wholly, Love Only and the Ten Commandments - given that we live responsibly in our communities - *the attitudes of the Beatitudes and the fruit of the Spirit are the checks and balances we need for our behavior each day*. Against these there is no law. When others are operating in the list of behaviors to avoid, we are to maintain Jesus' Beatitudes attitudes and operate in the fruit of the Spirit. When we are being treated badly, we are to respond with words and actions that can be fruitful for them – whether or not they choose to hear them. That takes patience and humility, the opposites of pride, control, resentment, rivalries and divisiveness. Would you like to be blessed? Consider a life lived in these attitudes:

Matthew 5:2-12; 43-48

2 And he opened his mouth and taught them, saying: 3 "Blessed are the poor in spirit, for theirs is the kingdom of heaven. 4 "Blessed are those who mourn, for they shall be comforted. 5 "Blessed are the meek, for they shall inherit the earth. 6 "Blessed are those who hunger and thirst for righteousness, for they shall be satisfied. 7 "Blessed are the merciful, for they shall receive mercy. 8 "Blessed are the pure in heart, for they shall see God. 9 "Blessed are the peacemakers, for they shall be called sons of God. 10 "Blessed are those who are persecuted for righteousness' sake, for theirs is the kingdom of heaven. 11 "Blessed are you when others revile you and persecute you and utter all kinds of evil against you falsely on my account. 12 Rejoice and be glad, for your reward is great in heaven, for so they persecuted the prophets who were before you. .... 43 "You have heard that it was said, 'You shall love your neighbor and hate your enemy.' 44 But I say to you, Love your enemies and pray for those who persecute you, 45 so that you may be sons of your Father who is in heaven. For he makes his sun rise on the evil and on the good, and sends rain on the just and on the unjust. 46 For if you love those who love you, what reward do you have? Do not even the tax collectors do the same? 47 And if you greet only your brothers, what more are you doing than others? Do not even the Gentiles do the same? 48 You therefore must be perfect, as your heavenly Father is perfect.

Thankfully, through Jesus, the Father sees us as perfect. It is quite a difficult task to love the unloving, but that is what unconditional love does. That is what God does. That is what he is growing us up to do. Little by little. Success by success. Glory by glory. More and more. Are you growing? That is all that matters!

2 Corinthians 3:18

And we all, with unveiled face, beholding the glory of the Lord, are being transformed into the same image from one degree of glory to another. For this comes from the Lord who is the Spirit.

Romans 8:26-29

26 Likewise the Spirit helps us in our weakness. For we do not know what to pray for as we ought, but the Spirit himself intercedes for us with groanings too deep for words. 27 And he who searches hearts knows what is the mind of the Spirit, because the Spirit intercedes for the saints according to the will of God. 28 And we know that for those who love God all things work together for good, for those who are called according to his purpose. 29 For those whom he foreknew he also predestined to be conformed to the image of his Son, in order that he might be the firstborn among many brothers.

But how can we be perfect? If we invite him into our heart, he will perfect us little by little. God looks at the heart. He looks at our hearts of stone and asks us to let him in to help. If we agree, he gives us a soft productive regenerated heart, his heart for us. In one sense, we will be perfect in the eyes of the Father because of our faith in Jesus. In another, he also tells us that with him now in us, having his heart for us, as one with him, he will support us eternally, perfect us over time, conform us to his image, transform us by the renewing of our minds, give us the mind and attitudes of Christ and give us the desires of that new heart - because the desires of the old one were selfish.

Jeremiah 17:9-10

9 The heart is deceitful above all things, and desperately sick; who can understand it? 10 "I the Lord search the heart and test the mind, to give every man according to his ways, according to the fruit of his deeds."

Ezekiel 36:26

And I will give you a new heart, and a new spirit I will put within you. And I will remove the heart of stone from your flesh and give you a heart of flesh.

Psalm 37:4

Delight yourself in the Lord, and he will give you the desires of your heart.

Your heart after his, *the desires of your heart will become his desires for you* - because his ways are way better than ours, bring us life to the full and make our joy complete. Personal holiness!

It's all about Love or Not Love. It's not so much about The Law, about what's right and what's wrong, though The Law was given to help us know the difference. All behaviors will fit into one of two categories: Love or Not Love. God's behavior has always and will always fit into just one category, that of Love. He IS Love. That's all that he does, and all that he will ever do. Acceptors must more and more become Love-ers. Rejectors need our help if they will ever stop being Not Love-ers, and become Acceptors.

****

Father, your kingdom come and will be done, on earth as it is in heaven. Fill us with your Spirit and train us up in your ways. Thank you for replacing our selfish hearts of stone. May our new regenerated hearts be fully after yours, that the desires of our hearts be the desires you have for us. That our will would fully spring from your will for us. Therefore, may whatever we ask here in your Presence be in your character and attributes, that our new hearts ask for what you desire us to ask. May we abide in you as you abide in us and, like Jesus, only do and say as the Father wills. Father, make us one as you are one, you in us and us in you, dwell in us and accomplish your Works. Keep us always intimate with you, that you grow us to abound in grace, faith, love, mercy, forgiveness, hope and truth.

Father, I thank you that you are moving in the hearts, souls and minds of every man, woman and child on the whole earth; that we each have every opportunity to come to know you, trust you and love you – as it is in heaven.

Draw us closer and closer to you, strengthening us in love and understanding, that we become more and more like you and one with you.

We agree with you! That we be one as you are one - you in us and us in you - that your kingdom come, that your will be done on the whole earth as it is in heaven. Therefore, O God, conform our hearts, souls and minds and place your desires for us within them. Therefore, transform us by the renewing of our minds. Therefore, clarify our thoughts, that our words and actions be in accordance with your will for us. Therefore, bind and loose on earth as in heaven, according to your will. Therefore, teach us, train us, guide us and unite us to more productive service in your ways, in your will, one with you. Therefore, give us Wisdom, Self-Control and Patience that we be reliable witnesses reflecting your glory in the various expressions of love.

Chapter Fifteen

The Problem Was Solved Before The Beginning

Before the beginning, Jesus said that he would leave heaven when the time came to offer us rescue from our Rejecting. He would come to earth and take responsibility for both what God is responsible for and what mankind is responsible for. What God is responsible for, there is nothing to apologize for. Responsible for giving us life and freedom? Yes. Done in error? No way! We are the ones who choose selfish interests and hellish interests, and we alone are responsible for them.

1 Peter 1:20
He was foreknown before the foundation of the world but was made manifest in the last times for the sake of you.

Philippians 2:6-7
6 who, though he was in the form of God, did not count equality with God a thing to be grasped, 7 but emptied himself, by taking the form of a servant, being born in the likeness of men.

Psalm 40:7-10
7 Then I said, "Behold, I have come; in the scroll of the book it is
written of me: 8 I delight to do your will, O my God; your law is
within my heart." 9 I have told the glad news of deliverance in the
great congregation; behold, I have not restrained my lips, as you
know, O Lord. 10 I have not hidden your deliverance within my heart;
I have spoken of your faithfulness and your salvation; I have not
concealed your steadfast love and your faithfulness
from the great congregation.

Hebrews 10:5-6
5 Consequently, when Christ came into the world, he said, "Sacrifices
and offerings you have not desired, but a body have you prepared for
me; 6 in burnt offerings and sin offerings you have taken no pleasure.

Isaiah 65:1

I was ready to be sought by those who did not ask for me; I was ready to be found by those who did not seek me. I said, "Here I am, here I am," to a nation that was not called by my name (who do not have the reputation of living in my Presence and according to my character and attributes).

Hebrews 10: 15-17

15 And the Holy Spirit also bears witness to us; for after saying, 16
"This is the covenant that I will make with them after those days, declares the Lord: I will put my laws on their hearts, and write them on
their minds," 17 then he adds, "I will remember their sins and their
lawless deeds no more."

John 15:13

Greater love has no one than this, that someone lay down his life for his friends.

John 10:17-18

17 For this reason the Father loves me, because I lay down my life that
I may take it up again. 18 No one takes it from me, but I lay it down of
my own accord. I have authority to lay it down, and I have authority to take it up again. This charge I have received from my Father."

Psalm 89:27

And I will make him the firstborn, the highest of the kings of the earth.

Hebrews 2:11-15

11 For he who sanctifies and those who are sanctified all have one
source. That is why he is not ashamed to call them brothers, 12 saying,
"I will tell of your name (your reputation and the availability of your Presence, character and attributes) to my brothers; in the midst of the
congregation I will sing your praise." 13 And again, "I will put my
trust in him." And again, "Behold, I and the children God has given
me." 14 Since therefore the children share in flesh and blood, he himself likewise partook of the same things, that through death he might destroy the one who has the power of death, that is, the devil,
15 and deliver all those who through fear of death
were subject to lifelong slavery.

Make no mistake about it: God had you in mind before he ever created the universe. He placed you in Christ Jesus before he gave you life on earth. His desire was that you grow up as an imager of his Son and be one with God. His offer? To take you in as an eternal member of his family. Jesus, the God-Man, came, took responsibility for both and taught us how to overcome Enemy influence.

Ephesians 1:4-6
4 even as he chose us in him before the foundation of the world, that we should be holy and blameless before him. In love 5 he predestined us for adoption to himself as sons through Jesus Christ, according to the purpose of his will, 6 to the praise of his glorious grace, with which he has blessed us in *the Beloved.*

2 Timothy 1:9
who saved us and called us to a holy calling, not because of our works but because of his own purpose and grace, which he gave us in Christ Jesus before the ages began

1 Corinthians 2:7
But we impart a secret and hidden wisdom of God, which God decreed before the ages for our glory.

Ephesians 2:10
For we are his workmanship, created in *Christ Jesus for good works, which God prepared beforehand, that we should walk in them.*

Romans 9:23
in order to make known the riches of his glory for vessels of mercy, which he has prepared beforehand for glory -

Romans 11:2a
God has not rejected his people whom he foreknew.

John 17:24
Father, I desire that they also, whom you have given me, may be with me where I am, to see my glory that you have given me because you loved me before the foundation of the world.

Psalm 16:11
You make known to me the path of life; in your presence there is

fullness of joy; at your right hand are pleasures forevermore.

Acts 2:28

You have made known to me the paths of life; you will make me full of gladness with your presence.'

Romans 8:29

For those whom he foreknew he also predestined to be conformed to the image of his Son, in order that he might be the firstborn among many brothers.

John 6:44

No one can come to me unless the Father who sent me draws him. And I will raise him up on the last day.

John 6:37

All that the Father gives me will come to me, and whoever comes to me I will never cast out.

God made the choice to give life to all and then let us choose to love him back or reject him. He takes responsibility for that. But God will not manipulate or coerce us into loving him and behaving well. Love given out of fear is not love after all. No, it is fear. Fear is the opposite of love, and one of Satan's favorite tools.

The scripture says that where the Spirit of the Lord is there is freedom. And it has always, always, always been true. To do otherwise would be coercion. Like his, our approach must be Patient as we Gently and Kindly use fruit of the Spirit language in Peace and Love, in Goodness, Perseverance and Self-Control – that one day their Joy may be full.

2 Peter 3:9

The Lord is not slow to fulfill his promise as some count slowness, but is patient toward you, not wishing that any should perish, but that all should reach repentance.

Some of us, however, use half-told-truths to pressure people in the hopes that their mind might come quickly to faith. One of these is, "Jesus is the only way, believe in him or you will be going to hell."

The "Believe or Else Method" does not balance their heart with their mind in the decision, and minds pressured into decisions tend to rethink those decisions later. As they later wonder, and perhaps doubt, who will be there if they change their mind?

Some, considering the pressured argument above, will block us out thinking to themselves "That's not fair! Why should I believe in such a strict and punitive God? What about people, like jungle people, who have never even heard about Jesus?!!! What about children who die young?!!!"

Though it is a half-told-truth, it *is true*: Jesus *is* the only way. The only way *through* to the Father.

John 14:1-7

"Let not your hearts be troubled. Believe in God; believe also in me. 2 In my Father's house are many rooms. If it were not so, would I have told you that I go to prepare a place for you? 3 And if I go and prepare a place for you, I will come again and will take you to myself, that where I am you may be also. 4 And you know the way to where I am going." 5 Thomas said to him, "Lord, we do not know where you are going. How can we know the way?" 6 Jesus said to him, "I am the way, and the truth, and the life. No one comes to the Father except through me.

Jesus is the *gate*, the *only* gate through which heaven is accessible. Still, a portion who do not know Jesus *will* come to the Father *through him* because he *is* fair and just, for example with children who die young and jungle people who have never had the opportunity to hear of him.

Psalm 116:6

The Lord preserves the simple; when I was brought low, he saved me.

Romans 10:14

How then will they call on him in whom they have not believed? And how are they to believe in him of whom they have never heard? And how are they to hear without someone preaching?

Still, some will not know him because *we* drove them away with a heavy-handed approach. In these, it is *us* that they are rejecting. *We* the ones blocking their interest in the love of God, when we *should* be the ones *piquing* it.

Scripture shares that he has made conditional allowances for those who, by no fault of their own, do not know him. As *The Way*, the only way *through*, he has made *conditional ways* available according to his great mercy and grace.

Romans 9:15

God can have compassion and mercy on whomever he chooses

What about the girl born into a Muslim family in Iran who has been trained to ignore Jesus, but then - drawing the girl to himself - God helps that child to live a life pleasing to him? In ignorance, does this child eventually go to hell?

Still, we must also keep in mind that he has been using creation to help *all* know that he really *does* exist, *drawing* them to consider himself. Looking upon their heart, he considers their actions:

Romans 1:20

"For since the creation of the world God's invisible qualities - his eternal power and divine nature - have been clearly seen, being understood from what has been made, so that men are without excuse"

1 Samuel 16:7

But the Lord said to Samuel, "Do not look on his appearance or on the height of his stature, because I have rejected him. For the Lord sees not as man sees: man looks on the outward appearance, but the Lord looks on the heart."

John 15:22

If I had not come and spoken to them, they would not have been guilty of sin, but now they have no excuse for their sin.

Let us be careful lest a threatening approach turn them away from listening to us. We simply do not know what will be decided or when.

Jesus will judge, not us – so share the information as God leads in fruit of the Spirit language and let them decide for themselves without pressure. For some it will take a lifetime:

Luke 23:39-43
39 One of the criminals who were hanged railed at him, saying, "Are
you not the Christ? Save yourself and us!" 40 But the other rebuked
him, saying, "Do you not fear God, since you are under the same
sentence of condemnation? 41 And we indeed justly, for we are
receiving the due reward of our deeds; but this man has done nothing
wrong." 42 And he said, "Jesus, remember me when you come into
your kingdom." 43 And he said to him, "Truly, I say to you, today you
will be with me in paradise."

Some people choose to Reject God because of the half-told-truth they heard from a Christ follower who thought it compelling: "The Father sent the Son to die for us!" They say, "What? The Father sentenced his own son to death?!!!" They wonder, "What kind of Father would send his own Son to his death for stupid humans! I can't believe in such a being!" But what the pastor or teacher or Christ Follower forgot to say is that Jesus was *also* free to choose, that he *offered* to come, that he *chose* it - and that the Father agreed that he would go when the appropriate time came. That is a very different thing!

I sometimes wonder about how the Father felt the day that Jesus was beaten and was hanging there on that cross, and I wonder how Jesus might have felt going through it, and at the very end of it all. I cannot comprehend the love the Father has for us to have allowed it. I cannot comprehend the love that Jesus has for us to have come down here and done such a thing, *knowing* what was going to happen.

Still, Adonai waits for us to accept or reject this gift. The possibility of the Joy of eternal life with him requires a decision on our part and actions that follow that are consistent with that decision.

We are the ones who choose to eat the modern-day forbidden fruit anyway when the Tempter arrives. We do that with our rationalizing minds. We will never overcome our minds until we allow him to balance them with a soft new heart after his. It always comes down to matters of the heart:

Acts 13:22
And when he had removed him (Saul), he raised up David to be their king, of whom he testified and said, 'I have found in David the son of Jesse a man after my heart, who will do all my will.'

Jeremiah 29:13-14
13 You will seek me and find me, when you seek me with all your heart.
14 I will be found by you, declares the Lord, and I will restore your fortunes and gather you from all the nations and all the places where I have driven you, declares the Lord, and I will bring you back to the place from which I sent you into exile.

Psalm 51:10
Create in me a clean heart, O God, and renew a right spirit within me.

Psalm 37:4
Delight yourself in the Lord, and he will give you the desires of your heart.

Matthew 6:33
But seek first the kingdom of God and his righteousness, and all these things will be added to you.

Chapter Sixteen

In The Attitudes Of The Beatitudes With Fruit Of The Spirit Language & Actions

1 John 2:3-6
3 And by this we know that we have come to know him, if we keep his commandments. 4 Whoever says "I know him" but does not keep his commandments is a liar, and the truth is not in him, 5 but whoever keeps his word, in him truly the love of God is perfected. By this we may know that we are in him: 6 whoever says he abides in him ought to walk in the same way in which he walked.

Matthew 11:28-30
28 Come to me, all who labor and are heavy laden, and I will give you rest. 29 Take my yoke upon you, and learn from me; for I am gentle and lowly in heart, and you will find rest for your souls. 30 For my yoke is easy, and my burden is light."

Matthew 11:28-30 NIV
28 "Come to me, all you who are weary and burdened, and I will give you rest. 29 Take my yoke upon you and learn from me, for I am gentle and humble in heart, and you will find rest for your souls. 30 For my yoke is easy and my burden is light."

In 1 John 2 above, John tells us that if we abide in Jesus, we will walk as he walked, or more clearly, we will *become* like him. In Matthew 11 above, Jesus tells us that he is gentle, lowly and humble in heart. Other translations use the words humble in spirit, lowly in heart, and gentle not arrogant.

In Matthew 5:2-12, in what is traditionally called The Sermon on the Mount, *Jesus himself tells us* that we will be blessed if we *become* like him. In verse 5, many translations offer that the word "gentle" is a better translation than "meek". What we therefore find is a connection between Matthew 5 and Matthew 11 and that it is his desire for us to *become like him in gentleness and humility*.

Matthew 5:2-12

2 And he opened his mouth and taught them, saying:
3 "Blessed are the poor in spirit, for theirs is the kingdom of heaven.
4 "Blessed are those who mourn, for they shall be comforted.
5 "Blessed are the meek, for they shall inherit the earth.
6 "Blessed are those who hunger and thirst for righteousness,
for they shall be satisfied.
7 "Blessed are the merciful, for they shall receive mercy.
8 "Blessed are the pure in heart, for they shall see God.
9 "Blessed are the peacemakers, for they shall be called sons of God.
10 "Blessed are those who are persecuted for righteousness' sake,
for theirs is the kingdom of heaven.
11 "Blessed are you when others revile you and persecute you and
utter all kinds of evil against you falsely on my account. 12 Rejoice and
be glad, for your reward is great in heaven, for so they persecuted
the prophets who were before you.

Jesus said, "Take my yoke upon you and learn from me, for I am gentle and lowly (humble) in heart, and you will find rest for your souls." He was lowly, poor in spirit, humble, gentle and a man of sorrows. A portion of his yolk for us as we *become more and more like him* are these attitudes of his.

Like Jesus, we may be simultaneously poor in spirit and joyful because we know the Father will never cease to be actively drawing every person closer and closer to himself, that none should perish. Knowing he is using all things for good, the Joy of the Lord is our strength! (Romans 8:28-29, 2 Peter 3:9, Nehemiah 8:10b)

Have you noticed that Jesus' attitudes in the Beatitudes build upon one another even as they promise blessing? If we will consider the order of his promises to bless, we may see that there is a progression that may be characterized in prayer. *That more and more we become like him in our attitudes…*

Jesus' Attitudes: The Attitudes to "Be In"

- *Be poor in spirit, be humble, don't think so much about yourself!*
- *When you mourn, be comforted by a Big Picture understanding of why you are here, that life is short and that eternity with God awaits.*

- *Be meek: gentleness as a way of life.*
- *Hunger and thirst for righteousness. Pray as Jesus taught us to pray: Give us justice against our adversaries, O God, and send your laborers to them that they repent and come into right relationship with you. Do your works in us and make us effective laborers, too! Flow your gentle righteousness through us to others and accomplish your will.*
- *Be merciful, and receive mercy!*
- *Be pure in heart, overcome the temptations of anger.*
- *Be a peacemaker, child of God!*
- *When you are persecuted for righteousness' sake, as God flows his gentle righteousness through you to others; when others revile you and persecute you and utter all kinds of evil against you falsely on his account; rejoice and be glad, for your reward is great in heaven, for so they persecuted the prophets who were before you!*

… that we *better and better* respond to others in fruit of the Spirit language and actions:

O Adonai, my spirit is lowly as I ache for the spiritually lost. Knowing it is you in me that strengthens and saves, help me to be humble of heart as I mourn for them. Forgive me if I am not gentle with all who have been deceived. As I see the injustice of this world I hunger and thirst for righteousness, help me not to enter into temptation, but to be merciful with the unrighteous. If I will live pure in heart, becoming more like you, I will be a peacemaker. Though I may be persecuted for righteousness' sake, when others revile me and persecute me and utter all kinds of evil against me falsely on your account, help me to respond in the fruitful words and actions that your Holy Spirit will provide. Deliver us from the evil we would otherwise do, O God!

As Jesus continues in verse 13, he tells us not to behave as the world behaves, or respond as the world responds. Rather, that we glorify him by *living* in the attitudes of the Beatitudes, and therefore with language and actions that develop fruit of the Spirit:

Salt and Light

13 "You are the salt of the earth, but if salt has lost its taste, how shall its saltiness be restored? It is no longer good for anything except to be thrown out and trampled under people's feet. 14 "You are the light of the world. A city set on a hill cannot be hidden. 15 Nor do people light

a lamp and put it under a basket, but on a stand, and it gives light to
all in the house. 16 In the same way, let your light shine before others,
so that they may see your good works and give glory to your Father
who is in heaven.

Christ Came to Fulfill the Law

17 "Do not think that I have come to abolish the Law or the Prophets;
I have not come to abolish them but to fulfill them. 18 For truly, I say
to you, until heaven and earth pass away, not an iota, not a dot, will
pass from the Law until all is accomplished. 19 Therefore whoever
relaxes one of the least of these commandments and teaches others to
do the same will be called least in the kingdom of heaven, but whoever
does them and teaches them will be called great in the kingdom of
heaven. 20 For I tell you, unless your righteousness exceeds that of the
scribes and Pharisees, you will never enter the kingdom of heaven.

Anger

21 "You have heard that it was said to those of old, 'You shall not
murder; and whoever murders will be liable to judgment.' 22 But I say
to you that everyone who is angry with his brother will be liable to
judgment; whoever insults his brother will be liable to the council; and
whoever says, 'You fool!' will be liable to the hell of fire. 23 So if you
are offering your gift at the altar and there remember that your brother
has something against you, 24 leave your gift there before the altar
and go. First be reconciled to your brother, and then come and offer
your gift. 25 Come to terms quickly with your accuser while you are
going with him to court, lest your accuser hand you over to the judge,
and the judge to the guard, and you be put in prison. 26 Truly, I say to
you, you will never get out until you have paid the last penny.

Lust

27 "You have heard that it was said, 'You shall not commit
adultery.' 28 But I say to you that everyone who looks at a woman with
lustful intent has already committed adultery with her in his
heart. 29 If your right eye causes you to sin, tear it out and throw it
away. For it is better that you lose one of your members than that your
whole body be thrown into hell. 30 And if your right hand causes you

to sin, cut it off and throw it away. For it is better that you lose one of
your members than that your whole body go into hell.

Divorce

31 "It was also said, 'Whoever divorces his wife, let him give her a
certificate of divorce.' 32 But I say to you that everyone who divorces
his wife, except on the ground of sexual immorality, makes her commit
adultery, and whoever marries a divorced woman commits adultery.

Oaths

33 "Again you have heard that it was said to those of old, 'You shall
not swear falsely, but shall perform to the Lord what you have
sworn.' 34 But I say to you, Do not take an oath at all, either by
heaven, for it is the throne of God, 35 or by the earth, for it is his
footstool, or by Jerusalem, for it is the city of the great King. 36 And
do not take an oath by your head, for you cannot make one hair white
or black. 37 Let what you say be simply 'Yes' or 'No'; anything more
than this comes from evil.

Retaliation

38 "You have heard that it was said, 'An eye for an eye and a tooth for
a tooth.' 39 But I say to you, Do not resist the one who is evil. But if
anyone slaps you on the right cheek, turn to him the other
also. 40 And if anyone would sue you and take your tunic, let him have
your cloak as well. 41 And if anyone forces you to go one mile, go with
him two miles. 42 Give to the one who begs from you, and do not
refuse the one who would borrow from you.

Love Your Enemies

43 "You have heard that it was said, 'You shall love your neighbor and
hate your enemy.' 44 But I say to you, Love your enemies and pray for
those who persecute you, 45 so that you may be sons of your Father
who is in heaven. For he makes his sun rise on the evil and on the
good, and sends rain on the just and on the unjust. 46 For if you love
those who love you, what reward do you have? Do not even the tax
collectors do the same? 47 And if you greet only your brothers, what
more are you doing than others? Do not even the Gentiles do the
same? 48 You therefore must be perfect,
as your heavenly Father is perfect.

For over 30 years I have been working with people from all of the world religions - in twenty countries spanning five continents. I can honestly tell you that they all agree about this: whether or not you believe Jesus is the Son of God, your life and the lives of those around you will be better if you live as he directed. All of the world religions agree that Jesus was a great prophet. All believe that walking in his attitudes will result in a better life for you and for those with whom you interact. All recognize that walking in these attitudes tends to produce (what we call) fruit of the Spirit. All, that is, except the religious extremists.

For over 30 years I have been working with people from all of the world religions - in twenty countries spanning five continents. I can honestly tell you that they all agree about this: whether or not you believe Jesus is the Son of God, your life and the lives of those around you will be better if you live as he directed.

If our attitudes are not those he describes in the Beatitudes, we will frequently find ourselves battling against the flesh and blood before us, yet Paul reminds us that our battle is not against flesh and blood, but with the principalities and powers in the heavenlies *for the souls* of the flesh and blood!

Ephesians 6:10-18
For we do not wrestle against flesh and blood (people), but against the rulers, against the authorities, against the cosmic powers over this present darkness, against the spiritual forces of evil in the heavenly places.

As we progress more and more in being able to live and walk each day in Jesus' attitudes, the attitudes of the Beatitudes, we become more and more dangerous to God's Enemies - for the benefit of the people before us. Those who do not understand that our battle is really against the spiritual forces of evil are often seen utilizing manipulate to control strategies in their war against people.

My wife and I have moved many times over the last 40+ years and have therefore attended many churches. As it turns out, God placed us in these that we might observe and have intimate knowledge of the cause of three church splits and, in others, how his ways avoided them. In each case the splits were caused by hierarchical pastors warring against flesh and blood. In the others, which flourished without splits for four and five decades, iron continually sharpened iron in Unity and respect – by rejecting the use of hierarchy and manipulate to control strategies. If we will reject these and instead live and walk in Jesus' attitudes with language and actions in the fruit of the Spirit, we may always expect to find greater unity, synergy and therefore greater Kingdom productivity.

Matthew 12:25

Knowing their thoughts, he said to them, "Every kingdom divided against itself is laid waste, and no city or house divided against itself will stand.

Manipulate-to-Control Relationship Busters (Fight or Flight)
Judgement, Anger, Accusation, Condemnation, Shaming, Demanding, Ultimatums, Intimidation, Threatening, Coercion, Retaliation, Abuse of Power, Going Silent, Pride, Give to Get, Lies, Deception, Self-Focus, Rationalization, Rejection, Trickery, Covetousness, Expectations: Which really just set us up to get Angry at someone's failure.

Be In Jesus' Attitudes – Attitudes That Bless

- Be poor in spirit, be humble, don't think so much about yourself!
- When you mourn, be comforted by a Big Picture understanding of why you are here, that life is short and that eternity with God awaits.
- Be meek: gentleness as a way of life.
- Hunger and thirst for righteousness. Pray as Jesus taught us to pray: Give us justice against our adversaries, O God, and send your laborers to them that they repent and come into right relationship with you. Do your works in us and make us effective laborers, too! Flow your gentle righteousness through us to others and accomplish your will.
- Be merciful, and receive mercy!
- Be pure in heart, overcome the temptations of anger.
- Be a peacemaker, child of God!
- When you are persecuted for righteousness' sake, as God flows his gentle righteousness through you to others; when others revile you

and persecute you and utter all kinds of evil against you falsely on his account; rejoice and be glad, for your reward is great in heaven, for so they persecuted the prophets who were before you!

What are your eyes, face, body language, volume and tone saying?
Are you trying to Threaten and Intimidate,
or Nurture and Facilitate?

When we walk in Jesus' attitudes, we will more easily learn and practice the Discipline God will provide us as we gain the Self-Control his Spirit offers. Then, we will find that the Discipline we gain aids us in being sacrificially supportive of others as he Joyfully encourages us. As our sacrificial service to others results in the Joy of the Lord, he will grow in us even more strength for our future activities *with* him, together: win/win after win/win after win/win!

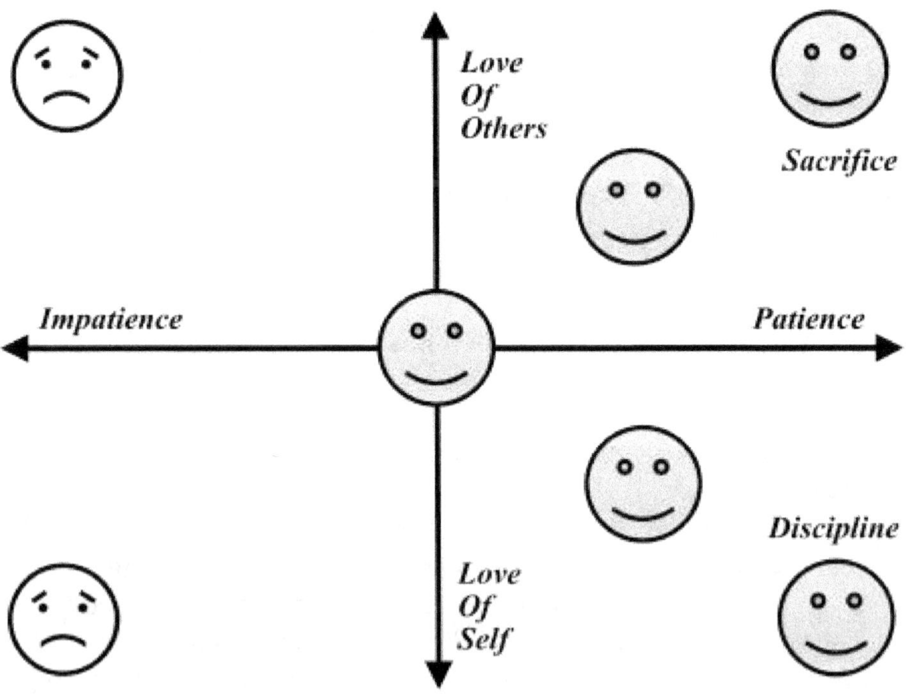

If you live a life pleasing to God, your life and the lives of those around you will be better.

Chapter Seventeen

Fight, Flight and Dialogue

By now, most of the people reading this book will have experienced the sweetness of the innocent child. Perhaps you have seen the excitement in their eyes as they learned to crawl and walk and talk. We must remember that we were all once innocent wide-eyed children who had our innocence stolen away by the actions of others. I try to remember that during each consultation, each mentoring session, with husbands and wives, in my daily public interactions and with my family.

God's fruit of the Spirit ways (Galatians 5:22-23) lead us to language and actions in the attitudes of the Beatitudes (Matthew 5:2-12). These lead us to say and to do in ways consistent with *his* character, that give *us* a reputation for walking in his will, that bring Peace that surpasses all understanding, and a quiet confidence borne of him.

As we encounter people each day, we will all do better if we will remember that the people and pressures of this world have a way of hardening us into difficult adults. Pain is real. The powers of evil work hard each day to send into hiding the very best parts of us – and bring out the worst. The Holy Spirit is our Encourager and Helper as he *flows through us* to Encourage and Help others. Our Joy may be made full if we will only follow the leadings and promptings of God! Cultivating an ear for his voice results in more frequent "flow throughs" for the benefit of others. As they are thankful, these lead to Joy and Peace that surpass all understanding.

Still, as we step out in faith confident that it is him directing us, we will not always find thankful hearts and receptive minds. Self-focus and unforgiveness are common. Years of hardening often result in automated responses for Fight or Flight. What will we do as they rationalize that they must respond with some form of attack, or perhaps instead withdraw and isolate themselves?

It will again be helpful if we will remember that both of these actions are borne of some form of Fear. Take a little time to reflect and ask the Father to show you which one you tend to use most. Consider when and where you use each. Now ask him to help you understand why.

The reality is that he would prefer we use neither. God does not use Fight or Flight, neither are loving. That which is "not love" is "not God". Rather, we are to use non-confrontational Dialogue.

The nine fruit of his Spirit bring us the Peace, Patience and Perseverance to stand our ground with Kindness and Goodness. Him in us and us in him, he provides us the Self-Control we need to Gently speak truth in Love. Though they still have the right to choose to Accept or Reject, we will find Joy in either as we remember that God has availed it all for good!

Romans 8:28
And we know that for those who love God all things work together for good, for those who are called according to his purpose.

James 1:2-4
2 Count it all joy, my brothers, when you meet trials of various kinds,
3 for you know that the testing of your faith produces steadfastness.
4 And let steadfastness have its full effect, that you may be perfect and complete, lacking in nothing.

1 Timothy 2:3-4
3 This is good, and it is pleasing in the sight of God our Savior, 4 who
desires all people to be saved and to come to the knowledge of the truth.

2 Peter 3:9
The Lord is not slow to fulfill his promise as some count slowness, but is patient toward you, not wishing that any should perish, but that all should reach repentance.

Philippians 4:7
And the peace of God, which surpasses all understanding, will guard your hearts and your minds in Christ Jesus.

1 John 1:4
And we are writing these things so that our joy may be complete.

Kindly and Gently share the information God has prepared in advance for them to hear. Then, with a posture of humility and the attitudes of the Beatitudes, wait for them to respond. Perhaps Fight or Flight, but ask God to intercede that they instead choose Dialogue. Whatever they choose, that is their right. It may not go as we would hope. It could even get messy. Nonetheless, God will use even this for good. Do we trust him and his word? Was it him who prompted our actions? Were they shared in the fruit of the Spirit? Regardless, he will use it for good - though it may well be later when we are not around. He has lots of people ready to do his will, maybe we were just setting up the next person! But for now, keep in mind:

Matthew 5:11-12
11 "Blessed are you when others revile you and persecute you and utter all kinds of evil against you falsely on my account. 12 Rejoice and be glad, for your reward is great in heaven, for so they persecuted the prophets who were before you.

In hindsight, did you fall victim to your old Foolish ways? I have watched people raise their voice in attack as they shared what they claimed to be God's will, but there wasn't any fruit of the Spirit to be found in it. Still, they claimed that God did it. I have even heard them quote other scripture to justify their actions. This is why it is so important to understand what God will do and what God will not do. God who *is* Love cannot act *without* Love. One of the scriptures I have heard quoted is:

Galatians 2:20
I have been crucified with Christ. It is no longer I who live, but Christ who lives in me. And the life I now live in the flesh I live by faith in the Son of God, who loved me and gave himself for me.

They try to say that it was God in them who did it. That it must have been what Jesus wanted. That the Spirit led them to say/do it. But it is simply not possible for God to behave badly. No fruit of the Spirit? Not God. We may as well say, "It is no longer I who sin, but Christ who sins in me!"

"It is Christ Himself, not the Bible, who is the true word of God. The Bible, read in the right spirit and with the guidance of good teachers, will bring us to Him. We must not use the Bible as a sort of encyclopedia out of which texts can be taken for use as weapons."
C. S. Lewis

Fruit of the Spirit will always be found where God is. Even the hardest of truths will be shared with Peace, Patience, Kindness, Gentleness, Goodness, Perseverance and Self-Control. Him in us and us in him, speaking the truth in Love, with the hope of Joy, though it may be sharper than a two-edged sword.

Hebrews 4:12
For the word of God is living and active, sharper than any two-edged sword, piercing to the division of soul and of spirit, of joints and of marrow, and discerning the thoughts and intentions of the heart.

What if we were to just stay away from aggressive people and isolated people? They can be so difficult! Though we notice that the person hardened by unforgiveness is not a kind or generous person, may we remember that they were once an innocent child whose heart became hardened by the trials of life. What they are doing with the loss of their innocence may ruin them. Lack of forgiveness and the spiteful actions that result are often their greatest obstacle.

Who will be understanding toward them? Who will share with them *God's* ways? Who will *continue to* participate with the Father as he draws *all* people to himself? *What* we do is not as important as *how* we do it and *with whom*. Are you willing to do it *with* him? In Wisdom?

Deep within the heart of God is a desire that we would know his voice and hear it. Trust his voice through frequent experience and be obedient by faith. Finding Joy in him as he Helps us overcome temptation and deliverance from evil, he gives us the Patience, Perseverance and Self-Control to Kindly and Gently offer a better way in Peace and Goodness. In Dialogue, not in the *Fight or Flight* that cause separation, isolation and rocky relationships:

(Name), we're doing it again. If we don't pause and reconsider,

we're headed for a Fight or Flight response that will cause distance between us again. Instead, I choose Dialogue. Can we try to talk about this again? You are certainly a Wise person in most areas of your life, and I am blessed to have you in my life. Still, in this one area, we continue to suffer.

Once again you are choosing to avoid doing what you agreed to do, and what you know is consistent with God's ways and God's will. To me, to continue to do what you are doing looks like Foolishness. There is just no Wisdom in it, but you have every right to continue to choose it if you wish. Nonetheless, I cannot be a part of it, and I cannot stand silently by as you continue to put the quality of our relationship at risk because of it. Relationships are built upon Trust. Trust is torn when promises are broken. The distance this puts between us is something I am powerless to change.

We are not to enable bad behavior with each other, so I must speak up. I am not saying this in Judgement, but rather Love that says it hurts when you choose this over what you have agreed is best. There is no desirable future that can possibly come from it. You know it, and you are the only one with the power to change it. Will you commit yourself to what this means to us?

While it may be difficult to always flow in the fruit of the Spirit, these are the skills that God will develop in you *if you will continue* to ask for his help. He will use it for good. Though it may require many renditions of the same approach with them over a long period of time, we must remember that this is exactly what God is doing with us! As the Father does his Works within us, and as our skills improve, more and more people will choose Dialogue, be thankful and grow with us in intimacy and Love. So be sure to tell them that it was him, explain how they too can do it and give him all glory!

God's desire is to lead us through each day in one-ness with him that none should perish. Being taught by him to grow to reflect his character and attributes to others more and more is a lifelong process! (2 Corinthians 3:18: little by little, success by success, glory by glory; Romans 8:29: conformed to the image of his Son.)

1 John 2:28

And now, little children, abide in him, so that when he appears we may have confidence and not shrink from him in shame at his coming.

Chapter Eighteen

Friendships: Deep, Growing and Playground

I don't know about you, but I have a number of very deep friendships. People that I can safely tell anything to, people that can safely tell me anything, and who we trust to counsel each other from time to time.

God provides people like this to us in addition to himself. That the *collective wisdom* would be helpful for all. It's one of the reasons we need to be developing these kinds of friendships. In these, we find a depth of love and care that we can trust – and it sometimes takes years to develop. Its foundation starts with a belief that you can be trusted. Do you trust God?

The Enemy tells us that God cannot be trusted, but if you will give him a chance, and some time, you will find that he is the most trustworthy friend you will ever have. A lifetime friend. Jesus said it himself, "I call you friend." (John 15:15). There will be no one you will ever trust more.

But if you believe that he is *not* trustworthy, it will be because you have accepted the pack of Enemy lies discussed in our opening chapters.

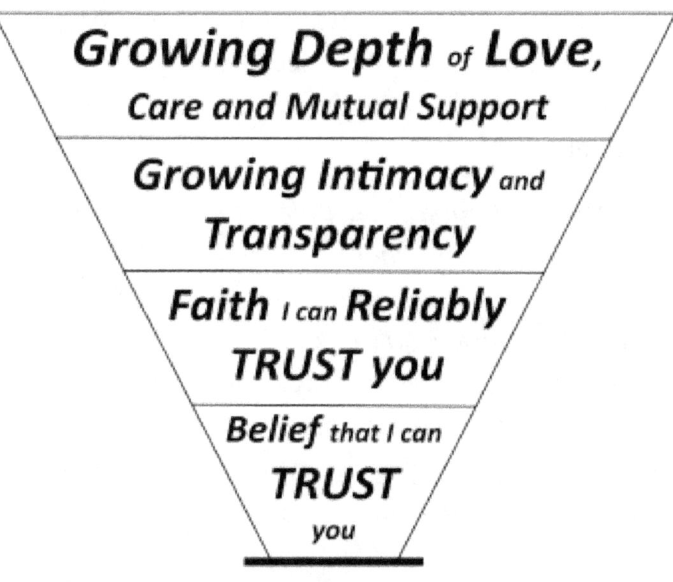

Fight or Flight will keep you from ever having deep friends like this. God included. Dialogue is the secret to deep friendships, but we must go slow. We must develop *mutual* trust little by little. A one-sided relational trust will not last long. If you risk too much transparency too quickly you will likely end up hurt, as they begin to assume too much about what they may expect from you. Or maybe it will be that it is a bit overwhelming to them, and you will raise their suspicions - about what it is that you may be trying to get from *them.*

Offering transparency little by little is a risk worth taking, though it takes more time. If they prove trustworthy with the information, you can share a little more. As in the chart above, belief that I can trust you moves me toward faith that I can reliably trust you. As time goes by and I realize that you are not using what you have learned against me, I will find a growing intimacy developing - through trust and dialogue. Each trusting the other a little bit more and a little bit more, we develop a growing depth of trust, love, care and mutual support. It must, however, be a two-way process. *Both* must be on the path to greater transparency or the process will end. This is critical.

God offers us this two-way process, and he is faithful to do it. Are you trusting him for it? Little by little? As described in chapters 8, 9 and 16? Give him a chance to show you, *little by little*. You won't have any luck if you go after big things with him right away. He will know that you are trying to use him. Too far too fast won't work. It never works with *anybody*. Slow and steady wins the race – and in this case, it builds a solid relationship. Two-way. Are you growing in transparency with him as your life proceeds?

This is a glimpse into the later chapter titled: Stay Tuned In To The Kingdom Channel:

For me, it was helpful to transition into a transparent all-day conversation by recognizing that he is truly watching our every move and is hopeful to talk with us about whatever we are doing or contemplating. For those who think of him like a penitent, punishing boss complaining about our every mistake, this would be counterproductive. But for those of us who see him as he really is - an encouraging life coach cheering us on to success after success, little by little, bit by bit, more and more and glory by glory (2 Corinthians

3:17-18) - we find ourselves learning to talk with others the way he talks with us: truthfully, in Jesus' attitudes of the Beatitudes and with fruit of the Spirit language and actions. Failing him less and less because more and more we are in him, and in creative collaboration with him.

****

Where might we best find people with the potential for growing friendships that can become deep friendships? The obvious places are the places you frequent. Work, church, a place where you "play" or maybe workout. I play pickleball, it has been a recent source of new playground friends that are becoming growing friendships.

It has sometimes also been that God introduced me to a person he wanted me to help in their time of need. As I helped them, they naturally wanted more of my time and support, and this created relational opportunities for conversation. All I did was let the process begin, trust God to lead me in my words and actions and from time to time share any concerns that were arising that perhaps they were trying to go too far too fast – to take advantage of me. These conversations required that I remained in the attitudes of Jesus, with a desire for fruit that the Spirit was leading me to develop with them. That took Dialogue. I needed to prove I was trustworthy, too, and that I was not using what I knew about them against them in judgement, anger, condemnation or shaming.

Feeling taken advantage of, I did not Fight or Flight: separate, isolate, go silent, get angry, or judge and condemn them. No. It must be Kind and Gentle Dialogue desirous of Peacemaking. That is the answer. In the attitudes of Jesus. Do this, and you will see fruit develop – or not. Then you will know if they are really using you and don't care about you – just what you have to give - or if they will share sincerely and try to make it right. Then listen for God's leading and say and do accordingly. Just like Jesus. As a talmid of Jesus *becoming* more and more like him. Only saying and doing what the Father gives you to say and do.

****

In my experience, when people lose trust they tend to back off and put space between themselves and that relationship. But is that what God led them to do? Or was it an automated fight or flight response? However God leads, that will be best for *us* to do. It could be that he is giving you an opportunity to practice Dialogue. Most often, it is the better way to handle it. Dialogue in the attitudes of Jesus that desire producing fruit of the Spirit results.

In the beginning as you practice this, you will fail often – and maybe fall back into your old ways. This may be because the person you are trying to Dialogue with has chosen fight or flight and you have been once again hurt in the trying. Don't let it bother you, God forgives you – so forgive them too and do or say as he leads next! Call it practice. Embrace the preparation for your use next time!

****

Now when I meet people and begin to realize that they are not trustworthy, I ask God to help me know what he has in mind for me to do. Is it for me to cut them off? It could be that I just need to keep walking in the attitudes of Jesus and surprise them with Kindness, Goodness, Gentleness, Perseverance and Self-Control. There are so many people lost and alone out there. So many walk around each day in attitudes of protection that isolate them from others *on purpose*! This world is not just about me or you. It's about us. When Jesus said, "Our Father in heaven, hallowed be your presence. Your kingdom come. Your will be done." He said "us", everything after that is "us", "us", "us"!

And so we need to come alongside those whom he "gives us" and give them a chance. Jesus said, "My yoke is easy. My burden's light." He's not going to give you a relationship you can't handle. And so, what you really need to be asking him is, "Is this one for me?"

Am I to Persevere in caring? Am I to surprise them with the Father's love? Is my heart after the Father? Is his heart, saying, "Rick, this one's for you."? As I've been willing, I've developed some deep, deep friendships with people I never thought possible. Some of these are folks I've mentored in halfway houses. They've killed people. They've been drug addicts. They've robbed and beaten people. They've been prostitutes. (So it was too, talmid, for your Rabbi Jesus.)

They're all hurting to have done what they've done and lived how they've lived. And when I get to know their story from childhood on I get to better understand why they are as they are: the parents they had; the abusers they had known; the friends of similar backgrounds that they chose in familiarity and for commiseration; the coping mistakes that they had made. The harm that the Enemy was happy to identify for them so that they too could say, "Yeah, God can't be good to have let this stuff happen to me. I'm just going to live my life my way."

In them I see another person who simply receded into their heads. Who lost their heart more and more as their mind made choices for coping and protection from all the rejection. And as the pain went on and on and on, and the heart couldn't handle it anymore. How they finally decided that it was time for a halfway house, an at-church program, or some other option.

I've been blessed to have some very deep friends develop from those mentoring relationships. Friendships that are over 10 years old. These friends have succeeded. They are doing well and we are doing well together as friends. But you don't know if one of these are your neighbor, someone at work or somebody that you happen to run into. I've learned that oftentimes it's not a "happen to run into". It's a God created coincidence. I call them God incidences.

Keep your antenna up for what the Spirit is up to. Leading and guiding you into situations where you can love like the Father loves. His yoke on you easy. His burden light. He won't give you more than you can handle. He won't give you people that are beyond your understanding. Whatever you know and understand is enough for whomever he gives you. And if you'll help them to realize that God is good and why evil exists on this earth, you'll be taking the first steps with them on a journey that opens up an amazing, wonderful life. Not just for you, but for them.

Chapter Nineteen

The Plan Has Always Been The Reason Why

Whether Acceptor or Rejector, actions consistent with our choice will follow. Jesus, The Son, Our Savior, The Reconciler of us to The Father, Emmanuel (God with us), the Sacrificial Lamb, the Atoning Sacrifice – is the ultimate Acceptor willing to act consistently with his choice, with a heart of love in alignment with that of his Father.

But what was Jesus' name before he came to earth, before he was born of Mary?

In the gospel of John, he wrote, "In the beginning there was The Logos." The Logos is a Greek word translated as The Word in most of our Bibles, but there is so much more to it. This word has a history that goes back 600 years before John. It was coined in Ephesus, the same place where John wrote his gospel, and its meaning for them would have been quite different in that day. This is the way the great theologian David Pawson described it roughly 50 years ago:

> In Ephesus, in 568 BC, Heraclitus, a keen observer and the founder of science, was always asking "Why?". He said that we must all train our senses of sight and hearing and touch to observe what is going on around us and then ask the question, "Why does that behave the way it behaves?". Ask it about the weather, the clouds, human beings, animals. "Why do they behave like that?" He coined the phrase, "the reason why", but not being an English speaker, he called it "the logos". And he said, "The logos is the reason why." You must always look for "the logos" in anything. So when you study life, bios, look for the bio-logos. We call that biology. Studying the weather, look for the meteor-logos: meteorology. When you study the animals, look for the zoo-logos: zoology. Every branch of science is looking for "the logos", "the reason why" things are as they are. So if we are students of the way the human psyche behaves we call it psyche-logos: psychology. Or as students of the way society behaves we call it sociology, socio-logos. Every branch of science is based upon

Heraclitus' logos: the reason why. But the snag with science, is that each only look at a very small part of reality, and develop their own jargon and language - which cuts off the flow of communication between everybody else.

John was saying that we must ask the reason why for all of it at once. What is the reason why it is *all* here?

John, in Ephesus, knew full well that the people of Ephesus, as well as the whole region, knew the history of this man Heraclitus. For them the Logos, capital "L" to indicate a person, would very clearly indicate his meaning be that *the reason why for it all was in existence before any of it was made*.

The three main translation options for logos in the Greek include "the reason why", "the plan" and "the word". Try the other two on for size below:

John 1:1-5
1 In the beginning was The Reason Why, and The Reason Why was with God, and The Reason Why was God. 2 He was in the beginning with God. 3 All things were made through him, and without him was not any thing made that was made. 4 In him was life, and the life was the light of men. 5 The light shines in the darkness, and the darkness has not overcome it.

John 1:1-5
1 In the beginning was The Plan, and The Plan was with God, and The Plan was God. 2 He was in the beginning with God. 3 All things were made through him, and without him was not any thing made that was made. 4 In him was life, and the life was the light of men. 5 The light shines in the darkness, and the darkness has not overcome it.

The answer to "why" about all of it at once is Jesus. He is "The Logos", "The Reason Why", "The Plan" for reconciling us back to The Father, and "The Word" of God.

All of creation belongs to the Son. He is The Reason Why we are here. That The Reason Why would be the one to come, take responsibility for God and Man as the God-Man and reconcile us to the

Father. That the Father would raise him up to be the King of Kings and Lord of Lords over the universe for all eternity. But first the finite *period of offering* would take place so that we might all have an opportunity to Accept our Savior or not. To love him or not. To choose God or not. The *finite period* ends for each individual as their earthly death occurs, and finally for all with the returning of his Son, to bring justice to us all and to restore the fallen world to what he originally intended – us reigning in participation *with him* always.

The Reason Why offered to go before the beginning, The Reason Why the Father agreed to send his Son. The Reason Why the universe and humanity could be created, God knowing full well that we would be Corrupted by a Corrupt spirit we call Satan. The Reason Why for Christmas. The Reason Why for Easter. The Reason Why justice will eventually be implemented on a largely unjust humanity. The Reason Why we are able to know with certainty that this life is short and finite and worthwhile – The Reason Why eternity with God is again available. Infinitely.

The Father has made a gift of the whole world to The Reason Why, his sacrificial love as God-Man took responsibility for God's responsibility and our responsibility. The Reason Why our minds must know more than the facts in the scripture. The Reason Why is the heart of God. The heart of the Father. The heart of the Son. The heart of the Spirit given to us. The author and perfecter of our faith. The One who made our spirit and soul for joy-filled eternity with him.

Why would a holy and loving God allow such evil to take place against his people, or against any person for that matter? The Reason Why! The Plan! A *finite offering period* that ends, brings justice and then joyful eternity for the Acceptors. I don't know about you, but enduring the evil of Rejectors for such a short time seems a small price to pay.

1 Peter 5:10-11

10 And <u>after you have suffered a little while</u>, the God of all grace, who has called you to his eternal glory in Christ, will himself restore, confirm, strengthen, and establish you. 11 To him be the dominion forever and ever. Amen.

James 4:14
- yet you do not know what tomorrow will bring. What is your life? For you are a mist that appears for a little time and then vanishes.

Psalm 144:4
Man is like a breath; his days are like a passing shadow.

Psalm 102:3
For my days pass away like smoke,
and my bones burn like a furnace.

Psalm 39:4-5
4 "O Lord, make me know my end and what is the measure of my
days; let me know how fleeting I am! 5 Behold, you have made my
days a few handbreadths, and my lifetime is as nothing before you.
Surely all mankind stands as a mere breath!

Psalm 103:15-16
15 As for man, his days are like grass; he flourishes like a flower of
the field; 16 for the wind passes over it, and it is gone,
and its place knows it no more.

Psalm 90:12
So teach us to number our days that we may get a heart of wisdom.

These days we do a disservice to those with whom we would share the love of God. We give them the facts and the logic and then fight to persuade them for saving faith. Would it not be better to first share with them the love of God for us before the foundation of the world? From a heart of Wisdom? Would it not be better to share that all-encompassing, always drawing, gently pursuing love? Why not also entice their mind and ask them if they have ever wondered why there is evil in this world? Otherwise, many will not ask but will *go on wondering*. With thoughts like these out of the way, they might more quickly trust their heart and appreciate The Plan, The Way, The Truth, The Life, The Reason Why – and with a newfound sense of awe want to know more. If Love himself has led you to share, then Love himself will have prepared them in advance for you. So love wholly and love only.

The eternal consequences in view, C. S. Lewis said it right: All day long we are, in some degree helping each other to one or the other of these destinations. It is in the light of these overwhelming possibilities, it is with the awe and the circumspection proper to them, that we should conduct all of our dealings with one another, all friendships, all loves, all play, all politics.

****

Years ago at the age of 4 months, our grandson suffered brain damage at the hands of a reckless anesthesiologist during a simple surgery. He still cannot walk or talk or reach out to hold our hands. I have additional stories I could relate about others in my family. You likely have stories that you could share.

I hold no grudges. I simply remember that it is all over in the blink of an eye. One day I will hear my grandson speak, and I'll walk with him – and we will have eternity with which to do it. I will take no joy in the great number of Rejectors (perhaps the anesthesiologist and others who have harmed me) who will not be joining us there. But I do find myself very thankful that we will all be safe once the *finite period of offering* is over. *Time infinite* with God and all the other Acceptors is worth the short time we suffer here.

No matter who the Enemy and his cohorts have taken from you. No matter what they have done to you and yours. No matter the depth of the pain and suffering they have inflicted upon you – used of the Enemy to try to turn you away and into a Rejector like them. Remain an Acceptor. God is just. The heavenly reunion awaits. Eternity together. Joy to the full in life everlasting. Together.

Father, thank you for your forgiveness of our failings each day! Train us up in your ways that we follow your forgiveness and keep our promises with those who fail us each day. Clarify our thoughts, that we not enter into the temptation to continue in our own ways or return to our former ways. That all our thoughts, needs, words and deeds accomplish your will for us, one with you, you in us and us in you. Teach us, Train us, Lead us, Guide us. Dwell in us, Father, and do your Works. Our hearts after yours, doing all your will. Forgive us our sins in the same way that we forgive those who sin against us. If we are unforgiving, or forgive with subtle threats, intimidation, coercion or shaming to try to manipulate and control people, how can we expect your forgiveness? Teach us to forgive like you, graciously and without manipulation. Forgive us for crossing the line and pressuring people to do what we want. May we also forgive others who do the same to us.

Teach us and train us to recognize when we are being tempted to coerce or manipulate others that we may instead learn to offer, share, describe and explain our position without malice, anger, shaming, coercion, manipulation, the raising of our voices or in veiled threat. Thank you, Father, for doing your Works in us. Thank you that you are perfecting us little by little, glory by glory. Thank you, Jesus, that the Father sees us as perfected in you. Thank you, Spirit, for leading and guiding us in the will of the Father. Precious are you, O God, thank you that you know the plans you have for us, plans for our peace and welfare. None to harm us. Have your way in our lives, always and everywhere!

Jesus came that all might be saved. In praise and worship, we are here to participate with him in saving some: willing participants in creative collaboration.

1 Corinthians 9:22b-23
...I have become all things to all people, that by all means I might save some. 23 I do it all for the sake of the gospel, that I may share with them in its blessings.

Chapter Twenty

If They Had Known The Reason Why…

1 Corinthians 2:8
None of the rulers of this age understood this, for if they had, they would not have crucified the Lord of glory.

The Hebrew Tanakh, our Old Testament, is full of prophecies, references and descriptions regarding the God-Man Jesus, the Messiah who was yet to come. But most of these references regarding The Reason Why, The Plan, The Way, The Truth and The Life were ingeniously scattered throughout over thousands of years so that the rulers of this age would not understand their *collective* meaning and importance. For if Satan had known, they would have never conspired to kill him.

Adonai planted this trail of treasure for the ultimate telling and explanation by Jesus himself after his resurrection. Using them, and in the continuation of his 3 years of teaching prior, he described God's plan for humanity from the beginning of time. That we might understand the meaning of life and the love God has for us all, that we would rejoin his family. He answered the age-old questions: Why am I here? What's it all about?

God's desire has always been for a people who would *choose* to love him *freely*. Not under compulsion. Not in fear. But as they came to know his love for them. As they came to know his ways.

One scholar, J. Barton Payne, has found as many as 574 verses in the Old Testament that somehow point to or describe or reference the coming Messiah. Alfred Edersheim found 456 Old Testament verses referring to the Messiah or His times. Conservatively, Jesus fulfilled at least 300 prophecies in His earthly ministry.
GotQuestions.org

For 40 days with his talmidim after his sacrificial death and resurrection, Jesus explained these hidden references and our redemption by him for the past, present and future sins of all mankind.

Luke 24:13-35

On the Road to Emmaus

*13 That very day two of them were going to a village named
Emmaus, about seven miles from Jerusalem, 14 and they were
talking with each other about all these things that had
happened. 15 While they were talking and discussing together,
Jesus himself drew near and went with them. 16 But their eyes
were kept from recognizing him. 17 And he said to them, "What is
this conversation that you are holding with each other as you
walk?" And they stood still, looking sad. 18 Then one of them,
named Cleopas, answered him, "Are you the only visitor to
Jerusalem who does not know the things that have happened there
in these days?" 19 And he said to them, "What things?" And they
said to him, "Concerning Jesus of Nazareth, a man who was a
prophet mighty in deed and word before God and all the
people, 20 and how our chief priests and rulers delivered him up
to be condemned to death, and crucified him. 21 But we had hoped
that he was the one to redeem Israel. Yes, and besides all this, it is
now the third day since these things happened. 22 Moreover, some
women of our company amazed us. They were at the tomb early in
the morning, 23 and when they did not find his body, they came
back saying that they had even seen a vision of angels, who said
that he was alive. 24 Some of those who were with us went to the
tomb and found it just as the women had said, but him they did not
see." 25 And he said to them, "O foolish ones, and slow of heart to
believe all that the prophets have spoken! 26 Was it not necessary
that the Christ should suffer these things and enter into his
glory?" 27 <u>And beginning with Moses and all the Prophets, he
interpreted to them in all the Scriptures the things concerning
himself.</u> 28 So they drew near to the village to which they were
going. He acted as if he were going farther, 29 but they urged him
strongly, saying, "Stay with us, for it is toward evening and the
day is now far spent." So he went in to stay with them. 30 When he*

was at table with them, he took the bread and blessed and broke it and gave it to them. 31 And their eyes were opened, and they recognized him. And he vanished from their sight. 32 They said to each other, "Did not our hearts burn within us while he talked to us on the road, <u>while he opened to us the Scriptures</u>?" 33 And they rose that same hour and returned to Jerusalem. And they found the eleven and those who were with them gathered together, 34 saying, "The Lord has risen indeed, and has appeared to Simon!" 35 Then they told what had happened on the road, and how he was known to them in the breaking of the bread.

Luke 24:36-49

Jesus Appears to His Disciples

36 As they were talking about these things, Jesus himself stood among them, and said to them, "Peace to you!" 37 But they were startled and frightened and thought they saw a spirit. 38 And he said to them, "Why are you troubled, and why do doubts arise in your hearts? 39 See my hands and my feet, that it is I myself. Touch me, and see. For a spirit does not have flesh and bones as you see that I have." 40 And when he had said this, he showed them his hands and his feet. 41 And while they still disbelieved for joy and were marveling, he said to them, "Have you anything here to eat?" 42 They gave him a piece of broiled fish, 43 and he took it and ate before them. 44 Then he said to them, "These are my words that I spoke to you while I was still with you, <u>that everything written about me in the Law of Moses and the Prophets and the Psalms must be fulfilled</u>." 45 <u>Then he opened their minds to understand the Scriptures,</u> 46 and said to them, "<u>Thus it is written, that the Christ should suffer and on the third day rise from the dead, 47 and that repentance for the forgiveness of sins should be proclaimed in his name to all nations, beginning from Jerusalem</u>. 48 You are witnesses of these things. 49 And behold, I am sending the promise of my Father upon you. But stay in the city until you are clothed with power from on high."

Luke 24:50-53
The Ascension
50 And he led them out as far as Bethany, and lifting up his hands
he blessed them. 51 While he blessed them, he parted from them
and was carried up into heaven. 52 And they worshiped him
and returned to Jerusalem with great joy, 53 and were continually
in the temple blessing God.

And then, on Pentecost, it was *their* turn…

Acts 2:22-24; 36-41
22 "Men of Israel, hear these words: Jesus of Nazareth, a man
attested to you by God with mighty works and wonders and signs
that God did through him in your midst, as you yourselves
know— 23 this Jesus, delivered up according to the definite plan
and foreknowledge of God, you crucified and killed by the hands
of lawless men. 24 God raised him up, loosing the pangs of death,
because it was not possible for him to be held by it.... 36 Let all
the house of Israel therefore know for certain that God has made
him both Lord and Christ, this Jesus whom you crucified." 37 Now
when they heard this they were cut to the heart, and said to Peter
and the rest of the apostles, "Brothers, what shall we do?" 38 And
Peter said to them, "Repent and be baptized every one of you in
the name of Jesus Christ for the forgiveness of your sins, and you
will receive the gift of the Holy Spirit. 39 For the promise is for
you and for your children and for all who are far off,
everyone whom the Lord our God calls to himself." 40 And with
many other words he bore witness and continued to exhort them,
saying, "Save yourselves from this crooked generation." 41 So
those who received his word were baptized, and there were added
that day about three thousand souls.

Acts 8:26-40
26 Now an angel of the Lord said to Philip, "Rise and go toward
the south to the road that goes down from Jerusalem to Gaza."
This is a desert place. 27 And he rose and went. And there was
an Ethiopian, a eunuch, a court official of Candace, queen of the
Ethiopians, who was in charge of all her treasure. He had come to

Jerusalem to worship 28 and was returning, seated in his chariot, and he was reading the prophet Isaiah. 29 And the Spirit said to Philip, "Go over and join this chariot." 30 So Philip ran to him and heard him reading Isaiah the prophet and asked, "Do you understand what you are reading?" 31 And he said, "How can I, unless someone guides me?" And he invited Philip to come up and sit with him. 32 Now the passage of the Scripture that he was reading was this:

"Like a sheep he was led to the slaughter
and like a lamb before its shearer is silent,
so he opens not his mouth.
33 In his humiliation justice was denied him.
Who can describe his generation?
For his life is taken away from the earth."

34 And the eunuch said to Philip, "About whom, I ask you, does the prophet say this, about himself or about someone else?" 35 Then Philip opened his mouth, and beginning with this Scripture he told him the good news about Jesus. 36 And as they were going along the road they came to some water, and the eunuch said, "See, here is water! What prevents me from being baptized?" 38 And he commanded the chariot to stop, and they both went down into the water, Philip and the eunuch, and he baptized him. 39 And when they came up out of the water, the Spirit of the Lord carried Philip away, and the eunuch saw him no more, and went on his way rejoicing. 40 But Philip found himself at Azotus, and as he passed through he preached the gospel to all the towns until he came to Caesarea.

Now it is *our* turn. Spread the good news with Joy! I don't know about you, but I can easily imagine Jesus grinning from ear to ear as he was putting it all together for his talmidim! I can further imagine them looking at each other like a modern-day sports team that had just won Olympic gold. I see them, hands raised, jumping up and down celebrating with Jesus in victory! The Joy of the Lord is truly our strength!

Acts 2:28

You have made known to me the paths of life; you will make me full of gladness with your presence.'

Nehemiah 8:10b

... for the joy of the Lord is your strength."

Chapter Twenty-One

Individualistic Or Talmidic?

Still defiant, the forces of Evil continue to wage war against The Plan to expand God's kingdom to include the earth as it does heaven. Now they *know* the plan. Like a mass murderer on death row who continually appeals for a stay in his execution, they are committed to stalling theirs for as long as possible. For when the *finite period of offering* comes to its *global* end, so, too, will *they* come to their own *eternal* end. Certain things must come to pass before Jesus returns to make all things new, so his Enemies are working hard to stave off their occurrence.

It is no secret that this cosmic war is going on. Within each nation of the earth, the battle for the souls of people continues. We see it all around us. Nations are battling nations for the domination of the earth. Yet it seems we are all so caught up in our daily lives that we hardly realize that we, too, are playing a part in that battle. God is in the process of reclaiming and restoring Acceptors to his family for eternity, as in the Eden where he started!

The Creator of the universe has made it clear through The Reason Why, The Plan for salvation, that our *personal* choices play a part in the *global impact* and affect *our* eternal destination. Yet we continue to think small. Upon self. Upon wants, needs and desires. Expanding *our* families and *our* kingdoms, even as we greatly desire Eden. At least I know I do. I tried to make myself one once. It was a fine home with a backyard patio and gardens I could escape to when the weather was nice. Inside there was everything I needed to play with, feel safe and secure in, and be well fed. I drove back and forth from it to church every Sunday.

But it was Foolishness, for though I had many friends and a good family, I actually felt like I was alone and hiding out there - in a mere representation of what God himself provided at Eden in the beginning and offers to us eternally again now. I was listening to the sounds of the world as it tried to drown out the heavenly music.

The Grand Finale will eventually be played, and our *finite period of offering* will end. The King of kings and Lord of lords is coming for us. If we understood this, *all* would be on the side of the Lord of glory. Yet the cosmic battle rages on here *among* us.

Though he lived, died and lives again, the rulers of this age have not given up. So many continue to be deceived by the powers of darkness. Just as all scripture advises, we are not *watching* the war, we have taken a side *in* it.

Which side are you on? Yours? I know I was.

There are actually *three* sides to choose from. His, the Enemy's, and yours. Though I was on *my* side, God led people to open up the scriptures to me. In the Old Testament, it was called *fulfilling the Torah*. Rabbis fulfilled the Torah by opening up the meaning of the scripture so that the people could understand *how* to live a life pleasing to Adonai.

Jesus was the ultimate rabbi in his ability to fulfill the Torah. In fact in one sense, he *is* the fulfillment of the Torah. He is the Messiah who came to make life right for all mankind. Following his resurrection he *initiated* the opening of our understanding starting with his talmidim, and then them to us - that *we* might be able to fulfill the Torah as well. That is to say, open up the meaning of *all* scripture – including the New Testament – so that people can understand *how* to live a life pleasing to Adonai.

****

These days we admonish people to read their Bibles each day, but many are having difficulty with understanding. Like the story of Philip and the Eunuch, we need to have the scriptures opened up to us if we will *comprehend* how to live the God-led life with hearts after our Father. Like the two who encountered Jesus on the road to Emmaus, our hearts will burn as the scriptures are opened up to us. Jesus availed himself for 40 days after his resurrection to point out the treasures in the Torah and connect the dots so that they in turn could do the same for others. And us for still others as well.

Unfortunately, much of what a portion of our present-day pastor/teachers do is to provide head knowledge for our choosing in a particular *life application*. These take the individualistic *Hellenistic* approach rather than the *talmidic* approach, and it may be the biggest reason that the church in the USA has been in decline for so very many decades. I have endeavored here in *Life, Love and Leading* to offer the talmidic approach.

One of the ways to overcome our heads is to place ourselves in the context of scripture. That is, to insert ourselves into the time of the writings so as to better understand the meanings being given to them in their day. When we understand the context, we will derive far greater meaning than just reading the text as translated for us. Translation allows for interpretation, and we have so many English translations trying to be helpful these days that many of them are saying slightly different things than what was meant in the original Hebrew, Aramaic or Greek context.

I heartily suggest the 16 DVD series *That The World May Know*. In the nearly 100 episodes, Ray Vander Laan takes you along on 20-30 minute tours of biblical locations and incorporates the cultural context of the day. Please also consider Dr. Michael Heiser and the many books and organizations he has partnered with to awaken us and open up the scripture to us.

Harken back, you will find great Joy in the learnings!

Chapter Twenty-Two

A New Beginning Outside Of Eden

Genesis 5:3
When Adam had lived 130 years, he fathered a son in his own likeness, after his image, and named him Seth.

Unlike Adam and Eve, we were not born with adult size bodies walking and talking with God. No, we were born screaming and crying for the milk we needed to fill our empty bellies.

Adam and Eve never had to demand that God give them food. Rather, they were born into a system of care that provided for their every need. God could just step back and take joy in watching his children *en*joy, that was until they indulged with the fruit of that one tree.

Outside of Eden, the first births began to take place. Not just of people, but of a variety of cultures. The first parents had to figure out how they were going to raise the children that *they* had created. So they contrived a system of care. That, my friends, was the birth of the Family Culture. Culture is a term that we consultants use all the time. It dictates, often without words. It determines and specifies *correct* behavior. By it we know the lay of the land. No, the law of the land. Do this, don't do that. In their selfishness, I wonder how loving it was? I wonder where Cain and Abel learned the behavior that scripture explains followed their arrival on the scene? I wonder when the Family Culture came to include "Do what I say, or else."?

The Father never threatened "or else" to Adam and Eve, that would have been coercive. Rather, he shared the information they needed to know and left them alone to make their choice. But Adam and Eve could not give information to the babies under their care. They would first have to teach them to talk. Like most modern-day parents, they figured it out as they went, and I'll bet they made plenty of mistakes.

The Family Culture started with what Adam and Eve taught, and then Abel killed his brother Cain. Quite an inauspicious start.

Outside of Eden, we went from leading a family, to many leading families, to many leading nations, to nations warring with each other. Satan taught us leadership in *his* image, in the World Operating System, according to what *we* want, and then our parents started passing it down through the generations.

Sadly, so many of us are stuck in the gears of Satan's World Operating System, some with a God focus, when we could rather be liberated by God's Unity Operating System *in us*, with a world focus. That none should perish.

Check out the extremely well written 1946 book Animal Farm by George Orwell for an example of how our best group intentions always end up with individuals taking over as they are Corrupted by the power of Authority. The book tells the story of a group of farm animals who rebel against their human farmer, hoping to create a society where the animals can be equal, free, and happy. Ultimately, however, the rebellion is betrayed by the very pigs that they put in power to keep them free. The farm ends up in a state as bad as it was before, under the dictatorship of a pig named Napoleon who eventually said:

"All animals are equal, but some animals are more equal than others."

There is a popular phrase being used these days by leaders who have moved in the direction of collective leadership, but who do not want to fully comply: First among equals.

They say, "Sometimes somebody just needs to take charge and make a decision when none seems forthcoming in consensus." This is a very dangerous precedent that moves them backwards toward the re-use of hierarchical Authoritarian leadership. Like the pigs who were able to lobby for and receive power, "First Among Equals" will eventually return their "farms" to a state worse than what they had before. With the best of intentions, believing that they will make their organizations more productive utilizing the power of Caesar, they make themselves the boss. They say, "Time is of the essence!". But when expedience and productivity are more important than Collective Wisdom & Relational Unity, winners and losers will be the relational result. And that type of result breeds Division.

As we will see later in the Love and Leading sections, If I am in him and he in me, taking action outside of Unity is to allow myself to break off in disunity and assume a portion of *his* authority. Acting on our own is not reflective of him and his ways. Yet it is our tendency to do just that "for the greater good", to "get it done", to "serve him". But he is not glorified in it.

The only productivity Adonai (our triune God) really cares about is the development of life saving relationships. When our number one priority is relationship building, he will make us useful to develop more and more talmidim who will develop more and more talmidim, who will develop more and more talmidim. The strengthening of people and relationships then broadens the trustworthy leadership base such that greater productivity and higher quality efforts invariably result.

As Authoritarians utilize Leverage to feign the building of consensus, iron sharpening iron opportunities are stifled and the growth of qualitative productivity is scuttled. This will always occur when the risk of stating differing perspectives could mean the loss of that person's status or eventually even their employment. The allegiance to family security being primary, who would risk affecting the well-being of their family? Unfortunately, authoritarians know this and use Leverage to maintain Control.

When Authority is allowed to develop, speaking freely will eventually be associated with risk. Honoring and valuing the collective Wisdom, all may speak up safely because no one person has the Authority to fire. When all are committed to the sharing of the collective Wisdom, our only risk is in not using fruit of the Spirit language in the attitudes of the Beatitudes – Jesus' attitudes. Fruit of the Spirit language in Jesus' attitudes facilitates Unity. When we behave otherwise we are moving down the path of self-selecting our way out all by ourselves.

While Authoritarian "Time is of the essence!" actions are certainly expedient with one person as Boss/Sr. Pastor/CEO/President/Chairman, the quality of their considerations will most certainly be lacking a full perspective. Though answers may be given and decisions made quickly, errors will most certainly be made as well. We must resist "Something must be done! Lead, follow or get out of the way!" – or the ongoing relational damage will eventually decimate our Unity and scuttle our progress - whether in families, organizations or nations.

When we use Authority, Unity and the collective Wisdom offered to us by God, are not our number one priority.

****

Who was the *first* boss? This is a very important question because it would have been the very first time that one person took control to direct the actions of another. This is something that the Father never did, but that humanity has been doing ever since.

To refresh your memory, he never said that one could or should have dominion over another.

Genesis 1:26-31

Then God said, "Let us make man in our image, after our likeness. And let them have dominion over the fish of the sea and over the birds of the heavens and over the livestock and over all the earth and over every creeping thing that creeps on the earth." So God created man in his own image, in the image of God he created him; male and female he created them. And God blessed them. And God said to them, "Be fruitful and multiply and fill the earth and subdue it and have dominion over the fish of the sea and over the birds of the heavens and over every living thing that moves on the earth." And God said, "Behold, I have given you every plant yielding seed that is on the face of all the earth, and every tree with seed in its fruit. You shall have them for food. And to every beast of the earth and to every bird of the heavens and to everything that creeps on the earth, everything that has the breath of life, I have given every green plant for food." And it was so. And God saw everything that he had made, and behold, it was very good. And there was evening and there was morning, the sixth day.

Members of God's family, he had no desire for any of us to take Authority over people - and no authority was ever given. But we have since taken it and that means that we took it from him – because all authority was (and really still is) all his. Though he has allowed us to assume it during our *finite period of offering*, eternity is in view and coming soon. As someone once said, "The death rate is hovering right around 100%.".

Maybe we can infer some things about how "boss" came to pass without going too far afield. As with most things our Adversary devises for Deception, it originally looked like a good idea. Let's take a look at how it might have happened. The beginning of "boss". Imagine it with me.

Go back to when Adam and Eve found themselves outside of Eden and on their own. Soon after Eden, babies began to be born and parents led their families. Now let's fast forward five hundred years. I wonder how many babies had been born by then? I wonder what the population of the earth had become. I wonder how far the children had spread in search of land of their own to have dominion over.

I don't know about you, but I can imagine both loving families staying in close contact nearby each other and disintegrated families that spread far and wide to get away from each other.

When I think of the conflicts between Cain & Abel, Isaac & Ishmael, Jacob & Esau and Joseph & his brothers it is not hard for me to consider it likely that during the first thousand years some family members would become openly hostile to other family members. Since distance would increase safety, I can further imagine that many of the hundred thousand or hundreds of thousands of people in the world population eventually knew absolutely nothing of each other. Though they were relatives.

Now let's take into consideration that some would likely be hunter/gatherers and some would likely be farming/ranching types. And let's say that back then you and I ended up as farming/ranching neighbors without any grievance against each other. And that for whatever reason you were quite successful at it and I wasn't. And that then some devastating type of weather event occurred and that you, in your greater skill, figured out how to survive it. For the most part, you and your livestock and your plants survived, but mine did not, so I could no longer feed my family.

It's not much of a stretch of the imagination to think that I might have come to you in my emergency and asked for your help. It is also quite possible that you would be willing to help. It might just have gone something like this:

Me: "If you will provide for us, we will in turn happily provide you our labor. We promise to be as supportive of you as you will be of us. We also offer you our land in return so that there will be enough property to feed both of our families."

You: "Works for me. You can start right away. Here are some provisions for your family. See you in the morning."

So my family goes out with you every day to help. We go here and there while you do this and that. Then, as time goes by, you begin to notice that what we have been doing for you here and there is what caused our farming/ranching operation to fail.

You, in your greater skill, suddenly realize that you have made a big mistake in letting me do as I've always done. So you, of course, put a stop to it. You tell us that we can no longer do as we see fit, but that we must only do what we are told, the way we are told to do it, and that if we do not work according to your direction that we will be banished from your property and no longer fed. You explain that, in the best interest of all of us, you know better.

Suddenly, you became the first boss! And you were a good boss, too. You did what the Father did in the Garden of Eden. You laid out the ground rules and promised separation if we did not follow. Well done! All good! Quite fair! And guess what, my family and I followed you in your direction from then on!

The land that was formerly mine became productive, and I didn't mind that it became yours because I clearly did not know what I was doing. Having learned from you, I was thankful and not in the slightest bit resentful that you came to own what was once mine. My family was better off *and* had a secure future. Win-Win!

Hey, Good Boss, this is working out pretty well for you! So when you notice that another neighbor is having difficulty, you offer him the same deal I have, and he agrees! Wow, over time you become the owner of lots and lots of land! Well done, Good Boss!

OK, so let's jump ahead another hundred years to find that you and your descendants have accumulated plenty of other parcels. By then my children's children and their families are working for your children's children and your family, and you and I are long gone. As a matter of fact, none of your family know any of my family now because your family lives over there and the rest of the families live in homes on our former properties. Once we had learned what to do, all your foreman (hired from my family) had to do was stop by each place each week to keep it all friendly and to collect your share.

OK? Can you imagine that, Good Boss? There are lots of possibilities as to how it really went, but this one will suffice for our purposes.

So let's take it a step further in the next chapter. This probably happened in some way, too. Just like on any old TV Western from the 1960's. (Get the popcorn!)

Chapter Twenty-Three

Soon After the Beginning: I Need a Military!

The foreman has told your family that there is a neighbor, a mile or more away on a property that you do not own, who has been allowing his pigs to get into the small stream and wallow around. He told your family that they are contaminating the water before it comes onto your land and it is affecting the health of your cattle and sheep. It also makes it impossible for the neighbors on the land you own to get a drink from the stream while they're working during the day.

He tells your family that he has been talking with this neighbor about better ways to handle wallowing his pigs, but that they have not been willing to accomplish what needs to be done. They get their water above stream from the pigs, so it isn't an issue for them. Further, your family learns that the neighbor simply doesn't care, has no motivation to act and that this has been going on for far too long!

Well now *your* family is motivated. Something must be done! One of your descendants joins my descendants and they head on over there to talk it through. An offer to help is even given, but it doesn't go well. The neighbor just tells them to get off of his land and leave them alone. So our descendants tell them to solve the problem, or the next time they come back there will be enough people with them to MAKE it happen.

Just in case they still don't take appropriate action, your descendants get all of the families from the lands they now own together to consider options. As it turns out, one of the men from one of the families is quite a leader and he says that he is willing to organize a work party that could just possibly become an offensive force, if need be, to make the water safe for all. Everyone agrees that it may need to happen just that way. So they wait and see.

After a reasonable amount of time, and since no solution has been accomplished by the neighbor, this leader leads a large work party up to accomplish the solution. The other neighbor sees them coming and sends out a large group to turn back the work party. As you may expect, the leader of your larger work party exhorts your people to go on the offensive and your leader leads your people to victory in The Battle For Safe Water. To keep the peace, your leader banishes the other neighbor's family and commands them to stay away so that there won't be any more trouble.

As with any good TV Western, the other neighbor's family goes to the families on the adjacent lands they own and convinces them to help take their land back. They pull together a much larger group than the previous one and come back to retake the land they lost.

As you may suppose, after the victory at The Battle For Safe Water, your family appointed the winning leader from your side as the Lead Protector and he kept assembled an occupation group that included scouts to watch for any trouble that may come. Sure enough, when the scouts saw the neighbor clan returning, they informed the Lead Protector and twice the neighbor's number of people showed up for The Battle To Keep Our Water Safe.

****

Sometime in history the first boss and military general arrived on the scene, and bosses and generals may easily be described as having been a good idea in some ways. However, the Tempter has used the concepts to Deceive us into inappropriate uses and over thousands of years has embedded the military chain of command and *Authority* into almost every area of what is now our World Culture.

Outside of Eden we learned the Enemy's Operating System and Hierarchical Structure, his goal being to unite us in *defiance* of God's Unity Operating System and Structure. The one who went Rogue in The Beginning has been engraining in us that there is simply no other way ever since.

His World Operating System uses the hierarchical Military Chain Of Command methodology to Manipulate, Leverage and Control people. Our Culture has *become* his. The battle between Good and Evil continues, not only between people, but between *nations* who now wield their armies and monies in Manipulate to Control strategies designed to influence their *world* neighbors.

A portion of our churches function in this way, too. As we evolved into use of the hierarchical World Operating System, we in a manner of speaking, began warring with each other over *whose* doctrine is best.

Claiming a *More Authoritative Knowledge*, we have been Dividing ourselves again and again down through the ages. We have become competitive businesses that operate through Military Chains Of Command nationally, utilizing Boards/Elders/Councils hierarchically *over* staff and congregants locally. First among equals, some more equal than others, we have evolved into *Religions* doing battle.

There is only one doctrine – God's – and it is explained by the totality of the Bible and the contexts in which it was written.

As the centuries have passed, we have created our own Doctrines (Sub-Doctrines really) due to our pride and the condescending belief that we have a special area of superior scripture knowledge - and have used these to Divide ourselves from each other over them - gaining power and Authority over others through Division.

But "Our Doctrine is better than Your Doctrine" is not consistent with his doctrine, because his (the totality of the Bible) draws us together in Unity and ours separate ourselves from each other into sides by our selection of, and focus upon, specific scripture.

Our use of Doctrine in very subtle Divide and Conquer strategies helps us win people over to our side. Doctrines are for the Proud and the Pharisaic. They are used to adjust his doctrine so as to have a justification for dividing us, one from another. Supposedly for our own good!

Religions cause Divisions. My doctrine must be his. It is clear that:

- *There is only one doctrine, the whole Bible with no emphasis upon any portion, lest in reducing the whole I cause infirmity in myself and others.*
- *Since Adonai is God and his ways unfathomable to the minds of humans, I cannot know the exact whats, whens, whys or hows of what he was/is thinking, doing or going to do.*
- *While scripture is instructive, I cannot fully comprehend it.*
- *What is most important is that we confess that we all have areas of ignorance while we seek to join each other in John 17 Unity.*
- *None better than another, the collective wisdom he offers us together is sufficient for the advancement of the Kingdom of God on earth.*

As iron sharpens iron, we would do well to instead walk and talk focused upon Unity in Goodness, Kindness and Peace; with the Grace, Patience and Self-Control he will provide us, as we Gently speak in Love. When iron sharpens iron, it is not necessary to make sparks. When iron sharpens iron, Disunity should never be any portion of the result.

Chapter Twenty-Four

When Will We Learn *AND* Remember?

We have been fooled since The Beginning. So God put an end to it and started over after the flood, but we continually fall back into it – trusting in ourselves and our own ways.

Genesis 8:20-21
20 Then Noah built an altar to the Lord and took some of every clean animal and some of every clean bird and offered burnt offerings on the altar. 21 And when the Lord smelled the pleasing aroma, the Lord said in his heart, "I will never again curse the ground because of man, for the intention of man's heart is evil from his youth. Neither will I ever again strike down every living creature as I have done.

Genesis 9:1
And God blessed Noah and his sons and said to them, "Be fruitful and multiply and fill the earth.

Genesis 11:4
Then they said, "Come, let us build ourselves a city and a tower with its top in the heavens, and let us make a name for ourselves, lest we be dispersed over the face of the whole earth."

Genesis 11:8
So the Lord dispersed them from there over the face of all the earth, and they left off building the city.

God told them to multiply and fill the earth, but they decided to build a city for themselves and stay. So God disinherited them, dispersed them, and later started all over again, *again*. With Abram.

Genesis 12:1-3
1 Now the Lord said to Abram, "Go from your country and your kindred and your father's house to the land that I will show you. 2 And I will make of you a great nation, and I will bless you and make your name great, so that you will be a blessing. 3 I will bless those who

bless you, and him who dishonors you I will curse, and in you all the families of the earth shall be blessed."

Deuteronomy 32:8-9

8 When the Most High gave to the nations their inheritance, when he divided mankind, he fixed the borders of the peoples according to the number of the sons of God. 9 But the Lord's portion is his people, Jacob his allotted heritage.

So God grew this great nation for himself from Abraham (Abram), Isaac and Jacob and called it Israel, but as the centuries went by, they looked at the nations around them and wanted to be like *them*. They liked the look of The World Operating System - the hierarchical Military Chain Of Command Operating System - and *again* Rejected God and his Unity Operating System whereby the collective Wisdom of the people listen for and discern the will of God, their *only* authority. The story is told in the book of 1 Samuel:

1 Samuel 8:4-22

Israel Demands a King

4 Then all the elders of Israel gathered together and came to Samuel at Ramah 5 and said to him, "Behold, you are old and your sons do not walk in your ways. Now appoint for us a king to judge us like all the nations." 6 But the thing displeased Samuel when they said, "Give us a king to judge us." And Samuel prayed to the Lord. 7 And the Lord said to Samuel, "Obey the voice of the people in all that they say to you, for they have not rejected you, but they have rejected me from being king over them. 8 According to all the deeds that they have done, from the day I brought them up out of Egypt even to this day, forsaking me and serving other gods, so they are also doing to you. 9 Now then, obey their voice; only you shall solemnly warn them and show them the ways of the king who shall reign over them."

Samuel's Warning Against Kings

10 So Samuel told all the words of the Lord to the people who were asking for a king from him. 11 He said, "These will be the ways of the king who will reign over you: he will take your sons and appoint them to his chariots and to be his horsemen and to run before his chariots.

12 And he will appoint for himself commanders of thousands and commanders of fifties, and some to plow his ground and to reap his harvest, and to make his implements of war and the equipment of his chariots. 13 He will take your daughters to be perfumers and cooks and bakers. 14 He will take the best of your fields and vineyards and olive orchards and give them to his servants. 15 He will take the tenth of your grain and of your vineyards and give it to his officers and to his servants. 16 He will take your male servants and female servants and the best of your young men and your donkeys, and put them to his work. 17 He will take the tenth of your flocks, and you shall be his slaves. 18 And in that day you will cry out because of your king, whom you have chosen for yourselves, but the Lord will not answer you in that day."

The Lord Grants Israel's Request

19 But the people refused to obey the voice of Samuel. And they said, "No! But there shall be a king over us, 20 that we also may be like all the nations, and that our king may judge us and go out before us and fight our battles." 21 And when Samuel had heard all the words of the people, he repeated them in the ears of the Lord. 22 And the Lord said to Samuel, "Obey their voice and make them a king." Samuel then said to the men of Israel, "Go every man to his city."

This was the beginning of the end for Israel. *Again*. No longer following God, they lost his protection and were scattered as they were conquered. When Jesus came, he re-established the Unity Operating System with his talmidim.

Luke 22:24-27

24 A dispute also arose among them, as to which of them was to be regarded as the greatest. 25 And he said to them, "The kings of the Gentiles exercise lordship over them, and those in authority over them are called benefactors. 26 But not so with you. Rather, let the greatest among you become as the youngest, and the leader as one who serves. 27 For who is the greater, one who reclines at table or one who serves? Is it not the one who reclines at table? But I am among you as the one who serves.

Who was greatest among them could only be important in the determination of who had the most power, and therefore the ability to use it. They were trying to determine the hierarchy of *who had Authority over whom.*

Mark 9:33-35

33 And they came to Capernaum. And when he was in the house he asked them, "What were you discussing on the way?" 34 But they kept silent, for on the way they had argued with one another about who was the greatest. 35 And he sat down and called the twelve. And he said to them, "If anyone would be first, he must be last of all and servant of all."

Mark 10:42-45

42 And Jesus called them to him and said to them, "You know that those who are considered rulers of the Gentiles lord it over them, and their great ones exercise authority over them. 43 But it shall not be so among you. But whoever would be great among you must be your servant, 44 and whoever would be first among you must be slave of all. 45 For even the Son of Man came not to be served but to serve, and to give his life as a ransom for many."

Colossians 2:8

See to it that no one takes you captive by philosophy and empty deceit, according to human tradition (Authority), according to the elemental spirits of the world (the World OS), and not according to Christ.

John 17:20-23

"... may they all be one, just as you, Father, are in me, and I in you, that they also may be in us, ... that they may be one even as we are one, I in them and you in me, that they may become perfectly one, so that the world may know that you sent me ..."

1 Corinthians 11:3a

But I want you to understand that the head of every man is Christ

Ephesians 1:22

And he put all things under his feet and gave him as head over all things to the church,

1 Thessalonians 5:12-13

12 We ask you, brothers, to respect those <u>who labor among you and are (watching) over you in the Lord</u> and admonish you, 13 and to esteem them very highly in love because of their work. Be at peace among yourselves.

Taken out of context, leaders have used the selective reading of 1 Thessalonians 5:12 above *to take Authority over congregants* in the Lord. As we have seen, the totality of scripture in context does not agree with their assertion.

Several decades after Jesus rose from the dead and ascended into heaven - unbelieving Israel, retaining its Corrupt Authoritarian power, was decimated.

Proverbs 29:18

Where there is no prophetic vision the people cast off restraint, but blessed is he who keeps the law.

Proverbs 29:18 NIV

Where there is no revelation, people cast off restraint; but blessed is the one who heeds wisdom's instruction.

We are no better than Israel. We use phrases like, "Time is of the essence!" to justify authoritarian individual decisive action. It sure is expedient, isn't it? With one person in Authority as the Boss/Sr. Pastor/CEO/President/Chairman, answers can be given and decisions made quickly! "Something must be done! Lead, follow or get out of the way!" Though the resulting relational damage decimates Unity in relationships, families, organizations and nations.

Clearly, Division from and Hierarchy over, is not the culture God desires for us. These cause conflict, loss of relationship, disunity and poorer decisions through singularity. The sins of the parents have been being passed down to the third and fourth generation for generations. For generations of generations, and this has been happening for thousands of years. It has become so deeply ingrained in our ***Man***agement Culture that we rarely imagine there could be any other way.

We've carried on with it for thousands of years because we think it works! It's expeditious! Who has time to sit around trying to build consensus when we could be *getting things done*?!!!

But God can unite us to more productive service if we will but submit to him as the only authority and come together in his Spirit of Unity across denominational lines. The Lausanne Covenant, signed in 1974 by the Christ Followers of over 150 nations, espouses such Unity and the synergy it will bring. The Leading section of this book describes a workable approach for the uniting of God's people to more productive service in any community. If we will start small together in our communities, we will be better able to spread such effectiveness into other communities as they take notice of our successes.

Synergy finds its foundation in the organizational climate. As long as our seminaries and Bible colleges teach organization under the hierarchical military chain of command, we will be unable to synergistically operate our churches in Unity - in God's Unity Operating System - with us as body parts and Christ the only Head.

There is a way to operate *everything* in The Unity Operating System. I have seen it work in businesses, churches and non-profits - as have other consultants and authors. These will be identified in the section on Leading. God is not only blessing these businesses and organizations as they operate currently, he will also bless those of us who are operating in them, *in him,* at the end of the *finite offering period*.

Chapter Twenty-Five

Like Saul?

1 Samuel 15:10-11, 23

10 The word of the Lord came to Samuel: 11 "I regret that I have made Saul king, for he has turned back from following me and has not performed my commandments." And Samuel was angry, and he cried to the Lord all night. ... 23 For rebellion is as the sin of divination, and presumption is as iniquity and idolatry. Because you have rejected the word of the Lord, he has also rejected you from being king."

It's not so much that he is in you, as that you are in him. Learn his ways and agree with him for the Works he is doing in you. Otherwise deaf, you will forget the lessons of the past, Reject his will in the moment and not accomplish what is in front of you.

Consider that a soldier or group of soldiers carry the weapons provided by the Commander for the purpose that the Commander has determined. Still, as soldiers go out, look around and see what is going on, they may think that another option should be considered. Armed with the weapons of the Commander, they have the *ability* to act upon their thoughts according to their own determinations.

At this point the question becomes whether or not the Commander has given them liberty to act according to their own understanding or not. Sometimes Commanders do this by suggesting contingency plans to be used if the original plan is falling apart. This was not the case for Saul. His orders were clear. He simply disobeyed them so as to enrich himself.

Matthew 6:24

"No one can serve two masters, for either he will hate the one and love the other, or he will be devoted to the one and despise the other. You cannot serve God and money.

1 Samuel 13:14

But now your kingdom (Saul) shall not continue. The Lord has sought out a man after his own heart, and the Lord has commanded him to be prince over his people, because you have not kept what the Lord commanded you."

Acts 13:22

And when he had removed him (Saul), he raised up David to be their king, of whom he testified and said, 'I have found in David the son of Jesse a man after my heart, who will do all my will.'

When we have become so in tune with our Commander and his contingency plans, we can often predict what he/she would have us do. When we are that in tune with God, it will be true for *us in him*, too. When we understand what "not love" is, we will know what God would *not* have us do in that split second. What remains will only be "loving actions" that often include sharing the "truth in love", that is, Gently and in fruit of the Spirit language.

This was the case for David, who even when there were no "orders" from God, knew what God would have him *not do*. His heart after the Father's, his spirit bore fruit *of* the Spirit.

The nine fruit of his Spirit bring us the Peace, Patience and Perseverance to stand our ground with Kindness and Goodness. Him in us and us in him, he provides us the Self-Control we need to Gently speak the truth in Love. Unlike true war, our battle options are typically quite simple. Our Commander does not tell us to kill or take prisoners. Neither of these are godly choices. God's ways are less expedient. His ways are to win them over to *his* side.

Our Commander tells us that it is not *them* that we are fighting. *It is them that we are fighting the Enemy for*!

Ephesians 6:10-18

10 Finally, be strong in the Lord and in the strength of his might.
11 Put on the whole armor of God, that you may be able to stand against the schemes of the devil. 12 For we do not wrestle against flesh and blood (people), but against the rulers, against the authorities, against the cosmic powers over this present darkness, against the spiritual forces of evil in the heavenly places. 13 Therefore take up the whole armor of God, that you may be able to withstand in the evil day, and having done all, to stand firm. 14 Stand therefore, having fastened on the belt of truth, and having put on the breastplate of righteousness,

15 and, as shoes for your feet, having put on the readiness given by the gospel of peace. 16 In all circumstances take up the shield of faith, with which you can extinguish all the flaming darts of the evil one; 17 and take the helmet of salvation, and the sword of the Spirit, which is the word of God, 18 praying at all times in the Spirit, with all prayer and supplication. To that end, keep alert with all perseverance, making supplication for all the saints.

On the battlefield of relationships, we do not battle against flesh and blood (people), but rather the Principalities and Powers (spirits) who are trying to kill, steal and destroy them. Our Enemy wants to steal possessions, destroy relationships and weaken resolve. He wants to eliminate any chance of hope in the existence of a just Commander.

The Enemy is warring against them <u>and</u> us so that we might pass Foolishness down to the 3rd and 4th generation of our children, so that they can pass it down to theirs, too. If he can interrupt the passing down of Wisdom, it will be Fools who instead pass down ignorance, grow Corruption and block vision – so that the people perish. (KJV Proverbs 29:18 Where there is no vision the people perish). If he succeeds in tempting us to leave our marriages, our children and their children's children will all be weakened. Statistics show the best way to cause difficulties in the future of adults is to tear apart the marriages of their parents while they are still young.

Pray for the children! Caught up in the physical, and focused upon getting their worldly wants, without Wisdom they will be out of touch with the Spiritual. Short-sighted, they will never even realize that they are entangled in the war for souls happening all around them – for the disintegration of families and nations. Most know *of* God, but how many *know* God and *his* ways and are his *talmidim*?

Proverbs 22:6
Train up a child in the way he should go;
even when he is old he will not depart from it.

John 10:10
The thief comes only to steal and kill and destroy. I came that they may have life and have it abundantly.

1 Timothy 2:3-4
3 This is good, and it is pleasing in the sight of God our Savior, 4 who desires all people to be saved and to come to the knowledge of the truth.

Psalm 23:6
Surely goodness and mercy shall follow me (characterize me) all the days of my life, and I shall dwell in the house of the Lord forever.

Philippians 4:7
And the peace of God, which surpasses all understanding, will guard your hearts and your minds in Christ Jesus.

1 John 5:13
I write these things to you who believe in the name (presence, power, character, attributes and reputation) of the Son of God, that you may know that you have eternal life.

Always the gentleman, God will not conscript us into his service. Rather, he *invites* us in. I am so thankful for the many people that chose usefulness to Adonai as he Gently drew me to himself. These people opened up the scriptures to me and helped me understand *how* to live a life pleasing to God. Therefore, it is my love for him that compels me to serve him in the war for souls and the introduction of others to his ways. For the passing down of Wisdom (rather than Foolishness) to the 3rd and 4th generation. That, *becoming* Wise, they see and hear clearly and live joyfully in him too. Eternally. Generation after generation.

****

When we see something wrong going on in any setting, it is appropriate to share with God our assessment of the situation and ask for his Direction in it. If, however, we instead allow the assessment to move towards Judgement, like Saul we will be moving according to our own *Prideful* will, and in that direction, we will select for some form of *Fight or Flight*. But neither of these coercions or manipulations are ever truly effective, and their use will most certainly cause some form of distance between us and the person or people involved.

Forgetting for the moment that we are not to Judge, we have *become* unavailable for the accomplishment of *his* will for them as participants *with* him. If we will instead remember the innocence of the young child and our recognition that the world has certainly hardened them in some way, we might rather have *compassion for their plight*. Choosing *Love* rather than *Not Love*, we *become* available to God for *his* will. Then, according to the situation, we ask God what we might do to be helpful.

It could be that we are *not* to act, but simply *agree* with him (pray) that his will be done in their lives (on earth as in heaven), all the while praising him because we know he is rallying *other* people to them. Or, perhaps he *would* have us *do* and/or *say* something in a fruit of the Spirit way that would be beneficial for them, so that they may be brought into understanding.

Do and/or Speak If So Led	Prayers of Agreement *For* Them	Compassion for Their Plight	***Assessment*** ⟷	Judgement - Separation - Isolation

⟵ Increasingly Available **In Light of Our Assessment, We Are *Becoming*** Increasingly Unavailable ⟶

As children we were taught to Judge and Separate as needed for our safety, but we are not children anymore. Are you available to reverse the Divisive trend God's Enemies are using against us? The Temptations for Prideful Divisions are ever-present. Comparison with others enlivens it within us. Don't fall prey to it!

Luke 18:9-14

9 He also told this parable to some who trusted in themselves that they
were righteous, and treated others with contempt: 10 "Two men went
up into the temple to pray, one a Pharisee and the other a tax
collector. 11 The Pharisee, standing by himself, prayed thus: 'God, I
thank you that I am not like other men, extortioners, unjust, adulterers,
or even like this tax collector. 12 I fast twice a week; I give tithes of all
that I get.' 13 But the tax collector, standing far off, would not even lift
up his eyes to heaven, but beat his breast, saying, 'God, be merciful to
me, a sinner!' 14 I tell you, this man went down to his house justified,
rather than the other. For everyone who exalts himself will be
humbled, but the one who humbles himself will be exalted."

****

No one can hurt us as deeply as our family and close friends. My worst behavior has been with my family members, and theirs perhaps with me. When things are going the best, the wheels come flying off the fastest. With our guard down, we are easily knocked off balance by someone's sudden reoccurring bad behavior. Surprised and Angered, our loss of Patience with it adds fuel to the fire.

The Enemy spirit is always looking for an opening through which Division may be initiated - and I have failed far too frequently in these! It is easy for us to feel misunderstood, mistreated, taken for granted, used and abused at these times - and lash out. This because we are being hurt by the very ones we love most. These are the most difficult of times, but embrace the Training!

If you will look into why it is you became so Angry, it will more than likely be because you had an expectation that was not met. Unmet expectations remind us that they once again let us down. That the behavior which has been agreed upon to end so many times – still hasn't. It is infuriating when they "continue to do" that which was expected to end. As you sit in Judgement, keep in mind that your heart has been pushed aside in favor of a Desire To Control. That God could easily provide you a list of these regarding yourself, and that his approach with you instead includes a Gentle and helpful assessment in fruit of the Spirit language - not Judgement. We are to do for them as he does for us and always choose fruit of the Spirit words and/or actions in the attitudes of the Beatitudes that will not damage the relationship.

We must be careful to be listening for the leading of his still small voice. If we step in to do or say what is *not ours* to do or say, we can be sure that it is *not* in his will and that we have tried to Control things in *our* will – perhaps in pride. These types of actions frequently do harm and will have unintended consequences. This is another reason why it is so important to be continually developing ears that hear in an all-day long conversation with him. Eyes that see and ears that hear are critical in the accomplishment of his will for us. In the war for souls.

Matthew 13:14-15

14 Indeed, in their case the prophecy of Isaiah is fulfilled that says: "'"You will indeed hear but never understand, and you will indeed see but never perceive." 15 For this people's heart has grown dull, and with their ears they can barely hear, and their eyes they have closed, lest they should see with their eyes and hear with their ears and understand with their heart and turn, and I would heal them.'

Give thought now to your own reoccurring bad behaviors. Those things that *you* "continue to do" that hurt the people you love - that damage Unity and weaken relationships. Ask God to help you see what needs to be changed in you so that you will be able to overcome it by the power of his Name (the power of his Presence, character, attributes and reputation). Ask Jesus to Teach you, the Spirit to Encourage and Lead you, and the Father to continue to do his Works in you. In the warring for souls. Change in us is best accomplished by *him in us*.

He knows my *name*. He knows my character, attributes and reputation. He knew where to start the healing in my life, and it started with Teaching me to forgive. He knows the many I have hurt and is available to Teach them to forgive also. He knows your name, character, attributes and reputation, too.

Our Adversary wants to harden our relationships with people, remembering *their* reputation. But people can change, and relationships may be strengthened. Maybe the ones you are not forgiving have changed marvelously. Maybe you will never know it because of your unforgiveness and, remembering the old data, the guard you keep high in every current interaction – such that you will never again truly know them.

This goes, too, for what occurs in other interactions. Once we have unjustly lost a job or possessions and our resolve is weakened, the Enemy aims to Destroy our trust and belief in *everyone*. His age-old trick says God's reputation is unjust because of the injustice we see. Then he cajoles us, "How can you believe in a Commander that allows such ills to survive, thrive and dominate your life - and the lives of the oppressed? Blame the Commander! Make yourself King!" He hopes to get us to say to ourselves, "Therefore, I will Command Myself."

But <u>he</u> is the Oppressor, not God. Pay close attention. One of the ways of the Deceptive is to Name Call others to Blame them for what they are actually doing *themselves*.

That is why it is so important that we know and can share why it is that God has allowed evil to exist: So that we may have both the time and opportunity to choose - that he may bring us home for eternity - once the brief yet finite *period of offering* has passed.

Dear Father, I don't want to be king anymore. Do your Works in me that your kingdom comes fully into my life. That your will be fully accomplished in my life, as in heaven. Thank you that I may participate with you as you draw all people to yourself! Help others overcome their memories of my former ways that our relationships may be restored. Help me to overcome their reputations, too! Though it may be a slow slog back to regaining trust, may we be committed to it.

Help us to remember that we were all once just innocent little children - until our innocence was stolen away and we initiated our protective measures in defense. Help us to see that many of these protective measures utilize offensive strategies that push people away from us. Teach us and Train us in your ways for the restoration of relationships!

Jesus, thank you for teaching me that the Father's way is best. Strengthen me in his ways that, like you, I not shirk the relational work you have for me. You endured this life, the Foolish, the Corrupt, the Obstinate, the Wicked, and much more. Finally, you endured the cross and the suffering required to benefit us all. That we may join you in your Father's house. Our Father's house! Thank you that your mind of Wisdom, the mind and attitudes of Christ, are always available to me.

O Helper, Encourager, Spirit of the Living God, Wonderful Counselor: lead me that I not enter into temptation. Show me what is mine to do and what is not mine to do. When I see something I want to do <u>for</u> you, may I always check it out <u>with</u> you. It may <u>not</u> be mine to do, you may have someone else in mind. I don't want to interfere. All I do, I want to do <u>with</u> you. According to <u>your</u> leading. Participating. Nothing on my own. May this be an entire day of communion <u>with</u> you. Led <u>by</u> you. Amen!

The Fruit of the Spirit & The Whole Armor of God in Conflict Resolution

"In this world you will have trouble." (John 16:33)

What do we do with the trouble before us? How do we present it to those involved?

The fruit of the Spirit are God's reference points for our behavior & the tools with which we are to contend. The whole armor of God is our protection when others attack us, absorbing the blows and taking the arrows *for* us. So love like He does and communicate like He does, knowing full well that they may choose to go their own way - and continue to lean on their own understanding. It may also be that *we* are the ones responding in Fear of losing control, and not with the respectful Wisdom that shares information for our mutual benefit. Often God's help is in the overlap, somewhere between our oppositions, and available for discernment.

There is a difference between unconditional love and enablement. Like God, we are to provide the information. Like God, we are to allow others to make their own choice, no matter how foolish - and continue to love them unconditionally. One of the expressions of that love is to allow them to go out and learn on their own what they have chosen not to learn from the wisdom of others. When we love unconditionally, we bathe them in prayer when they go their own way, asking God to intervene that they may *learn quickly*. Enablement *saves them quickly* such that they *learn little* and so *continue to repeat their folly*.

Unity Builders produce fruit of the Spirit in an attempt to create or maintain unity during conflict resolution. Respectful information sharing, care, and a relational focus are the motivating factors.

Unity Builders: In Humility & Love

The Spirit of the Lord offers freedom, so we:

◊ Inform with Gentleness

◊ Encourage with Kindness

◊ Explain with grace in Peace

◊ Share with compassion in Goodness

◊ Describe with hope the Joyful outcome available

◊ Train to produce Patience & Perseverance

◊ Coach to develop Self-Control

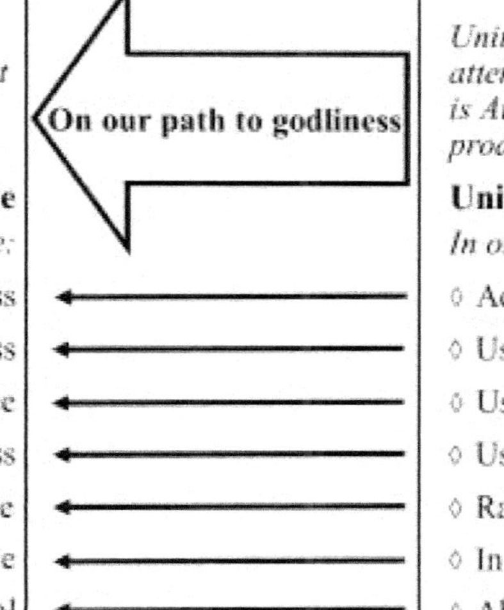

Unity Busters accuse, judge, condemn and shame people in an attempt to maintain or retake control over a situation. The focus is Autonomy & Control of others. Over time, this manipulation produces relational loss.

Unity Busters: In Fear of Loss

In our attempt to Control, we:

◊ Accuse, Judge & Condemn to Justify our Demands

◊ Use Blame, Anger and Malice to Threaten and Coerce

◊ Use Shame & Silence to subtly Threaten Abandonment

◊ Use our Voice to Threaten Vengeance, Retaliation, Retribution

◊ Rationalize that our divisive actions were caused by them

◊ In Pride & frustration, Lie & Deceive (…for their own good)

◊ Abuse whatever Power we may think we have

Chapter Twenty-Six

The Two-Way Conversation

Colossians 2:8
See to it that no one takes you captive by philosophy and empty deceit, according to human tradition (use of Authority and Hierarchy in the Military Chain of Command), according to the elemental spirits of the world (the World OS), and not according to Christ.

2 Corinthians 4:18
...as we look not to the things that are seen but to the things that are unseen. For the things that are seen are transient, but the things that are unseen are eternal.

What we see all around us is organizational structure that utilizes the World Operating System through the hierarchical Military Chain Of Command methodology. As this happens, it reinforces our value for strength and the use of Leverage in getting what we want. At some point most come to believe that Conflict is simply a necessary part of living in this world. As we look around and see so many others operating in similar orientations, it reinforces the belief that this is just the way it is.

"That's just the way it is.
Some things will never change!
That's just the way it is...
Awwww, but don't you believe them!"
Bruce Hornsby, The Way It Is, 1986

Learning *why* we Live and who will teach us *how* to Live, we will have a better chance at learning how to *Love* well. Only then might we *Lead* well – as we trust God and follow *his* leading.

It might accurately be said that the depth of our trust and understanding will bring us to the depth of our faith. And that the depth of our intimacy and therefore the depth of our love is based upon these.

I fell in love with my wife, not because of the facts that I learned about her, but because of the depth of understanding I gained in knowing her and the faith and trust that I found were safe with her.

The facts about her were very important, but facts can be misleading, too. As I came to know certain truths about her, I occasionally jumped to conclusions about her that were inaccurate. Had I not given her the opportunity to clarify my concerns, we would likely not have been married. And the joy that I have found in 40+ years with her would never have come to pass. Many have jumped to conclusions about God, as well. For so many, these conclusions have led to Judgement and a choice to Reject him.

Yet God invites us to bring these assessments and Judgements before him also, that he too might be able to clarify and explain what we do not yet understand. Commencing with his foundational love for us and how he had us in mind from before the beginning, he will be able to clarify for us layer by layer *why* things are as they are. We simply *must* start there if we are to understand, because if *we* don't understand, how will we ever give a satisfactory answer to those who tell us that they sit in Judgement of God and have Rejected him?

****

One of the things that has made me a successful consultant is that I have sought out Wise counsel for every area of my *own* life for as long as I can remember. These individuals hold tremendous expertise and Wisdom in many areas of specialization. As I gleaned from them I became stronger. I became more whole. I reduced the ignorance in my life, made fewer mistakes and found greater success.

When the same approach is taken with the Creator of the universe, we have an ongoing life teacher. If, however, we do not trust our teacher, we will not learn very much. Facts that make sense to us will be utilized. However, those that we do not understand, but allow to remain unstated, will never be resolved. Without communication we cannot learn and develop greater trust. Without trust, there can be no faith. Without faith there will be no love. The successful life is built upon faith and trust in God that has no doubt. God, whose character is perfect. Whose attributes are flawless. Whose unconditional love has no bounds. He is faithful, trustworthy and loving in essence. In John

17, Jesus described the successful life as lived *in him* with great trust, great faith and great love.

Blind Faith eventually brings doubt and weakens faith & trust because it is built upon foundational misunderstandings and incorrect assumptions. God is not asking us for Blind Faith. Rather, he demonstrates his trustworthiness and proves his love for us individually step by step, that we might gain trust, build faith and love him deeply. With the totality of our hearts, souls and minds.

When we step out in what we *believe* as faith, but then fail due to our incorrect assumptions and misunderstanding, doubt invariably creeps in. In some measure, we lose trust in the God we had faith in to continue our success. We blame him for our failure because we believe he is the one who was promising success and then didn't deliver. We were deceived, but it wasn't by him. Other actors were involved.

Through experience together and follow-up conversation, I know what I can count on my wife to do and to not do in any future context. God will do this for us also, but we must engage in the conversation.

We need a foundational understanding of who God is that develops such depth that we can know with confidence what he is willing and unwilling to do. Then we will know what we can always count on.

Unfortunately, there are many well-meaning teachers out there who have been taught in error by other well-meaning teachers down through the ages. We can easily go back through history and find well-meaning leaders doing ungodly things, starting ungodly precedents and then trace their passage down to us – refined, but still being retold with extremely subtle, yet foundationally major, errors. Scripture says that the failings (curses, errors, sins) of the parents are passed down to the 3rd and 4th generation. We see that in too many of our well-meaning pastor/teachers now.

Exodus 34:6-8

6 The Lord passed before him and proclaimed, "The Lord, the Lord, a God merciful and gracious, slow to anger, and abounding in steadfast love and faithfulness, 7 keeping steadfast love for thousands, forgiving iniquity and transgression and sin, but who will by no means clear the guilty, visiting the iniquity of the fathers on the children and the children's children, to the third and the fourth generation." 8 And Moses quickly bowed his head toward the earth and worshiped.

One of these major errors that was refined and retold for generations was that people should not have a Bible to read in their own language. That people need priests/pastors/teachers to tell them what the Bible says. It was an easy point to sell since for most people the Bible was not available in their native language anyway.

In those days, well-meaning people recognized the risk that would come with mistaken interpretation and decided that they should protect us from ourselves. A nice thought, but a big mistake. Putting the power of the scriptures into the hands of a few led to pride issues and many being corrupted in a similar manner as Satan. History identifies that people began to unknowingly follow priests/pastors/teachers rather than God. There is a very real risk for Corruption in such heady situations.

Still others who maintained their obedience to our Creator found themselves buried in so many individual requests for understanding that they simply could not serve them all. The birth of the Build-A-Bigger-Church Culture seemed necessary so as to gather the masses in one place each week to enable times of teaching and communion. Hardly the leader multiplication that Jesus described, Europe is now littered with huge empty cathedrals.

****

Jesus spent much of his time teaching in the small synagogues of "the triangle", that is, in the small villages of Bethsaida, Korazin and Capernaum.

In Jesus' day, a lone rabbi teaching in a synagogue was unusual. Rather, all of the rabbis from the insulas in the area (often five or more rabbis with hundreds of people in attendance) would gather in the synagogue to *conversationally* consider the appointed text of that sabbath day. *The people* were allowed to ask questions and weigh in on these discussions conversationally as well.

With several rabbis present, no one rabbi could steer the people in an unhealthy direction over time. In *conversational* style, God could send in his *Encouragers*, *Disruptors* and *Correctors* to contribute to the discussions and raise up issues and scripture for community deliberation. It was this setup that made it possible for Jesus (and later the apostle Paul) to speak *in any synagogue on any sabbath.*

Please note that history identifies that most of the people in the communities Jesus frequented had *thoroughly memorized* their Torah from a young age. Knowing that they could engage their teachers, they could be personally involved. Stimulating thoughts and memorable discussion on the related texts could then facilitate the deeper contemplations that lead to changed lives. The lone teacher setup is a heady situation that risks the people *becoming* teacher followers rather than talmidim of *Jesus*.

We would do well to reconsider our tradition of individuals teaching to gatherings by lecture. Rather, let's afford people conversational iron sharpening iron opportunities, and do so in a spirit that cultivates Unity. Our only requirement should be <u>hearts after the Father, humbly postured in the attitudes of the Beatitudes (Jesus' attitudes), and that thoughts be shared in true fruit of the Spirit language and actions</u>.

****

There is no evidence in the New Testament that we are to build buildings and then tell the people to come to us for talmidic teaching and training *en masse*. Talmidic training is best accomplished conversationally, the way Jesus did it. In his day, the people came to the synagogues on the sabbath to hear *multiple* rabbis discuss the scripture so as to *fulfill the Torah* for the people (*explain how to live a life pleasing to Adonai*). What's more, the people were allowed to join into the conversation as well.

Situationally, we must ask him whether or not it is in his will that we spend huge sums of money on building construction and then more still annually for maintenance when a large portion of those funds might just as easily, and might more effectively, go to activities in our communities and missionary work around the world.

While we now have the full Bible available in almost 700 languages, the remnants of the issue remain. Most people still *go* to church for *teaching en masse by one individual, void of illuminating discussion and therefore very little leader multiplication*. A movement back to house churches began quite some time ago, and the conversational approach that Jesus modeled is gaining traction once again. It is also extremely economical since huge investments in brick and mortar and annual maintenance are almost totally saved for mission purposes.

Do not assume that I am speaking against all large churches, I am not. Some have been able to start as house churches, grow into a movement of many house churches and then come together weekly or monthly in large scale settings for the benefits that large scale activity may bring to a community. Still others that were once mostly attractional large church gatherings have been able to reverse-implement the conversational house church concept, and are similarly engaging in large scale benefits to their communities. Remember, too, that Jesus spoke to gatherings of thousands and that God brought together over 3,000 on the day of Pentecost. If leaders will ask him his will for us *situationally*, and do so *collectively*, we will find that he will also answer us collectively and in Unity. There will be no doubt. (We will discuss this at greater length in the section on Leading.)

It must also be said that house churches run the risk of going off-track and becoming cultish, or perhaps a monastery where nice people may hide. A healthy house church will include conversational teaching with influence from others on the outside and be seeking leader multiplication so as to birth additional locations.

The house church movement is working because they are sharing what Jesus taught and explained conversationally. They can be a new beginning for the building up of trust and faith and love in oneness with him. Led by him. What became unavailable after Eden became available again through Jesus. Jesus came and took upon himself the responsibility for both God and Man as God-Man, that we all might become his talmidim.

Before the beginning God had the choice of either giving you life or never giving you life. And if he had never given you life, you would have never had the opportunity for an abundant life in loving relationship with him. Eternity with him would never have been more than a possibility that God himself chose not to allow you. This good and gracious and loving God chose to give you the chance, though it includes living among the many Rejectors.

God gave all people a chance at a love relationship with him for eternity. He is responsible for that. Much of humanity rejected him and did evil in the eyes of the Lord. We are responsible for that. In shared responsibility, the God-Man Jesus Christ came and paid the penalty for both. Did God make a mistake in creating humanity? No, but so many of us humans blame him for the existence of evil in the world anyway. They might cease to blame him if his talmidim will know his story well enough to be able to share it with them.

That none should perish.

Chapter Twenty-Seven

Train Us Up To Know Your Voice, O God!

God would like to lead us along the path of his ways to an abundant joy-filled life. Are you letting him?

Always the gentleman, God does not conscript us into his service. Rather, he invites us in with fruit of the Spirit language. It is my always growing love for him that then compels me to serve him and introduce others to him - that they too might live joyfully in him. Eternally.

God does not want to take authority over us, he wants us to give it. So if you will not give him authority over your life, neither will he try to take it. In unconditional love he says that you are free to choose him as your God or any other person or thing, including yourself. You have been given the right to choose, and gentleman that he is, he keeps his Word – during this *finite period of time*. The finite period of offering. After which he will come back and bring justice for all eternity.

Revelation 22:10-12
10 And he said to me, "Do not seal up the words of the prophecy of this book, for the time is near. 11 Let the evildoer still do evil, and the filthy still be filthy, and the righteous still do right, and the holy still be holy." 12 "Behold, I am coming soon, bringing my recompense with me, to repay each one for what he has done. 13 I am the Alpha and the Omega, the first and the last, the beginning and the end."

Like any good parent, God can function in both authority and intimacy. These are not mutually exclusive, and his primary desire is for intimacy with you. Intimacy with him brings Unity and Oneness. When there is Unity and Oneness with him there is no need for authority. He doesn't tell us what to do as King, he tells us what will be best as our loving Father - and when we eagerly comply in Love, we find Joy.

Like with my wife, and me for her, we know what to expect in any future context. Our character and attributes have been revealed to each other by our actions. We have a reputation with each other for consistently choosing these actions and behaviors.

Through the truth found in scripture and in conversational intimacy with him, God also makes clear what he will and will not do. His character is perfect. He is trustworthy. His attributes are flawless. He has consistently shown that his reputation is reliable. God's "name", the power of his Presence, character and attributes, have given him the reputation of being worthy, faithful, wise, perfect, unchanging, just, merciful, compassionate, gracious, loving, good, holy, glorious, trustworthy, righteous, omniscient, omnipotent, omnipresent and sovereign. Did I miss any?!!!

His foundational truth has the power to cast out fear and bring the abundant life. Jesus came and gave testimony that, if we will but return to God in conversational intimacy to be taught by him, we will find trust, faith, love, peace that surpasses understanding, life to the full and our joy made complete.

Luke 12:32

"Fear not, little flock, for it is your Father's good pleasure to give you the kingdom.

John 14:21

Whoever has my commandments and keeps them, he it is who loves me. And he who loves me will be loved by my Father, and I will love him and manifest myself to him."

John 14:23

Jesus answered him, "If anyone loves me, he will keep my word, and my Father will love him, and we will come to him and make our home with him.

Romans 12:2

Do not be conformed to this world, but be transformed by the renewal of your mind, that by testing you may discern what is the will of God, what is good and acceptable and perfect.

Micah 6:8

He has told you, O man, what is good; and what does the Lord require of you but to do justice, and to love kindness, and to walk humbly with your God?

Proverbs 3:11-12

11 My son, do not despise the Lord's discipline or be weary of his reproof, 12 for the Lord reproves him whom he loves, as a father the son in whom he delights.

Proverbs 16:25

There is a way that seems right to a man, but its end is the way to death.

Colossians 2:8

See to it that no one takes you captive by philosophy and empty deceit, according to human tradition (use of Authority in the Military Chain of Command), according to the elemental spirits of the world (the World OS), and not according to Christ.

James 4:8a

Draw near to God, and he will draw near to you.

James 1:17

Every good gift and every perfect gift is from above, coming down from the Father of lights, with whom there is no variation or shadow due to change.

Luke 11:11-13

11 What father among you, if his son asks for a fish, will instead of a fish give him a serpent; 12 or if he asks for an egg, will give him a scorpion? 13 If you then, who are evil, know how to give good gifts to your children, how much more will the heavenly Father give the Holy Spirit to those who ask him!"

Isaiah 56:7a

these I will bring to my holy mountain, and make them joyful in my house of prayer;

Philippians 1:6
And I am sure of this, that he who began a good work in you will bring it to completion at the day of Jesus Christ.

John 17:8, 13
8 For I have given them the words that you gave me, and they have received them and have come to know in truth that I came from you; and they have believed that you sent me. ...13 But now I am coming to you, and these things I speak in the world, that they may have my joy fulfilled in themselves.

1 John 1:4
And we are writing these things so that our joy may be complete.

John 15:11
These things I have spoken to you, that my joy may be in you, and that your joy may be full.

Ephesians 3:19
and to know the love of Christ that surpasses knowledge, that you may be filled with all the fullness of God.

Ephesians 4:13
until we all attain to the unity of the faith and of the knowledge of the Son of God, to mature manhood, to the measure of the stature of the fullness of Christ,

Psalm 23:6
Surely goodness and mercy shall follow me (characterize me) all the days of my life, and I shall dwell in the house of the Lord forever.

John 10:10
The thief comes only to steal and kill and destroy. I came that they may have life and have it abundantly.

2 Peter 3:9
The Lord is not slow to fulfill his promise as some count slowness, but is patient toward you, not wishing that any should perish, but that all should reach repentance.

1 Timothy 2:3-4

3 This is good, and it is pleasing in the sight of God our Savior, 4 who desires all people to be saved and to come to the knowledge of the truth.

Philippians 4:7

And the peace of God, which surpasses all understanding, will guard your hearts and your minds in Christ Jesus.

Mark 12:28-34a

28 And one of the scribes came up and heard them disputing with one another, and seeing that he answered them well, asked him, "Which commandment is the most important of all?" 29 Jesus answered, "The most important is, 'Hear, O Israel: The Lord our God, the Lord is one. 30 And you shall love the Lord your God with all your heart and with all your soul and with all your mind and with all your strength.' 31 The second is this: 'You shall love your neighbor as yourself.' There is no other commandment greater than these." 32 And the scribe said to him, "You are right, Teacher. You have truly said that he is one, and there is no other besides him. 33 And to love him with all the heart and with all the understanding and with all the strength, and to love one's neighbor as oneself, is much more than all whole burnt offerings and sacrifices." 34 And when Jesus saw that he answered wisely, he said to him, "You are not far from the kingdom of God."

He hasn't hidden himself in a few verses of the Bible, he has made himself known throughout. The many verses above are but a handful. Rejectors will have no excuse for not choosing him over themselves when their *personal finite time of offering* comes to an end.

How has he made it possible for us to have no doubt, and to learn to love so completely? *We will all be taught by God. (John 6:45)* He whispers this truth each day to each heart, soul and mind, drawing each of us to himself, that we might learn his ways and be strengthened. He teaches us directly from his Spirit to ours, through the scriptures, nature and other people. He has not missed anyone. He touches the heart of each person with his heart, even those isolated in the jungles of this world. He is continually available for direct communication conversationally when we seek after him with our whole heart.

Linguistic historians (etymologists) state that we first began to use the Latin word "conscience" around 1200 AD. It came from a "Christian ethic" and is a "mutual awareness" or "joint knowledge" of "what is right". Originally, it explained our ability to hear God's voice and know something *with God.*

Unfortunately, over the last thousand years our understanding of the word "conscience" has evolved to mean our *own* internal voice regarding what is right and what is wrong. Typical to the way he works, the Deceiver has managed to evolve its meaning very slowly over many hundreds of years to eventually exclude God.

In truth, our "conscience", even for those isolated in the jungles of this world, is *the Presence and still small voice of God!*

John 6:45

It is written in the Prophets, '<u>And they will all be taught by God</u>.' Everyone who has heard and learned from the Father comes to me.

John 14:10

Do you not believe that I am in the Father and the Father is in me? The words that I say to you I do not speak on my own authority, <u>but the Father who dwells in me does his works</u>.

Psalm 119:105

"You make known to me the path of life; you will fill me with joy in your presence, with eternal pleasures at your right hand."

Acts 2:28

You have made known to me the paths of life; you will make me full of gladness with your presence.'

1 Kings 19:11-13

11 And he said, "Go out and stand on the mount before the Lord." And behold, the Lord passed by, and a great and strong wind tore the mountains and broke in pieces the rocks before the Lord, but the Lord was not in the wind. And after the wind an earthquake, but the Lord was not in the earthquake. 12 And after the earthquake a fire, but the Lord was not in the fire. And after the fire <u>the sound of a low whisper</u>. 13 And when Elijah heard it, he wrapped his face in his cloak and went *out and stood at the entrance of the cave. And behold, there came a voice to him and said, "What are you doing here, Elijah?"*

Why is his voice "still small"? I believe it is because anything "bigger" could be interpreted by us as God *threatening* us to do what he wants or else. As we have seen, God will not threaten or coerce or manipulate. His still small voice is loud enough for us to "know" what he desires, and that is enough. If we will inquire of him he will tell us what we need to know. Sometimes, it may be to know the way of escape.

1 Corinthians 10:13
No temptation has overtaken you that is not common to man. God is faithful, and he will not let you be tempted beyond your ability, but with the temptation he will also provide the way of escape, that you may be able to endure it.

Philippians 4:6-8
6 do not be anxious about anything, but in everything by prayer and supplication with thanksgiving let your requests be made known to God. 7 And the peace of God, which surpasses all understanding, will guard your hearts and your minds in Christ Jesus. 8 Finally, brothers, whatever is true, whatever is honorable, whatever is just, whatever is pure, whatever is lovely, whatever is commendable, if there is any excellence, if there is anything worthy of praise, think about these things.

1 Peter 5:7-9
7 casting all your anxieties on him, because he cares for you. 8 Be sober-minded; be watchful. Your adversary the devil prowls around like a roaring lion, seeking someone to devour. 9 Resist him, firm in your faith, knowing that the same kinds of suffering are being experienced by your brotherhood throughout the world.

James 4:7
Submit yourselves therefore to God. Resist the devil, and he will flee from you.

2 Corinthians 10:3-5

3 For though we walk in the flesh, we are not waging war according to the flesh. 4 For the weapons of our warfare are not of the flesh but have divine power to destroy strongholds. 5 We destroy arguments and every lofty opinion raised against the knowledge of God, and take every thought captive to obey Christ,

There are three voices that we may "hear" in our heads: ours, the Deceivers' and God's. Whenever we have a thought in our mind that the still small voice of God would help us overcome, you can be sure that our Adversary will be right there with rationalizations to encourage us to go ahead and do it, like we deserve it, and that whatever bad might come from it will not be our fault. The Deceiver will likely have also enlisted other people to convince us to *continue to do it*, as well. He is trying to convince us that he is on *our* side, that the vote should be 2 to 1 and that the still small voice of God should lose. But the truth is that the Deceiver is only on *his own* side. What might we do?

James 4:7

Submit yourselves therefore to God. Resist the devil, and he will flee from you.

Nehemiah 8:10b

...And do not be grieved, for <u>the joy of the Lord is your strength</u>."

Are you in him and is he in you? Then submit yourselves to God and believe that the Deceiver must flee. By the power of the Presence of the Father, Son and Holy Spirit take every thought captive and accept the way out that God has prepared for you. Or not. It's up to you. The choice will be clear and simple. He is your strength in your time of need. The Deceiver and his minions may be sent away with the words, "Jesus Christ is my Lord and Savior. Be gone!" Then you will be able to "hear" what God is sharing with you more clearly – *but you will still have to choose what you will or will not do*.

Occasionally, when we are still not sure that we know what *to* do, he will make his silence obvious. The silence deafening, it is there to give us pause. That, because what we are continuing to contemplate is

Not Love, and is therefore something *not to do* - something he cannot approve of. In these moments, we will sense that this lesson and its consequences have occurred previously. Knowing all we need to know in the moment, he stands quietly by hoping that we will see clearly, remember the earlier lessons and decide accordingly – and if so, feel his approval as he celebrates over us.

Then we will see what the Father is doing and do likewise. Our eyes again on him, we will know his will, what to do and accomplish it. With compassion. With Love, Joy, Peace, Patience, Kindness, Goodness, Gentleness, Perseverance (Faithfulness) and Self-Control. The Spirit of the Living God leads us in the Self-Control *we* need when we would rather opt to control situations and outcomes, or give in to our passions.

Chapter Twenty-Eight

Stay Tuned In To The Kingdom Channel

There is no limit to the ways the still small voice of God may choose to communicate with us!

I often wake up in the morning with a song on my heart that he placed there. As I go through the day I always find that song to be a great encouragement, a sort of preparation for what he would have me *learn* today, or perhaps *do* in a situation that will unfold. Sometimes these are secular songs with catchy tunes and objectionable lyrics that I rewrite as the day goes by into songs of worship and praise. (By the end of 2025, many of these may be found for your use and free download at OneKingdomWorldwide.org)

He speaks to many of us through nature, children, looking at the night sky, and so many more. He loves us, he takes every opportunity to remind us that he is available. We must only be attentive to him. Pray without ceasing, inquire of him unceasingly, take every thought captive and ask him to teach you about it. An all-day long conversation with him will have many times of stillness, but be still and know that he is God! He is good, he knows the good plans he has for us. But first we must invite him in. All the way in. Heart, soul *and* mind.

Revelation 3:20
Behold, I stand at the door and knock. If anyone hears my voice and opens the door, <u>I will come in to him</u> and eat with him, and he with me.

John 14:23
Jesus answered him, "If anyone loves me, he will keep my word, and my Father will love him, and <u>we will come to him and make our home with him</u>.

John 14:10
Do you not believe that I am in the Father and the Father is in me? The words that I say to you I do not speak on my own authority, <u>but the Father who dwells in me does his works</u>.

Jeremiah 29:11-13

11 For I know the plans I have for you, declares the LORD, plans for welfare (peace) and not for evil, to give you a future and a hope. 12 Then you will call upon me and come and pray to me, and I will hear you. 13 You will seek me and find me, when you seek me with all your heart.

John 10:27-29

27 My sheep hear my voice, and I know them, and they follow me. 28 I give them eternal life, and they will never perish, and no one will snatch them out of my hand. 29 My Father, who has given them to me, is greater than all, and no one is able to snatch them out of the Father's hand.

2 Corinthians 10:5

We destroy arguments and every lofty opinion raised against the knowledge of God, and take every thought captive to obey Christ,

1 Thessalonians 5:17-18

17 pray (inquire, ask, petition, request) without ceasing, 18 give thanks in all circumstances; for this is the will of God in Christ Jesus for you.

Psalm 46:10

"Be still, and know that I am God. I will be exalted among the nations, I will be exalted in the earth!"

Gaining this conversational intimacy, this all-day long attentiveness, this ability to wear an earbud and microphone so to speak as you go through your day, requires a process. Cultivating an ear that hears God requires education, training and discernment to know when it is his Spirit speaking to our spirit and when it is a Rejector spirit attempting to deceive. We cannot use our minds to overcome, we overcome by *his* Spirit speaking to our spirit. Giving our hearts and minds over to his power and Presence, he trains us up in his character and attributes. One with him, him in us and us in him. He is Present for us, but are we present with him?

Matthew 13:13-17

13 This is why I speak to them in parables, because seeing they do not see, and hearing they do not hear, nor do they understand. 14 Indeed, in their case the prophecy of Isaiah is fulfilled that says:

“‘“You will indeed hear but never understand, and you will indeed see but never perceive.” 15 For this people's heart has grown dull, and with their ears they can barely hear, and their eyes they have closed, lest they should see with their eyes and hear with their ears and understand with their heart and turn, and I would heal them.’

16 But blessed are your eyes, for they see, and your ears, for they hear. 17 For truly, I say to you, many prophets and righteous people longed to see what you see, and did not see it, and to hear what you hear, and did not hear it.

Which are we? What do we allow to distract us from his still small voice? Where is our focus as we walk through each day? How can we hear and see what he has for us as we go through our day if we are giving attention to a steady onslaught of media sights and sounds? When will we be still and know that he is God? Periodically, or continually? Will we set ourselves up for success by eliminating these media distractions?

You who are easily discouraged have ears to hear, but your ears are listening to a foreign station while I am speaking to you on the kingdom frequency. You have eyes to see but are watching a channel that feeds your selfish disposition; you have lost your remote and until you find it, you are unable to switch to the kingdom channel to learn the secret clues of where the spiritual treasure is hidden. Ears and eyes that are always attuned to the worldly media remain ignorant of the secret knowledge of the Hidden Treasures of the kingdom.
You… the King and the Kingdom. Ed Caputo, Page 28.

Thank you, Lord, for the all-day conversational intimacy you make available to us! Starting each day with you is one thing, but walking through our entire day with you is quite another! Keep us attentive, O God!

"There is not in the world a kind of life more sweet and delightful than that of a continual conversation with God. Those only can comprehend it who practice and experience it, yet I do not advise you to do it from that motive. It is not pleasure which we ought to seek in this exercise, but let us do it from a principle of love, and because God would have us." Brother Lawrence in Dallas Willard, Hearing God (Intervarsity Press, 1999), p.15

For me, it was helpful to transition into a transparent all-day conversation by recognizing that he is truly watching our every move and is hopeful to talk with us about whatever we are doing or contemplating. For those who think of him like a penitent, punishing boss complaining about our every mistake, this would be counterproductive. But for those of us who see him as he really is - an encouraging life coach cheering us on to success after success, little by little, bit by bit, more and more and glory by glory (2 Corinthians 3:17-18) - we find ourselves learning to talk with others the way he talks with us: truthfully, in Jesus' attitudes of the Beatitudes and with fruit of the Spirit language and actions. Failing him less and less because more and more we are *in* him, and *in creative collaboration with him.*

I find that a life of little whispered words of adoration, of praise, of prayer, of worship can be breathed all through the day. One can have a very busy day, outwardly speaking, and yet be steadily in the Holy Presence... "Religion" isn't something to be added to our other duties, and thus make our lives more complex. <u>The life with God is the center of life</u>, and all else is remolded and integrated by it. Thomas R. Kelly, The Testament of Devotion

As we go through our day, sharing information as God does, we will be Gentle, Patient, Kind and Persevering in Goodness so that the information we share is void of manipulation or coercion. As the Holy Spirit helps us in Self-Control, we will offer a desired outcome to grow Peace, Joy and Love. Then, like God, we will remain available for dialogue and let them choose for themselves.

Worship him as you go, remembering that the Hebrew word for prayer includes a component of simultaneous worship. This cannot occur if you are *thinking* your way through the situations of each day.

In the original Hebrew, the concept of prayer is *continual conversational worship*. In this way, we involve him in everything we do all day long. Attentive to his Spirit, we are able to see, hear and perceive what he is Leading us to do. The Lord looks on the heart (1 Samuel 16:7), heart work brings balance to our thinking minds.

He calls us "friend", and walks with us as we walk with him, giving us peace that surpasses understanding throughout all our days – no matter what trouble the world throws at us. *Becoming* more like him, we will truly walk in the attitudes of the Beatitudes in a posture of gratitude that others will notice and appreciate - especially in adversity.

John 15:15
No longer do I call you servants, for the servant does not know what his master is doing; <u>but I have called you friends</u>, for all that I have heard from my Father I have made known to you.

Proverbs 17:17
A friend loves at all times, and a brother is born for adversity.

Philippians 4:6-8
6 do not be anxious about anything, but in everything by prayer and supplication with thanksgiving let your requests be made known to God. 7 And <u>the peace of God, which surpasses all understanding, will guard your hearts and your minds in Christ Jesus</u>. 8 Finally, brothers, whatever is true, whatever is honorable, whatever is just, whatever is pure, whatever is lovely, whatever is commendable, if there is any excellence, if there is anything worthy of praise, <u>think about these things</u>.

He is simply saying, "I am here. Talk to me. *Listen* for me and listen *to* me. You can trust me. I'll prove it to you. I will help you learn my ways, I will direct you, and you will succeed more and more in reflecting my love to those around you."

That last sentence is the make or break. "…, I will direct you, …" Are you willing to be directed?

Chapter Twenty-Nine

Nothing Clouds Our Vision Like Reality

Mark 11:23-25

23 Truly, I say to you, whoever says to this mountain, 'Be taken up and thrown into the sea,' and does not doubt in his heart, but believes that what he says will come to pass, it will be done for him. 24 Therefore I tell you, whatever you ask in prayer, believe that you have received it (are receiving it), and it will be yours. 25 And whenever you stand praying, forgive, if you have anything against anyone, so that your Father also who is in heaven may forgive you your trespasses. 26 But if you do not forgive, neither will your Father who is in heaven forgive your trespasses."

Please note that some manuscripts have translated it "have received it" and others have translated it "are receiving it". Nonetheless, *he* is the one doing it so whether we *have received it* or *are receiving it* – his will *will* come to pass.

Given what we have learned about Jesus only saying and doing what the Father told him, it is important to recognize that *what Jesus asked for, received and was receiving*, was *always* in alignment with the Father's will and timing. While Jesus believes without a doubt that the Father's kingdom will come and his will *will* be done, he is *only in the process of receiving it*. And so are we.

John 17:20-23

20 "I do not ask for these only, but also for those who will believe in me through their word, 21 that they may all be one, just as you, Father, are in me, and I in you, that they also may be in us, so that the world may believe that you have sent me. 22 The glory that you have given me I have given to them, that they may be one even as we are one, 23 I in them and you in me, that they may become perfectly one, so that the world may know that you sent me and loved them even as you loved me.

Two thousand years ago Jesus asked the Father that we be one as he is one. It has *not yet* fully come to pass, but it *is in the process* of occurring. *He is causing what as of yet has not been fully caused. When* it will be *fully caused* is up to *the Father's* timing - according to *his* will. The very will that we are asking and agreeing with him for. Not in our timing, but according to his.

His kingdom *is* coming, his will *is* in the process of being accomplished. We *are* participating with him to manifest and establish his kingdom on earth - in the hearts, souls and minds of people - as it is in heaven. He wants us to agree with him that it be done – and believe that we *are* in the process of receiving it. No matter the reality of what we *see.*

Just as Jesus said that he does not know the day or the hour of his return, we must realize that the timing of the accomplishment of the Father's will - that we are asking and agreeing with him for – is entirely up to him.

It is important to realize that in stating our agreement with him regarding his kingdom and will, we are somehow *participating with him to cause that which has not yet been caused, release that which has not yet been released and/or fulfill that which is in the process of being fulfilled.*

He asks us to ask, so we ask - because that is how he wants it. We don't know why he does it this way, but he does. Jesus told us to ask this way when he taught us how to pray. Must we understand how and why it is this way? I think not, but that it *is* this way is apparent from the words he taught us to *use.*

In continuous conversational worship (prayer), we are creative collaborators co-operating. Him in us spiritually and us in him spiritually, with us in the physical participating with him to bring the spiritual into earthly manifestation. Establishing his kingdom on earth as it is in heaven - in people - his will being done according to his timing. That all might come to know him, love him and join him, and thereby enter into the Family of God. That none should perish.

It is similarly so regarding him telling us to pray earnestly to the Lord of the harvest to send laborers:

Matthew 9:35-38

*35 And Jesus went throughout all the cities and villages, teaching in
their synagogues and proclaiming the gospel of the kingdom and
healing every disease and every affliction. 36 When he saw the
crowds, he had compassion for them, because they were harassed and
helpless, like sheep without a shepherd. 37 Then he said to his
disciples, "The harvest is plentiful, but the laborers are
few; 38 therefore pray earnestly to the Lord of the harvest
to send out laborers into his harvest."*

…and we are to be persistent in these prayers:

Luke 18:1-8

*1 And he told them a parable to the effect that they ought always to
pray and not lose heart. 2 He said, "In a certain city there was a judge
who neither feared God nor respected man. 3 And there was a widow
in that city who kept coming to him and saying, 'Give me justice
against my adversary.' 4 For a while he refused, but afterward he said
to himself, 'Though I neither fear God nor respect man, 5 yet because
this widow keeps bothering me, I will give her justice, so that she will
not beat me down by her continual coming.'" 6 And the Lord
said, "Hear what the unrighteous judge says. 7 And will not God give
justice to his elect, who cry to him day and night? Will he delay long
over them? 8 I tell you, he will give justice to them speedily.
Nevertheless, when the Son of Man comes,
will he find faith on earth?"*

Praying *for* our Adversaries as well:

Matthew 5:43-46

*43 "You have heard that it was said, 'You shall love your neighbor and
hate your enemy.' 44 But I say to you, Love your enemies and pray for
those who persecute you, 45 so that you may be sons of your Father
who is in heaven. For he makes his sun rise on the evil and on the
good, and sends rain on the just and on the unjust. 46 For if you love
those who love you, what reward do you have? Do not even the tax
collectors do the same? 47 And if you greet only your brothers, what*

more are you doing than others? Do not even the Gentiles do the same? 48 You therefore must be perfect, as your heavenly Father is perfect.

What happens when we ask the things that he has told us to ask? Why does it matter to him that we ask them? How does he respond when we do? Why does it work this way? Though I have some thoughts on the subject, scripture is not clear, so we do not know. In faith, we do not need to know, but have faith - we *do* need to be asking!

Thank you, Jesus, that you taught us how to pray. Your kingdom come, Father, your will be done. We agree with you and desire to participate with you for the coming of your kingdom on earth as it is in heaven. Strengthen us in the attitudes of the Beatitudes (Jesus' attitudes), that we Persevere to Patiently speak and act in Goodness, Kindness, Gentleness and Self-Control. In Peace that develops Joy and grows greater Love. Give us justice against our Adversaries, O God! Lord of the harvest, send laborers, bring our Adversaries to repentance and into a right relationship with you. May they repent, turn to you, be healed, and follow you all of the days of their lives. Thank you for your continual Presence, your Teaching, your Training, your Leading, your Guiding and for the Works you are doing in us. That we succeed in being effective laborers, sent by you, ourselves! We ask all these things here in your precious Presence and in agreement with your will. Amen!

****

Mark 11:23-25 above, John 14:12-14, John 14:26, John 15:16, John 16:23 and John 16:24 are some of the so called "proof texts" for those who have been Deceived into believing that we have the Power and Authority to make things happen on our own – because we think it would be *good* and believe that we have been given the right. But, if so, we are *leaning on our own understanding*, not the totality of the scripture - and are at risk of being one of the workers of lawlessness who will be told to depart from him.

Matthew 7:22-23

"On that day many will say to me, 'Lord, Lord, did we not prophesy in your name, and cast out demons in your name, and do many mighty works in your name?' And then will I declare to them, 'I never knew you; depart from me, you workers of lawlessness.'"

Which comes first? "I only say and do as the Father tells me?" Or, "Ask anything in my name and you will receive it?" The first precedes the second.

If we are one with him, we first focus ourselves on God's will and doing *it*. One with him, in his Presence, in his character and according to his attributes – we will be asking for what he wants us to ask for – and we will surely *receive it* or *be receiving* it. It *will* come to pass.

1 John 5:14-15 NASB

14 This is the confidence which we have before Him, that, if we ask anything according to His will, He hears us. 15 And if we know that He hears us in whatever we ask, we know that we have the requests which we have asked from Him.

Because we believe him for what his Spirit is telling our spirit to ask for, *it will come to pass*. It will. If Adonai tells us to throw this mountain into the sea *now*, it will be done by him *now* through the manifestation of his power *flowing through* us - *now*! Otherwise, though we may hope for something *now*, it may be that his will is that it occur in the future, and so *it is in the process* of being done by the manifestation of his power *as it is flowing now and will flow in the future*.

Mark 15:5

...apart from me you can do nothing

Romans 8:26-27

26 ...For we do not know what to pray for as we ought, but the Spirit himself intercedes for us with groanings too deep for words. 27 ... the Spirit intercedes for the saints according to the will of God.

Matthew 6:33

But seek first the kingdom of God and his righteousness,

****

If we step into a situation that is not in God's will but our own, we should not expect him to deliver - although sometimes he will. Most often, when he gives us what we want - that *he does not want* for us - it will be a learning experience that fails to accomplish what we had hoped it would. In it he Gently reminds us that our ways are not as high as his ways. Like any good father, he will allow us to test out our theories and then be there to help us learn how and why we failed.

I am thankful for a book by Lee Strobel called The Case for Miracles. A segment of our Christian population do not believe that they still occur, but the proof is there in the reading and the references. At the same time, I am sorrow-filled for the damage that another segment of our Christian population has done. They believe that they are able to heal "at will" because they have been given the Power and Authority to do so.

Yes, we all may be useful to God to heal - if he Directs it. I believe that I can be a vehicle for healing by the power of the Presence and the flow of the Spirit of God in any given situation – if he wills it. If power and authority have been given to us for our discretionary use and not situationally according to his will, then why don't we send teams into the hospitals to walk all the patients out happy, healthy and whole? Because the power and authority are not ours, they are *his* and are at *his* discretion!

His ways are higher than our ways. Use of his power and authority are *not* at our discretion. Power and authority are intimately intertwined *in* him to be Directed and Led *by* him as we participate *with* him.

Some who *have* participated with him in healings go on to believe that they have learned how to do it and have been *empowered* to do it. Unfortunately, I have watched as some of these people begin to say "I release" or "We release" healing for people that are not then healed. Initially, their words glorify themselves, not the One who would be doing the releasing. Then, when healing does not occur, they tarnish God's reputation as well as their own because he did not honor *their* releasing according to *their* will. Having stepped out in what they perceived as faith, they may easily end up causing those present to *lose* faith when healing does not occur. Some blame the individual for not being healed using rationalizations like, "You did not have enough faith to receive it.", thereby adding insult to the injury.

John 15:5
...apart from me you can do nothing.

God does not misfire. By whose will do they think they are healing? God's. But in my opinion they have been Deceived and are instilling doubt of both him and his followers into the lives of those present. As they sometimes successfully participate *with* him and sometimes fail while stepping out "in faith" *on their own*, they fail on their own. Tarnishing God's reputation, they provide doubters and skeptics the ammunition needed to suggest that the previous successes *in participation with him* ever occurred. You can be sure that the skeptics among us will publicize such failings as proof that the authentic healings never did.

One with him, he is the Vine, we are the branches. We can do nothing worthwhile without him. For him is under our power. With him is under his.

John 16:26
*In that day you will ask in my name (using the incantation, "...in his name"), and I do **not** say to you that I will ask the Father on your behalf;*

James 4:2b-3
2b... You do not have, because you do not ask. 3 You ask and do not receive, because you ask wrongly, to spend it on your passions.

If I am in a situation where prayer is requested for healing, I take great care to explain what may or may not happen. That if God tells me or someone else or all of us that he will heal them, then it *will* be done. Still, if I/we do not "hear" that he will, I/we will still ask him that it *be done* or *be in his process of being done* because he still might. God says that sometimes we do not receive because we do not ask.

Therefore, I/we will ask while also stating our agreement with him for *his* will to be done in his own way. We will ask that he do so for his glory and according to his will. So, if healing occurs, great! But if not, please be confident that he has a plan to use the infirmity for good.

Consider the large number of people we know about who have overcome an infirmity to do great things *with* God. Consider the even larger numbers of people who have been inspired by them to *also* accomplish other things with God. I am always careful to ask the infirm who request healing prayer to consider what good God might do *through* them for the benefit of others if he does not heal them.

If they will accept the issue, remember that this life is brief, that eternity is in view, and Peace and Joy that surpass understanding are available in the God-led life – they just might find themselves praising him later for what the infirmity has meant for *many* lives.

When we start from a solid foundation, knowing that he loves us, knowing that his care and his plans are *for* us, and then build brick by brick and board by board on top of that Foundation, we will find the abundant life that he promises. It is otherwise like trying to put a roof on top of a foundation that has no walls. When he is allowed to work with us to build walls around the foundation, he will not only build in us a solid main floor, but the opportunity to add a second floor and third and fourth and fifth.

Psalm 127:1-2

1 Unless the Lord builds the house, those who build it labor in vain. Unless the Lord watches over the city, the watchman stays awake in vain. 2 It is in vain that you rise up early and go late to rest, eating the bread of anxious toil; for he gives to his beloved sleep.

Isaiah 60:16b-17

...and you shall know that I, the Lord, am your Savior and your Redeemer, the Mighty One of Jacob. 17 Instead of bronze I will bring gold, and instead of iron I will bring silver; instead of wood, bronze, instead of stones, iron. I will make your overseers peace and your taskmasters righteousness.

Matthew 25:19-23

19 Now after a long time the master of those servants came and settled accounts with them. 20 And he who had received the five talents came forward, bringing five talents more, saying, 'Master, you delivered to me five talents; here, I have made five talents more.' 21 His master said to him, 'Well done, good and faithful servant. You have been faithful over a little; I will set you over much. Enter into the joy of your master.' 22 And he also who had the two talents came forward, saying, 'Master, you delivered to me two talents; here, I have made two talents more.' 23 His master said to him, 'Well done, good and faithful servant. You have been faithful over a little; I will set you over much. Enter into the joy of your master.'

Ephesians 3:20-21

20 Now to him who is able to do far more abundantly than all that we ask or think, according to the power at work within us, 21 to him be glory in the church and in Christ Jesus throughout all generations, forever and ever. Amen.

This is not meant to be a "prosperity" teaching, another Deception passed down through the ages. It is simply to say that God will provide, and often more and more than we could ever possibly imagine. Obedient to him in relationships, he will give us the materials we need to continue the expansion of his kingdom, in *his* peace, in *his* righteousness and in *his* will. Giving all glory to *him*!

Philippians 3: 12-15

12 Not that I have already obtained this or am already perfect, but I press on to make it my own, because Christ Jesus has made me his own. 13 Brothers, I do not consider that I have made it my own. But one thing I do: forgetting what lies behind and straining forward to what lies ahead, 14 I press on toward the goal for the prize of the upward call of God in Christ Jesus. 15 Let those of us who are mature think this way, <u>and if in anything you think otherwise, God will reveal that also to you</u>.

Chapter Thirty

Willing Participants In The Collective Wisdom

So many fail because they trust in their mind to work things out by its ability to think and logic things through. The mind is self-focused on its own, and some of our personalities are more predisposed to thinking than they are for matters of the feeling heart. That must be why Jesus spoke of the totality of the heart, soul and mind, and of the strength that he will give to us to overcome the Deceiver.

Thomas was one of the thinkers that could not logic his way through to believing that Jesus could have risen from the dead – even though he had trusted friends as witnesses who were recounting their experience of being with him. Unless they have matured and *become* balanced, this personality type tends toward only trusting what they can *see* and confirm.

John 20:24-25

24 Now Thomas, one of the twelve, called the Twin, was not with them when Jesus came. 25 So the other disciples told him, "We have seen the Lord." But he said to them, "Unless I see in his hands the mark of the nails, and place my finger into the mark of the nails, and place my hand into his side, I will never believe."

As children, with our brains already deeply engaged in accessing our daily needs and desires, while also working to master small and large motor skills - we were necessarily predisposed to calculation, logic and the intellectual processes. Then by the time we were teens, as we failed in any given area to satisfy our parents, many were pressed upon to "THINK!", "What are you doing?" "Use your head! Think it through!" If not by our parents, our mind-oriented culture otherwise came through loud and clear all the way through school.

Remembering the 4 basic personality types from which the multiplicity of types all spring, two are predisposed to thinking and logic and will easily take to the direction to "Think!". However, as they grow older, they will not easily find a balance with matters of the heart. These will tend to contemplate more like Thomas than John, the one whom Jesus loved. John was more balanced in his approach and could process what he was seeing and hearing through the combination of his heart and soul and mind.

Why might this have been so for John?

Consider that the two *other* basic personality types are predisposed to matters of the *heart* first. Having an inherent strength in the matters of the heart, they will better learn balance in a *mind-oriented* culture because they will *add* thinking and logic to their predisposition for heart related considerations.

Conversely, the two that are predisposed to thinking and logic will more easily ignore their heart because thinking is their strength. Unfortunately, in the mind-oriented culture of the USA, there are fewer people around to teach them how to *add* matters of the *heart*.

You may flip this around in cultures where the matters of the heart are primary over thinking and logic.

As stated previously, I have had the good fortune to spend time working in 20 countries. One of the things learned across five continents was that where food has historically been easy to access, a strong work ethic is unnecessary. In fact, having no one to compete against for food, these cultures are far more heart oriented. An example would be the people of most of the warm weather islands. One of the reasons that Hawaii is called Paradise is just so.

Historically, the land and the sea there have been so forthcoming with food that there was no need to compete with others for it. Given less interpersonal stress with regard to finding and competing for provision - strong families, strong relationships and strong communities were the norm.

In Hawaii, Mom and Dad were always around, and with no pressure to keep the kids fed or clothed, families had a lot more fun together! Trust comes easily in these situations, and that builds faith in one another, which then makes it easier to love and be committed *to* each other. Self-focus was historically far more rare and generosity far more common than what we might call *our* norm. This disposition toward trust made them perfect targets for unscrupulous outsiders who later bought massive land areas from them for next to nothing.

Modern day Hawaiians are telling their children that their ancestors were too soft-hearted, which is true in consideration of the outsiders who took advantage of them. However, they were not too soft-hearted with their own people. In fact, theirs was an amazing example of love and respect for one another, along with a tremendous history of music, dance and worship of the gods of their understanding. They very quickly came to accept the one true God when the missionaries arrived, and continue now to instead honor the Father, Son and Holy Spirit.

****

The local culture in which we are raised means everything to how we will view others, and the family culture we are raised in will therefore also reflect that culture to some extent. Does this help you make sense of how it is that our country formerly reflected such strong balanced families, but has evolved to become far less so? Our once agrarian nation of plenty is now a mostly urban competition of the faceless and the nameless. It is therefore much easier to rationalize the harm we will bring to those we do not know and may never meet. No wonder we have such a reduced willingness to trust anyone!

There is an old joke about a son who was up on the roof and afraid to jump down and the father who came to his rescue. The father told the son to jump down into his arms so that he could catch him. The son, afraid that the father might drop him, refused to jump. After many iterations of, "Don't worry, I'll catch you.", the father finally pleaded with the son to simply trust him. That as his father he loved him too much to let him fall. When the son had finally calmed down, dried his tears and had overcome his fear, he jumped toward his father's outstretched arms. At the same moment, the father stepped back and let him hit the ground. Shocked, the son looked up at his father who reprimanded, "Let that be a lesson to you, don't trust anybody!"

But trust is key. It was said previously that the depth of our relational trust will bring us to the depth of our faith relationally. And that the depth of our love for others is built upon our faith that we may continue to trust them with our hearts in any situation. Trust> Faith> Growing Intimacy> Love. All the Enemy needs to do to facilitate the tearing apart of relationships is persuade us to break Trust. That's what he did with Adam and Eve and the rest is history. Rather, God leads us in the maintaining of Trust and integrity in our relationships – and thereby Love grows.

The disintegration of the nuclear family is much discussed among most of us over the age of 60. The disintegration of our nation has naturally followed the disintegration of the nuclear family. We need each other in more ways than we may imagine. We are better together, him in us and us in him. But if we cannot trust each other the disintegration will continue.

****

God has given each of us unique things to "see", things to "know" and things to "understand" through perspectives and life experiences he uses for *our* good, for *our* preparation, for the helping of each other *collectively*.

Considering the four basic personality types from which all of the multiplicity of types spring, two "see" first with their hearts and two "see" first with their minds. We will not as easily find God by a search with our minds. Hearts of compassion, care and hope will more easily "see" what the mind cannot think, logic or judge.

The two basic personality types who "see" first with their hearts and seek confirmation with their minds will more easily come to know God. The two basic personality types who "see" first with their minds and then seek confirmation with their hearts will have a more difficult time coming to know God as they try to logic and judge what they "see". God makes all four useful to *participate with him and each other* in the search to understand why we are here and what it is all about.

Those who see first with their hearts will help those who see first with their minds to find God. Then, those who see first with their minds will come to be able to help those who see first with their hearts to better explain with their minds the love of Adonai, our triune God. Each may teach the other their strengths and bring a better balance for the benefit of the people in their lives. What we cannot "see" we do not appreciate, but once our vision is improved by the contributions of the others, we cannot imagine living together any other way. Collectively we will "see" better, "know" more and "understand" more fully how to follow the Father *collectively*, one in him and him in us.

Many of my best friends are on the opposite personality side and have well developed former "weaknesses". It is far more enjoyable sharing life with Thinkers with Heart and Hearts that can Think than with mostly one-dimensional folks. As God has shown us through experience together and follow-up conversation (as with my wife and I), we all know what we can count on each other to do and to not do in any future context. God helps us with this collectively too, but we must engage in the conversation to gain the benefit. In most of the USA, Thinkers need help in realizing that God would have them *check their heart* during decision making.

We see in Proverbs 29:18, *"Where there is no revelation, people cast off restraint; but blessed is the one who heeds wisdom's instruction."* If we will love God with all of our hearts, souls, minds and strength – we need the revelation of the Teaching of Jesus, the Leading of the Holy Spirit and the Father doing his Works *in us all* - to more *wholly* see. Only then will we be able to love wholly and love only *collectively*. We will be hearts and minds balanced in souls whose spirits fully relate to God by the power of his Holy Spirit. In this way, the multiplicity of personality types bring a beautiful tapestry, a wonderful orchestral quality and a rich life of helpful variety together. Each building upon the other, loving wholly and loving only.

As a child I remember listening to my father and his friends talking about their eventual retirement. One said they would spend it hunting, others said fishing, hitting the casino, golfing, woodworking and doing landscaping and gardening around their home.

Other than the casino, it was great to also hear that they had been doing these things with their children as they raised them. But with a slight modification, they could still be doing them during retirement with people of need in their communities.

These days many are finding great joy in doing these hobbies with troubled teens, rehabilitating felons and alongside lonely seniors. Jesus invited the apostles to become fishers of men. How about hunters of men, people taking a chance on men and woodworkers training up young men? The same could be said for bankers and lawyers and accountants.

What a waste it is when the collective Wisdom of the elders in our communities not only retire from their careers, but from engagement with those they could most easily support with their love of the Lord while doing activities that share their knowledge and skills. There is no more joyful and rewarding life than one of connecting with others in life-on-life opportunities. Like working with youth to share and show what it is like to be in relationship with the living God. Led by him, avoiding the pitfalls of life. Avoiding lives of isolation, sadness and perhaps even incarceration.

Matthew 5:13-16

13 "You are the salt of the earth, but if salt has lost its taste, how shall its saltiness be restored? It is no longer good for anything except to be thrown out and trampled under people's feet. 14 "You are the light of the world. A city set on a hill cannot be hidden. 15 Nor do people light a lamp and put it under a basket, but on a stand, and it gives light to all in the house. 16 In the same way, let your light shine before others, so that they may see your good works and give glory to your Father who is in heaven.

2 Peter 1:3-4 NIV

3 <u>His divine power has given us everything we need</u> for a godly life through our knowledge of him who called us by his own glory and goodness. 4 Through these he has given us his very great and precious promises, <u>so that through them you may participate in the divine nature</u>, having escaped the corruption in the world caused by evil desires.

O Adonai:

Sprinkle us like salt across our communities, each grain reflecting your light, that by your words and actions through us, as we participate with you, we illuminate their path home. That none should perish, but live eternally in the Joy of relationship with you.

1 John 2:3-6

3 And by this we know that we have come to know him, if we keep his commandments. 4 Whoever says "I know him" but does not keep his commandments is a liar, and the truth is not in him, 5 but whoever keeps his word, in him truly the love of God is perfected. By this we may know that we are in him: 6 whoever says he abides in him ought to walk in the same way in which he walked.

1 John 2:28
And now, little children, abide in him, so that when he appears we may have confidence and not shrink from him in shame at his coming.

****

As stated previously, the roaring lions among us are utilizing the zoological Landscape of Fear to silence those who disagree with them. Our fear having done so, they are gaining power and taking Control as they try to assume Authority over us. Our relationships now stifled, we have become extremely Divided in our politics, families, religions and governments.

We simply must learn how to speak up - in fruit of the Spirit language and actions - lest the disintegration of our families and nation continue.

As long as our conversations concede to those utilizing *Landscape of Fear* language, the trust required to develop strong workable relationships will be squelched. Fruit of the Spirit responses in Gentleness share the truth with them in Goodness, with Patience as we Persevere in Kindness, and with Self-Control as we speak from a spirit of Peace. Passionate conversations require the respect that facilitates true iron sharpening iron conversation. Fruit of the Spirit language gives them an opportunity to choose Dialogue and respect, though they may still Reject it and choose Fight or Flight.

When we are mature, balanced and united with him in our hearts, souls and minds, we may more effectively communicate with the lions of this world. Contemplate "*Life*" as you practice utilizing *fruit of the Spirit* language and actions. That you more and more *become* a talmid of Jesus, and therefore a more effective communicator doing the will of the Father. Respectfully, Perseveringly, Peaceably and Gently.

As a leader, are you a "mover and shaker" or a Gently influencing convincer, persuader and team builder?

Is your personality type that of the half that believe that the ends justify the means? Might it be that you are one of the roaring lions utilizing Landscape of Fear language and actions to accomplish your will the way you see fit? Are your ways like the ways of Judas and Peter mentioned in the chapter: Eyes That See and Ears That Hear.

The Father Directs our attention to a variety of matters every day. That we would consider them in light of the teachings of Jesus, with hearts after the Father's. That we would then be led into understanding by the Holy Spirit to agree with and to do God's will. That is: to draw all closer to him as we progress into Unity and the living of Joy-filled lives in the Family of God.

Learning to live the *Life* he has for us, submitting ourselves to his *Love* and Directional Guidance, we will be better able to Gently *Lead* by the power of the Holy Spirit, communicating Jesus' Teachings as the Father in us does his Works - accomplishing *his* will.

****

We are the ones who now must decide what we will do with the information that Jesus has Taught while the Father has been in us is doing his Works, and whether or not we will follow the Leading of the Holy Spirit. Accomplish your will in us, O God!

He is looking for willing participants in continuous conversational worship who will engage in creative collaboration – collectively – according to his Wisdom and his Will. By the Leading of his Holy Spirit. That none should perish.

I am happy to know that more and more are leading their small groups through this book, that disciples may become disciple-ers – developing talmidim of Jesus who will develop more talmidim who will then develop more and more talmidim. Leadership small groups and training teams such as these unite his people to more productive service. Lord of the harvest, send laborers!

Father, thank you that you Lead & Guide us for your influence upon all, that we may know you collectively, love you personally and accomplish your will - together! Thank you that you bring a joyful balance to our lives as we serve and share with each other. We greatly

desire to participate with you to establish, strengthen and multiply your people, O God! Do your Works in us that we not enter into the temptation to try to take control. Deliver all of us from the evil we would otherwise do leaning on our own understanding. We agree with you for your will your way. Unite your people to more productive service!
Amen!

Chapter Thirty-One

Never Talk About Politics Or Religion

In over 30 years of consulting and mentoring for businesses, churches and lives, I have found a common problem unique to each individual: We are only able to navigate the areas of ignorance in our life for so long before our foundational relational errors bring us to a dead-end wall. Or ceiling.

Those who *most successfully* navigate the world understand the inherent flaw in trying to manipulate and control others. Rather than responding in kind to a manipulator, they *instead offer safe information that allows them to make a choice* – free of manipulation or veiled threat. When one or more of those around them are resorting to their sophisticated manipulative skill set, they respond in ways that neutralize and inform that also share a preferred outcome – all without manipulation.

Though we may fail in it from time to time, our privilege is to participate *with* God in his drawing of those before us into a better relationship with ourselves and himself. What is paramount is our motivation, language and tone as we inform. I have often informed people of my Judgement of them and Demanded that they change because it was the "right" thing to do – and they owed it to me! It was never beneficial to them or me, nor at all effective in drawing them closer to God. These missed opportunities to participate *with* God in the building up of Unity and strong synergistic relationships instead brought greater Separation between us all.

Unless we endeavor otherwise, the *orientation* toward selfishness will continually impede our progress. Those who opt for the use of power and Authority to control those around them will periodically win, but often fail at crunch-time. Those who learn to deceive and slander in order to rise above will later learn that they eventually blocked their own upward mobility by the reputation that followed them. Those who take from others will have problems with the law. Those who judge and condemn in order to shame another into compliance with their view will find the size of their circle of friends and trusted co-workers diminishing. Those who cause Dissension and Division so that they might Divide and Conquer will find themselves isolated and alone, untrusted by others and therefore avoided.

Trust issues surround the self-oriented. They do not look for the win-win, but their own *self*-oriented win. At birth we were necessarily *self*-focused, not God and neighbor focused. But we are no longer children.

The self-focused have never learned how to talk respectfully about Faith, Family and the Governance we are all under. This is why they say we should never talk about politics or religion. This is true and correct because politics and religion are founded upon the Enemy principals designed to drag us into Argument that results in Division. Religion is a corruption of true Faith that leads to the corruption of government through Divisive Politics.

Faith, Family and Governance are different. These are matters of the heart, the necessary discussion of which must be founded upon our desire for Unity and according to the leading and iron sharpening iron activity of the One True God. Faith and Family focused, not self-focused, we are more likely to vote for people in Governance who will move us back towards operation as One nation under God, Indivisible, with Liberty and Justice for all. Operating in his Unity OS, his light will pierce the Darkness of the World OS. Scattered like grains of salt, each of us reflecting his light, his words and actions through us will participate with him in the illuminating of their path home. That none should perish but live eternally in the joy of relationship with him.

Matthew 5:13-16

13 "You are the salt of the earth, but if salt has lost its taste, how shall its saltiness be restored? It is no longer good for anything except to be thrown out and trampled under people's feet. 14 "You are the light of the world. A city set on a hill cannot be hidden. 15 Nor do people light a lamp and put it under a basket, but on a stand, and it gives light to all in the house. 16 In the same way, let your light shine before others, so that they may see your good works and give glory to your Father who is in heaven.

Matthew 6:33
But seek first the kingdom of God and his righteousness, and all these things will be added to you.

Proverbs 11:14 NASB
Where there is no guidance the people fall,
But in an abundance of counselors there is victory.

****

While the things that we know so very well are what we lean on to bring us success, it is the things that we do not know very well that trip us up and curtail it. Thinkers need Feelers to help identify these issues in their lives. As long as these remain misunderstood, they act like glass ceilings above us that we continually bump our heads against as we try to rise higher.

Though strong Thinkers may find their own way to the matters of the heart, the process is not typical for them. In Who Moved the Stone, Frank Morison is another strong Thinker atheist who tried to disprove the biblical account. As an ancient documents scholar who had made a career of proving the veracity of ancient documents through the investigation of other ancient documents, he theorized that he would be the perfect person to prove that the resurrection of Jesus did not occur. As he used all sorts of non-Bible ancient documents alongside the biblical account, he instead *proved* the biblical account: Jesus died and rose from the dead. His book is a courtroom drama capable of leading any logical Thinker to belief in Christ – if they will only take the time to carefully examine it.

We need to seek out others for Wise counsel, utilizing the collective Wisdom of God's people on our behalf.

None of us know everything. There is strength in numbers. Teams always accomplish more than individuals. The collective Wisdom found on teams brings greater success. The sum of the whole is logarithmically greater than the individual parts. (Yes, Rick, tell me something I don't know.) OK. Most of us do not know how to operate in *Unity* to do so. Most of us do not know how to play well together. Teams are frustrating to most people because they are not expedient. Most of us want to vote in order to expedite.

The old saying is that if you want to get something done, don't give it to a committee. One of the reasons for me is that committees seek a majority vote, and voting brings Division and Division adds to the politics, and politics are from Caesar, and their results are therefore tainted. *Not* so for those seeking God's will and discernment of the collective Wisdom in Unity.

When expedience and productivity are more important than Collective Wisdom & Relational Unity, winners and losers will be the relational result. And that type of result breeds Division.

Once Unity values are understood, put in place, practiced and in operation, most are amazed by the increasing quality of relationships, and therefore by the pace of progress and broad productivity God brings.

I believe you will find satisfaction about operating in Unity in the section on Leading. In it, we will discuss how Christ Followers may operate any entity, even the businesses they have been entrusted with by God, collaboratively. In Unity. One with him, him in us and us in him.

There is a big difference between Rules and Agreements. The saying "Rules are made to be broken." emanates from a lack of respect for the rule maker(s) due to disagreement about "the rule", which therefore ignites our emotion to rebel against Authoritarian Control.

Agreements, on the other hand, are freely made *together*, are understood by each, have a level of respect for the *relationship* that exists between the agreeing parties, and ignite the sense of loyalty and integrity that lead *us* to follow through on the agreement.

Rules are made to be broken, so the Ruler will always have rebels. But *agreements* are *Relational* commitments *to each other*. Agreements may be revised. Rules are rigid and beg rebellion because they are Controlling, and nobody wants to be Controlled. All want their say in the matter, but Rulers don't care about that. They just want their way.

****

Traditions are born of the passing down of understandings and misunderstandings that survive. Good ones *and* bad ones. The ways of the parents are passed down to the 3rd and 4th generation. So, too, have the errors of church leaders been passed down to the 3rd and 4th generation. For generations. For generations of generations. This is true for *every* religion.

The best of intentions may lead to the engraining of misunderstandings over time. Our forefathers bought into tiny Deceptions that have grown over the centuries to encompass large swaths of badly mistaken good intentions. So, too, was it true for their understandings in Jesus' day.

We have gotten past the belief that people shouldn't have a Bible that they can read, but now we have so many that they do not all agree in content. Some are written to simplify for the new believer, some for ease of reading, others for any number of reasons – but have they left the original meaning of the text behind in error? Which is closest to the original text? Which have lost the context? (Biblical scholars overwhelmingly recommend the ESV and NASB.)

When our bias for Authority is part of our foundational understanding, anything we create will use the Parallels OS (at best). Belief in our Authority gave us the confidence to rid the world of people who disagreed with us. It is responsible for the genocidal "cleansing" of the "Christian" Crusades against the Jews, in Hitler's Holocaust, against Bosnian Muslims and more recently by the Chinese against the Muslim Uyghurs.

God is Love. Anything that is "not Love" is not of God. Islam supports Mohammed's claim that he was told by God that they should subjugate (Control) women, that jihad and the murder of the infidels (the Jews) is in his will, and that violence and the threat of violence may be used to Control people - but it simply cannot be true. If we will be effective in discussing the issues of *Faith, Family and Governance*, we simply must educate ourselves in the problems of Religion (corrupted Faith) that have evolved to also Divide us politically over the past several thousand years.

The Jewish, Muslim and Christian faiths all originated with the very same family of people, at the very same time, under the very same God, with each believing the very same original Hebrew scriptures. Thousands of years later, the Hebrew people were divided by what

Jesus said and did, and then six hundred years later were divided again by what Mohammed said and did.

Since the very same original Hebrew scripture that is common to all three faiths says that God never changes, we know that Adonai said the same thing to all of us at the same time - giving us dominion over the earth, but never each other (Genesis 1, Genesis 9, 1 Samuel 8, Matthew 20, Mark 10, Luke 22).

Therefore, any claim that God now desires the killing off of the Hebrew people, the subjugation of women (or any person), or espousal of the use of intimidation or violence strategies that serve to Control people – simply cannot be of the one true and unchanging God they followed originally and claim to be following now. Allah, the god of Islam, must therefore be a Deception of the Enemy.

The Hebrew people were never a religion, they were simply a people of a given geography living in the relationship God initiated. "Religion" is a terminology made up by man around 1200AD because man needed a noun to describe the various "faiths" that had evolved since the time of Jesus.

Religion's etymology comes from the ancient word "religious". Religious means "strict adherence to a set of beliefs". By 1200AD there were so many different formalized sets of beliefs that we needed a way to describe them all. Religion is the noun we created for that.

Religions have come from the portions of mankind who believe that they can explain God and what God wants better than other people can. Religious (strictly adhering) people are therefore not following God, but rather the Proud who Divided us – and who instituted the various Religions.

God has not separated us; the Pride of mankind has Divided us through claims of having a superior knowledge. Therefore, Religions were birthed as people followed people. God has never asked us for anything other than a trusting personal relationship with him in The Family Of God. Following him and his ways alone.

By the way, the word religion in James 1:27 did NOT exist at that time. It is a mistranslation through anachronism. According to the originating language, what James actually said used the Hebrew word for "religious". That word, religious, DID exist at that time:

James 1:27
Strict adherence (religion) that is pure and undefiled before God the Father is this: to visit orphans and widows in their affliction, and to keep oneself unstained from the world."

In our desire to educate ourselves, it is important to note that:

- Genesis Chapters 15, 16, 17, 21, 22, 25 and non-religious Historians agree that the Muslims and Jews are *family* in a family feud that began with the birth of Ishmael and was intensified through the lives of the brothers Esau and Jacob about 4000 years ago.
- Nonetheless, when Israel returned from slavery in Egypt and conquered the land of Canaan (around 1300 BC), Edom (Esau's line) and Israel (Jacob's line) *lived separately but peacefully as neighbors* for hundreds of years. Historians identify that religion was not an issue between, and that there was actually *agreement* between them about God and his laws. One of these, "Don't eat pork.", came from *their original family foundation in the laws and traditions of their Hebrew heritage*.
- Israel (Jacob's line) and Edom (Esau's line) fought back and forth from about 930 BC, not over religion, but over their competing desire to raise animals and crops on the fertile lands. Those battles ended when Israel was conquered by Babylon in 587-586 BC and taken captive to Babylon.
- The writings of the Quran didn't begin until 610 AD. This book dredged up the *historical* family feud to restart and inflame it. This is the time of the birth of Islam. The Quran is the beginning of the Edomites (Muslim) belief that they should "Subjugate women." and "Kill the infidels (the Hebrew people) in jihad." Now Muslims call the USA "The Great Satan" and include us in their plans for jihad and subjugation.
    - For roughly 3,000 years, there was agreement between Israel (Jacob's line) and Edom (Esau's line) about God and his ways. "Subjugating women." and "Killing the infidels." goes against what the God of *their shared heritage* had been saying for thousands of years.

  - The god who in 610 AD began to command subjugation and jihad through Mohammed cannot be the same God. Caught up in the cosmic war between God and Satan, the writings of Mohammed are a deception from the devil, given to inflame a vulnerable people into remembering and acting upon the ancient yet formerly *resolved* feud between Esau and Jacob.
- The "Christian" Crusades against non-Christians were wrought by a Satan deceived people group. What happened then, and more recently in places like Bosnia and China, occurred in the same Deceptive way. They were *not* of God.
  - The Bible does not in any way encourage or command such things.
    - It is different in the Quran. The Quran is designed to keep the family feud alive and us in jihad.
    - The Christian Bible is a story of learning discipline to *overcome* anger and instead share *love* in Unity and the collective Wisdom God provides. Jesus and Mohammed are antithetical.

Further evidence:

- Genetic studies indicate that Palestinian Arabs have substantial genetic overlap with the Jews. They are family!
- Palestinians are considered to be the closest genetic neighbors to most Jewish populations, along with Bedouins, Druze, and southern European groups. In the history of the world, there has never been a "Palestine", Palestinian nation or Palestinian "state".
- The following link from one of many historical accounts will be helpful in support of your understanding, if you so desire: DailyHistory.org/Why_Were_the_Ancient_Israelites_and_Edomites_Enemies

Regarding the Philistines

- The Philistines originated as an *immigrant group* from the Aegean (that is Greece, and more than likely specifically the Mediterranean island of Crete) that settled in Canaan circa 1175 BC during the Late Bronze Age collapse. Over time, they gradually assimilated elements of the indigenous Levantine Semitic (Jewish) societies while preserving their own unique culture.
- In 604 BC, the Philistine polity, after having already been subjugated for centuries by the Neo-Assyrian Empire (911–605 BC), was finally destroyed by King Nebuchadnezzar II of the Neo-Babylonian Empire. Subsequently, the Philistines were compelled into exile in Babylonia, *where over time they lost their unique*

ethnic identity. By the late fifth century BC, *they vanished from both the historical and archaeological records as a distinct group*.

There is no evidence in the original scripture common to these three faiths that God espouses violence between us. There is no evidence that he has ever espoused the subjugation of women, or the Control of any people group. The *evidence* is that Jews, Christians and Muslims are all family of the God of the Hebrew lineage!

Yet what is common to many traditional Muslims today is that they are living portions of the Quran, the Hebrew Scriptures and the Christian New Testament! Therefore, it is not unfair to say this to them *in the attitudes of the Beatitudes and in fruit of the Spirit language and actions*: "If Allah is God, then follow him. Why do you waver between two or even three "religious" positions, trying to lead a "good" life according to *your own* way of thinking? Is it not hypocritical to disobey the Quran in the areas of subjugation and jihad, while agreeing with the Christian and Hebrew scriptures in the areas of civil morality?"

Is it not similarly so with our "Denominational Christians" our "Democrat Christians" and our "Republican Christians"? Each of these are Denominations, trying to live a "good life" separated and Divided into their own Doctrines and ways of thinking. Let's just be Followers of Jesus!

As we all pick and choose what we want to believe, we end up making little gods of ourselves trying to do "*right*". Living by a *code* of our *own* making, where *we* decide what "a good life" is, and that which is "virtuous". In that case, isn't God just a reference for us? Are we not living as our own gods as we pick and choose what we want to believe? "Strictly adhering" to our personal set of beliefs; have we not become a religion to ourselves?

We may gently and respectfully (1 Peter 3:15) share the following with people who believe according to their own way of thinking:

We do not follow "Allah", "Denominational or Non-Denominational Christians", "Democrat Christians" or "Republican Christians" as if they are the ones who best understand God. We believe that these are all deceptions from the devil in the cosmic battle between God and his Enemies. Because of these Divisions, we are at odds with each other – and Satan is laughing.

We DO believe, and have learned by doing it, that we were created for an amazing joy-filled life together, in a direct relationship with the One True God. We were not made for jihad according to Allah, or Division according to any "Religion" or "Denomination", - but for Unity, him in us and us in him (John 17). God is Love. Anything that is "Not Love" is "Not of God". Divisions between us are "Not Love".

****

In the Spirit of the Lord there is freedom (2 Corinthians 3:17). Any person, entity or nation that advocates for intimidation, violence or the threat of violence – using fear to Control people - cannot be of God. Though people still do it, supposedly according to God, today.

The belief in Authority and hierarchical structures gave us the Constantine church in Italy in AD 325 and every one of our "Christian" denominations ever since. Then came the birth of the non-denominations, and the growth of the political denominations - and the Enemy has Divided us further. History identifies that we have tried to multiply by Dividing ourselves. Pride bringing the Division.

Having taught us to take Authority, the Enemy incited Pride among us - that we might think we think best - to Divide us into religious denominations. And we are still Proud of our "better thought and understanding" in these today. But God can utilize these differences for good if we will but submit to him as the only authority and come together in his Spirit of Unity across denominational lines to operate in the Unity Operating System. The Lausanne Covenant, signed in 1974 by the Christ Followers of over 150 nations, espouses such Unity and the synergy it will bring.

The Leading section describes a workable approach for the uniting and aligning of God's people to more productive service in any community. (Beginning at the end of 2025, please see the Community Service and Support Network site at CSASNetwork.org) If we will start small together in our communities, we will be better able to spread such effectiveness into other communities and nations as they take notice of our successes. Now, fifty years later, its time has come!

****

President Ronald Reagan & Speaker of the House Tip O'Neill, and President Bill Clinton & Speaker of the House Newt Gingrich came together to accomplish great things for Americans and the world in their day - even though they came from opposing political parties and disagreed on many topics. These days our Pride and entrenched cultural bias for power and Authority have led a portion of our politicians to Divide themselves from each other - and us from amongst ourselves - so as to enshrine that very same belief in power over people that Jesus came to abolish. When God's people came together to birth this nation *in his ways*, we were set upon a course for liberty and freedom that made us a light on a lampstand for all the earth. Later, as God's people went the way of the World Operating System and Rejected his Unity Operating System, the beginning of our slide toward oblivion began. It can be reversed if we will only return to *him and his ways* – reuniting his people.

There is but One Church and One Kingdom of God in heaven and on earth – and Christ is our Head. The world's Religions and Political Parties are Divisions instituted by mostly well-intentioned people Deceived by the Enemy into believing that they have God more right than do others – and so must set themselves apart. These haven't stopped with the birth of denominations and non-denominations, but have continued on to even include the all-too-common splitting of one local church into two separate buildings within the *same* denominational or nondenominational community! The Unity Operating System has not only been discarded by most politicians, it has also been discarded by far too many of God's people!

I remember the visit from the pastor of a church Debbie and I visited early in our marriage. We had moved into a new city and were making our way around on Sundays to find a new church home. As that pastor spoke with us in *our* home, he tried to convince us that *his* church had it right. That their beliefs were *more right* than the others, and that if we cared to get it *all* right we would join *his* church. Do you see how this man's *right* view of himself was so *not right*? He was being Divisive of the broader body of Christ *in his own hometown*. We never went back.

How have we become so arrogant? We bought into tiny elements of Deception that sounded harmless enough *very slowly* – a little here and a little there - over many, many, many generations. The Deceptions and half-told-truths that have been passed down to us are similar to the traditions of the Pharisees who Jesus railed about. We have created our own Traditions, and some of them are simply not biblical. But God is still available to help us, even to help us use our many divisions for good, in Dialogue that unites his people to more productive service.

When we start with a foundational understanding of God's ways and model our behavior after them, Manipulate To Control behaviors go away. In the attitudes of Jesus, we produce fruit of the Spirit in support of each other.

While we will always have disagreements in our understandings of certain portions of scripture (Let iron sharpen iron!), may we Unite under God in the collective Wisdom he offers us. Unfortunately, like the Pharisees, we are all currently stuck in the Prideful ways of our various national Religions and Traditions *according to what we want God to want*. As we pressure each other for *what we think God should want*, the cosmic battle continues across nations. Peace eludes us as we tell others that our ways are the right ways. And the Enemy is laughing as he watches our nations collapse into the Chaos we have followed him into.

Utilizing the World OS, we assume *Authority and/or polity* will be needed to *expeditiously* overcome or isolate our opposition. Knowing his *Unity Operating System*, we look at our differences *collectively* and share in Wisdom and Unite as the picture and process forward becomes more clear.

It is inconceivable to simply abandon our Political Parties and Denominations. Rather, as is described in the Lausanne Covenant and will be further described in the Leading section, we must abandon our use of Authority and Hierarchical structures *in them* and Unite *across them*. When our Religious and Political Divisions give up their push for power and domination, abandon the Parallels OS, and align together with God and each other in his Unity OS and administrative structure - tremendous achievement will result. Otherwise, blinded by our Denominational and Party biases, the relational disintegration will continue.

All governments are founded first upon whether or not there is a belief in God, then the details of that belief are implemented based upon just what is believed. Atheistic governance is a great threat to all people, still so is governance Divided by Religion. Religion is a corruption of True Faith that leads to the corruption of governance through Divisive Politics. Let's be sure to point out the problems of Politics and Religion (corrupted faith), that we may then respectfully dialogue about Faith, Family and quality Governance. If our nation will ever heal, we must be willing to do this.

Dear God, awaken us to the Deceptions of Politics and Religion! Lead us by the power of your Spirit, taught and trained by you, as you continually do your works in us. Give us Wisdom. Unite us in True Faith under your governance and accomplish your will for us, O God. We ask these things here in your precious Presence, desiring that your will be done your way. Otherwise, if we "strictly adhere" to our personal set of beliefs, will we not have become a Religion to ourselves?

Chapter Thirty-Two

For The Children: Our Future

One of the ways and traditions we have is to not scare our children with talk of a devil trying to influence our behavior. There is a level of Wisdom here for the young, but those old enough to begin to understand need to start being prepared. If they are to be Led by the Spirit of the Living God as they mature, allowing the Father in them to do his Works, they must also be able to identify the voice of the Adversary who will try to confuse them and cause them to do wrongly.

Compelling research from the Barna group reveals that, on average, children now develop their worldview by age 13 and that 94% of decisions made for Christ happen before the age of 18!

Jesus said that his sheep know his voice and follow him. When should we start teaching our children how? Keep in mind that they were born coercing for milk, and that positive reinforcement will facilitate a more sophisticated use of manipulate to control strategies later. Even so, if what we offer them is our own personal view of what is right and wrong, they will eventually rebel against us *and* it as they age and doubt us. However if what we are teaching them is to trust the Teachings of Jesus, the difference between Love and Not Love, the Leading of the Spirit, and that the Father is available in them to do his Works - to help them and lead them to a life of greater Joy than they can otherwise know - they will have a better chance at finding their way along the narrow path.

If we would reveal the availability of the Father, Son and Spirit little by little they will grow to know *which* is the very voice of God.

Matthew 16:15-17

15 He said to them, "But who do you say that I am?" 16 Simon Peter replied, "You are the Christ, the Son of the living God." 17 And Jesus answered him, "Blessed are you, Simon Bar-Jonah! For <u>flesh and blood has not revealed this to you, but my Father who is in heaven</u>.

1 Corinthians 2:10
these things <u>God has revealed to us through the Spirit</u>.
For the Spirit searches everything, even the depths of God.

John 6:45a
It is written in the Prophets, '<u>And they will all be taught by God</u>.'

It's not as difficult or dangerous as you may think:

"Mommy, Daddy, did you see that?" "Yes, Johnny, that was you and God working together! Didn't it feel great to help those people like that?!!! Johnny, you're old enough now for me to help you understand something more about God and how he helps us know what to do and what not to do. Do you remember the other day when you and Bobby both wanted the same toy and you decided to let him play with it first? And last week when…"

"Susie, when you are angry you can always ask God to help you calm down. Did you notice the feeling you had when you were angry? I'm so proud of you that you didn't give in to it!" God helped you to overcome it! Did you notice that you were being helped to decide?

"Tommy, when we are working together with God we will never do anything to harm anyone else." If you ever feel like you are going to, ask God to help you overcome it. He is always right there with you, wherever you go, to help you…

"Sally, what do you want to be when you grow up? You know how we have been talking about how God loves you and is talking to you with his quiet voice to help you? Well, he wants to help you with what you will be when you grow up, too. If you will talk with him about your hopes and dreams, he will help you with your choices. As you talk with him to understand, he will make your life better than you can possibly imagine.

Jimmy, you're ready for us to start talking with you about how we live our lives in the attitudes of Jesus. These attitudes include humility, having sorrow for others, gentleness with others, a desire for God's righteousness to occur, having mercy on others, making peace with others, and an understanding that many people are going to treat us badly. These attitudes will help us say and do things that will grow relationships of love, joy, peace, patience, kindness, goodness, gentleness, perseverance and self-control. As your parents, we are going to start helping you see when you are living in this way and when you are not. We're also going to start helping you understand how to communicate with people who are using Manipulate To Control behaviors. If you will be willing to do this with us, you will be able to be at Peace even when there is trouble. The more you learn to live in Jesus' ways, the better your life will be!

But what we have been trained to do is talk with them about how to navigate this life. About right and wrong and nice and mean: "Don't shout, don't hit, give that back, that's theirs, they had it first, wait your turn, you have to learn to share. Don't steal. Work hard. Be good. Be honest. Be reliable." But to what? To whom? What about Wisdom? What about what *God* has to say about it?

Just as we tell them not to play on a busy street, as they age we should tell them not to risk sexual activity before marriage and potentially complicate their lives with the temptation of an abortion. We should tell them that the Enemy tempts *everyone* with *something* to try to seduce them into acts of Rejection of the ways of God. It will often seem harmless enough in the beginning, but if you give in to it, it will develop a hold on you over time.

It's easy enough to say that what I am tempted with is not such a bad thing, but that way of thinking has led us down a very slippery slope to a sort of cultural belief now that *everything* is OK. People say, "God made me this way, there's nothing wrong with what I am doing." and use him as an excuse to delve in. But what if we all thought that way and indulged?

- I like sex with children, so I…
- I like to beat the sense into people who do me wrong, so I…
- I like to drive fast, so I expect people to get out of my way…
- I like torturing animals, so I…
- I like the feeling I get from heroin, so I…
- I like making people bleed, so I…
- I like to murder people who I think shouldn't be here, so I…
- I like sexual relationships with people of both genders, so I…
- It helps to beat my spouse when she treats me bad, so I…
- I like sex with certain kinds of animals, so I…

- I like to steal things from wealthy people because…
- I like to set things on fire, so I…
- I hate people in authority, so I…

God has spelled out what he thinks about all of this in the Bible. If we aren't paying attention to what he has to say about these and other things, why should our children? Which will *they* then *become*: the Wise, the Foolish or the Corrupt?

Many of us point fingers at other people's kids, but what about ours? Our parents regret some of the things they built into us, and now we have made mistakes with our kids too. Worldwide, our troubles come from the poor training of our children and the selfishness in them that survives. "Christian" politicians are products of families who have belief systems which should be fully informed by their Christology as they go through life. Take care, lest *you* be the one who misleads them!

Matthew 18:5-6

5 "Whoever receives one such child in my name receives me, 6 but whoever causes one of these little ones who believe in me to sin, it would be better for him to have a great millstone fastened around his neck and to be drowned in the depth of the sea.

Matthew 18:14

So it is not the will of my Father who is in heaven that one of these little ones should perish.

As we have aged and matured, we have come to recognize the bad things that we built into our children and are now trying to circle back, hoping that we may help them avoid building these into their children, God's children, our grandchildren.

The lifestyle of the parents, their ways, are passed down to the 3rd and 4th generation.

What *are* your ways? What are *you* teaching them? *Whose* ways are you teaching them to follow? What are they *observing* around you? Will they navigate this life according to *your* teachings or his? Will they know his voice and be Led, or be debating whether or not to follow *yours*?

The teenage years are so vulnerable! As they take notice of the temptations and enticements in the world around them, it's so very difficult to heed the warnings of parents. Often, unbeknownst to their parents, they are seduced into trying things suggested by the ones they call friends. Then, if they are additionally deceived by others into doubting the Wisdom of their parents, the stage is set for them to distance themselves further and further from God's Wisdom.

1 Corinthians 15:33
Do not be deceived: "Bad company ruins good morals."

Such was the case for my sister, who ran away from home at the age of sixteen. As the attempts of parents and siblings failed to bring her back, she was led further and further astray into the freedom she thought she could handle. Years later, after the effects of the drugs she was eventually also led into ruined her life, she committed suicide in another state. The note she left with sorrow and regret and apology was of little solace to those she left behind. While this is one of the more tragic story endings, many teens are lost into lives lived in judgement, anger, separation and isolation.

Pray for the children! As they venture out and stand by a tree entering into temptation - fueled by anger that the Enemy will help them to call just - they will scarcely imagine the life that they may be *self-selecting* their way into.

Pray for the children! They don't know what they don't know, only what they have been taught by us. Then, as they grow up, will look at where they think we went wrong and go their own way. Rather, raised up One with him, may they follow Adonai, their life-long Navigator!

Pray for the children, they are the parents and politicians of tomorrow!

Proverbs 22:6
Train up a child in the way he should go;
even when he is old he will not depart from it.

The Enemy has been working to accomplish the exact opposite in us as children. That we not *become* talmidim, but the blind leading the blind. That we pass Foolishness and Selfishness down to the 3rd and the 4th generation. That our children's marriages be torn apart by Selfishness, and their children's children, too. That our societies crumble and our nations fall into chaos:

Raise up a child in Selfishness and surround them with Foolishness,
that they too will remain so, and stray from the ways of God,
so that when they are old they will not depart from it –
and will raise their children in the same way.

Over the generations, our children's lack of understanding of the ways of God have led to disunity in the family unit and therefore disunity in our nation. Our Father has revealed it to you. Who will reverse the trend? Who also will teach that what we have is enough, with plenty to share!

I don't want to get to heaven and hear, "Rick, I didn't want you to spend so much on yourself. There were needy all around you. There were investible people all around you. As I invested in you, I desired that you would invest in them. Money and time I gave you. Both in abundance."

The average American has more wealth
than 90% of the rest of the world.

Compared to the rest of the world, we are living in Paradise. My work in twenty countries has driven that truth home. Like Hawaii, mentioned previously, our land has been so forthcoming with food that there is little need to compete with others for it. But we want more, much more. And so we compete.

"You've got to look out for number one!" "I've got mine, they can get theirs." "Work hard, play hard!" "The one with the most toys wins!" It is no wonder we have such a reduced willingness to trust anyone.

Our nation of plenty is now a competition between the faceless and the nameless for *more*. And our children, though living in plenty, are the losers. Because the time it takes for *more* is so very much.

Like Hawaii, there would be less interpersonal stress if we would be content with *only* having wealth greater than 90% of the world. Moms and Dads would be able to be around so very much more, and families could have a lot more fun together! Trust comes easily in these situations, and that builds faith in one another, which then makes it easier to love and be committed *to* each other. If we would choose contentment, strong families, strong relationships and strong communities could once again be the norm.

Philippians 4:11-13 NIV
11 ...I have learned to be content whatever the circumstances. 12 I know what it is to be in need, and I know what it is to have plenty. I have learned the secret of being content in any and every situation, whether well fed or hungry, whether living in plenty or in want. 13 I can do all this through him who gives me strength.

I would have done much better in my life if I had known about contentment and fruit of the Spirit behavior early on. But foundationally, I would have also needed to develop a deep understanding of Colossians 3, Galatians 5, Romans 1 and the Beatitudes (Matthew 5:2-12). Then, having been trained to *check my heart* when Judgement, Condemnation and Anger were welling up inside of me, I would have been better able to defuse Enemy attempts to Divide and Conquer my healthy relationships.

I know a man who, as a late teen, was indoctrinated into a "church" for many years. Mind Control and sexual Abuse were part of their leader's ways. If this boy had been raised to distinguish between the voice of God and that of the Enemy, and to understand Colossians 3, Galatians 5, Romans 1 and so forth with regard to how to identify the people and behaviors to avoid, he may have never had to go through such a tragedy. We can help our children not become prey to people like these by helping them know God, his voice and what are and aren't his ways.

Life gets pretty simple when our behavioral attitudes are Jesus' attitudes (the Beatitudes), utilizing language and actions for production of fruit of the Spirit, and our path is led by him in our choices. Once I learned this, his yoke truly became easy and his burden light because *he* was the one doing his Works in me. Through me. As a participant in what *he* was doing. Now my peace truly surpasses understanding and my joy is full.

Life is extremely complicated when we spend it thinking about how to get what we want with or for our family, friends and associates. Life is a series of wins and losses that way. His ways are higher than our ways and bring Joy, even while in this world we will have trouble (John 16:33).

Life gets pretty simple when our behavioral attitudes are Jesus' attitudes, utilizing language and actions for production of fruit of the Spirit, and our path is led by him in our choices.

How have we gotten our teaching so far out of order? Slowly. Very slowly. Over generations of generations. It will become clear to you as the Father who dwells in you continues to do his Works, through the Help and power of the Holy Spirit, and according to the Teachings of our Lord Jesus Christ. Ask him for insight. Ask him for Wisdom.

Matthew 7:7-11

7 "Ask, and it will be given to you; seek, and you will find; knock, and it will be opened to you. 8 For everyone who asks receives, and the one who seeks finds, and to the one who knocks it will be opened. 9 Or which one of you, if his son asks him for bread, will give him a stone? 10 Or if he asks for a fish, will give him a serpent? 11 If you then, who are evil, know how to give good gifts to your children, how much more will your Father who is in heaven give good things to those who ask him!

Luke 11:11-13

11 What father among you, if his son asks for a fish, will instead of a fish give him a serpent; 12 or if he asks for an egg, will give him a scorpion? 13 If you then, who are evil, know how to give good gifts to your children, <u>how much more will the heavenly Father give the Holy Spirit to those who ask him!"</u>

The Father has given the Son to us, a gift to the whole world. He followed that up by providing the Holy Spirit to Acceptors for his replenishing supply! As parents, will your children be a gift to this world or be a part of the Rejector problem? Self-focused or Father focused?

It is important to recognize that the evil that will be done in this world in the future will come from a portion of the children being reared by the parents of today. Will some be yours?

Well intentioned, but poorly informed, the evil that comes will have come through us; will have been raised by us; and to some degree, will have been led astray by us.

Chapter Thirty-Three

Seek The Truth
The Truth Will Set You Free

John 8:31-36
31 So Jesus said to the Jews who had believed him, "If you abide in my
word, you are truly my talmidim, 32 and you will know the truth, and
the truth will set you free." 33 They answered him, "We are offspring
of Abraham and have never been enslaved to anyone. How is it that
you say, 'You will become free'?" 34 Jesus answered them, "Truly,
truly, I say to you, everyone who practices sin is a slave to sin. 35 The
slave does not remain in the house forever; the son remains forever.
36 So if the Son sets you free, you will be free indeed.

Some of the great Thinkers of the world never came to grips with God. As has been explained previously, they need the Feelers of this world to open their hearts and bring balance to the logic of their human minds. Many atheists and agnostics, with the best of intentions, end up making themselves little gods trying to do "right". Living by a *code* of their own making, *they* decide what "a good life" is and that which is "virtuous".

This was true for Marcus Aurelius, a Roman emperor who lived a hundred years after Jesus, and was the Caesar of his day. A renown Thinker, he held himself up like a wise and all-knowing god himself, he rationalized:

"Live a good life. If there are gods and they are just, then they will not care how devout you have been, but will welcome you based on the virtues you have lived by. If there are gods, but unjust, then you should not want to worship them. If there are no gods, then you will be gone, but will have lived a noble life that will live on in the memories of your loved ones."

An example of the self-focused individualistic Hellenists of his day, he also said:

"Begin each day by telling yourself: Today I shall be meeting with interference, ingratitude, insolence, disloyalty, ill-will, and selfishness - all of them due to the offenders' ignorance of what is good or evil... If someone is able to show me that what I think or do is not right, I will happily change, for I seek the truth, by which no one was ever truly harmed. It is the person who continues in his self-deception and ignorance who is harmed."

How did Marcus Aurelius define what "good" is, what "evil" is, what a "noble life" is, what a "virtuous life" is and what it means to "live a good life"? Following his rationale, and with now over seven billion people walking the earth, should we all be as *little gods* and do the same? If we do, we might find seven billion definitions for each.

He would have done well to consider his own words: "If someone is able to show me that what I think or do is not right, I will happily change, *for I seek the truth*, by which no one was ever truly harmed. It is *the person who continues in his self-deception and ignorance who is harmed*."

The *truth* is, the teachings of Marcus Aurelius foment Chaos among us as seven billion people live as their own gods defining and debating what is good, evil, fair, right, wrong and wise – who would each then also pass these determinations down to their children. Each reasoning on their own like 7 billion Marcus Aureliuses trying to decide together what is right what is wrong, what is better what is best. The blind leading the blind in their own understandings. Some with the best of intentions, some not so much.

But Jesus did show us (including Marcus Aurelius), in fact he modeled it, defining it for us as: Love wholly and Love only with hearts after the Father. In lives lived in freedom, in fruit of the Spirit language and actions, with the attitudes of the Beatitudes.

Dictators with the line of thinking of Emperor Marcus Aurelius still exist throughout the world today. Though Marcus Aurelius was a "good man", most dictators typically are *not*. Their people are not free, they are not able to "live a good life", and these nations are not disguising their attempts to spread their Control strategies into other nations across the world. As we consider our own actions and who we will next elect, keep in mind that these politicians will also represent us in the *worldwide* battle between good and evil as it continues – and will until Jesus comes back. Are we in the USA doing our part to influence world leaders for the benefit of the freedom of their people?

There is only one arbiter of what is "good" and "true", and he avails the abundant life of Joy. Jesus: who is respected worldwide for his teachings and Wisdom, even by those who do not consider him God. He showed Marcus Aurelius and all the rest of us the things we have been doing that *are not right*, but Marcus Aurelius did not *happily change* as he said he would. As Emperor, no one was above him. No one smarter. His way the best way. The only way. As the *final* Authority. Is this true of you and what you Control as well?

Most of our politicians were once children raised in "Christian" families whose beliefs should have been informed by their Christology. But what does it mean, to so many of them, to be Christian as politicians? Authority, power and use of the Military Chain of Command!

Truly, the sins of the parents have been being passed down to their children and children's children for generations of generations – and look where it has gotten us! Who will reverse the trend? The consequences of our actions are being allowed to play out:

Isaiah 1:2-5, 15-21a, 23

2 Hear, O heavens, and give ear, O earth; for the Lord has spoken: "<u>Children have I reared and brought up, but they have rebelled against me</u>. 3 The ox knows its owner, and the donkey its master's crib, but Israel does not know, <u>my people do not understand</u>." 4 Ah, sinful nation, a people laden with iniquity, offspring of evildoers, children who deal corruptly! They have forsaken the Lord, they have despised the Holy One of Israel, they are utterly estranged. 5 Why will you still be struck down? Why will you continue to rebel? The whole head is sick, and the whole heart faint. ...15 <u>When you spread out your hands, I will hide my eyes from you; even though you make many prayers, I will not listen; your hands are full of blood</u>. 16 Wash yourselves; make yourselves clean; remove the evil of your deeds from before my eyes; cease to do evil, 17 learn to do good; seek justice, correct oppression; bring justice to the fatherless, plead the widow's *cause. 18 "Come now, let us reason together, says the Lord: though your sins are like scarlet, they shall be as white as snow; though they are red like crimson, they shall become like wool. 19 If you are willing and obedient, you shall eat the good of the land; 20 but if you refuse and rebel, you shall be eaten by the sword; for the mouth of the Lord has spoken." 21a How the faithful city has become a whore, [become unchaste] she who was full of justice!... 23 Your princes are rebels and companions of thieves. Everyone loves a bribe and runs after gifts. They do not bring justice to the fatherless, and the widow's cause does not come to them.*

Luke 13:34
O Jerusalem, Jerusalem, the city that kills the prophets and stones those who are sent to it! How often would I have gathered your children together as a hen gathers her brood under her wings, and you were not willing!

Adonai, precious is your Presence. I don't want to be Emperor anymore. Your kingdom come. Yes, Lord, bring it. Manifest it, establish it, make it as real on the whole earth as it is in heaven. I agree with you and submit to you for the expansion of your kingdom, not mine. Your will be done, because mine is inferior to yours and yours is best for all – best on earth as it is best in heaven. May the whole world be fed today, with both physical and spiritual food, and forgive as you forgive. Help us that we not enter into temptation, deliver us from Evil! Give us justice against our Adversaries, O God! May they repent, turn to you, be healed, and follow you all of the days of their lives. Send laborers, O God, and lead us to succeed in being ones ourselves!

Such a brief and simple prayer. Yet it encompasses the whole world!

Genesis 15:6
And he believed the Lord, and he counted it to him as righteousness.

James 5:16

Therefore confess your sins to each other and pray for each other so that you may be healed. The prayer of a righteous person is powerful and effective.

Matthew 6:33

But seek first the kingdom of God and his righteousness, and all these things will be added to you.

Therefore, ask him to flow *his righteousness* through you in your *becoming*. Receive the abundant life that he offers, living in *his* righteousness, that your prayers *become* powerful and effective. For the whole world!

Chapter Thirty-Four

Listen For The Sake Of The Children, For The Sake Of Yourself!

Deceived, we think we know what we are doing, but we do not. We are not that smart. But there is One who is. One who is available to help us.

Will you help children to be Taught by Jesus and Led by the Holy Spirit, with the Father in them doing his Works? That they be influenced by him to Accept and be a part of the solution? A gift to others? These are key points about the Christian faith! What will *you* pass down to the 3rd and 4th generation? This is some of the most important work of your life.

Matthew 18:10, 14
10 "See that you do not despise one of these little ones. For I tell you that in heaven their angels always see the face of my Father who is in heaven. 14 So it is not the will of my Father who is in heaven that one of these little ones should perish.

Matthew 18:5-6
5 "Whoever receives one such child in my name receives me, 6 but whoever causes one of these little ones who believe in me to sin, it would be better for him to have a great millstone fastened around his neck and to be drowned in the depth of the sea.

God so loved the world that he made a gift of his Son. Made in his image, we are to do the same with our children. Raise your children to know his voice, and to be able to tell the difference between his and that of the Enemy. Let them know *that in heaven their angels always see the face of my Father who is in heaven* (Matthew 18:10b). Brought up with him and in him, Taught by Jesus, Led by the Holy Spirit, with the Father in them doing his Works - they will be a gift to the world. Gentle giants for Jesus.

Otherwise, the evil that will be done in this world in the future will have come through us; been raised by us; and have been, to some degree, led astray by us.

Matthew 18:1-4

1 At that time the disciples came to Jesus, saying, "Who is the greatest in the kingdom of heaven?" 2 And calling to him a child, he put him in the midst of them 3 and said, "Truly, I say to you, unless you turn and become like children, you will never enter the kingdom of heaven. 4 Whoever humbles himself like this child is the greatest in the kingdom of heaven.

Matthew 6:24

"No one can serve two masters, for either he will hate the one and love the other, or he will be devoted to the one and despise the other. You cannot serve God and money.

If you choose to be a portion Caesar, divided between alignment with God and the ways of the world, your development of personal holiness will be scuttled. Turn and live as his child. Be trained in loving *by* him, for living *like* him. Choose for your eternal benefit. Or not. For the benefit of others. Or not. By the power of the living God or by your power. He is gracious enough to let you choose for yourself. Gentleman that he is, he doesn't threaten you, but he does advise you. He doesn't call you names, only his child. He is both standing by and living within and is offering a yoke that is easy and a burden that is light. So that he might do his Works in you to give you the Joy of *creatively participating* in his will. Or not.

We have slowly been Deceived to the 3rd and 4th generation for generations of generations. Is it not now time to reopen the book for greater clarity? The scripture says, "I give you all authority…" so we take Authority over what we think we should take Authority over. But that is a selective reading that allows us to keep/have/take control over *people*. *Christ* is the Head, not us. We are all just Body parts following him in the will of *our* Father.

As Christ Following Thinkers think, they are predisposed to selecting scripture to justify controlling behavior, and if we will be persuaded that they are right – we will train up our children in it. As Christ Following Feelers feel, they are predisposed to selecting scripture to justify the enabling of bad behavior, and if we will be persuaded that they are right – we will train up our children in it.

Living as a child of the Father, are you asking him for *his* Direction, or have you gone Rogue? Children of the Father, we do not have the right to tell our siblings what to do, even as we are entreated to share information with them through fruit of the Spirit language and behavior. Even in our business environments there is a way to follow this way, child-like *with* him, inquiring *of* him, in *his* ways. (We will discuss this at length in the Leading section.)

Jesus told us that he only says and does what the Father tells him so that we would do likewise - and then he followed through in it all the way to the cross.

Mark 14:33-36

33 And he took with him Peter and James and John, and began to be greatly distressed and troubled. 34 And he said to them, "My soul is very sorrowful, even to death. Remain here and watch." 35 And going a little farther, he fell on the ground and prayed that, if it were possible, the hour might pass from him. 36 And he said, "Abba, Father, all things are possible for you. Remove this cup from me. Yet not what I will, but what you will."

How about us? Are we listening no matter how difficult his will sounds or seems? In *creative collaboration* are we offering him our thoughts and asking him for greater clarity – that we might better understand his will? That we might be *willing participants* accomplishing his will *together*? Are we willing to follow through even when those around us are pushing back?

When conflict comes what will you do? How will you respond? By what process will you decide? Personal holiness? How will you communicate it? Are Jesus' attitudes in fruit of the Spirit language and actions the way you roll?

Is God telling you to use judgement, condemnation or shaming in order to influence and persuade others to bring about his will? I can tell you that he is not. He is telling you to humbly produce fruit of the Spirit when you inform, influence and attempt to persuade others. Communicating in Love, Joy, Peace, Patience, Kindness, Goodness, Gentleness, Perseverance (Faithfulness) and Self-Control will never include judgement, condemnation, shaming or divide and conquer. That is a strategy straight from hell.

Divide and conquer typically ends with a democratic vote and is followed by the use of Authority according to the ways of Caesar. If you have winners and losers in the aftermath of a decision you can be sure that you didn't Persevere to Patiently utilize all of the information brought forward with Goodness, Kindness, Gentleness and Self-Control. In Peace that developed Joy and grew a greater Love. His ways bring Unity. Our ways, the ways we have been taught by the powers of Darkness and Deception throughout the ages, produce the power and Authority of the world. Don't go Rogue and join them! Christ is the Head. The only power and authority you have come from what *he* asks you to do in *his* Power and in *his* Authority, Taught by Jesus, Led by the Holy Spirit, with the Father in you doing his Works.

With him is under his power. For him is under ours.

And there is the great Deception. That we cannot know the will of God the Father in all things. That we must think and logic and consider and decide for ourselves and exercise *our Authority*. But Jesus never did that, and he said that we would do greater things than he. We CAN only say and do what the Father tells us through the Teaching and Training of Jesus, by the Help and power of the Holy Spirit, as the Father who dwells in us does his Works.

Occasionally, when we are not sure that we know what *to* do, he will make his silence obvious. The silence deafening, it is there to give us pause. That, because what we are continuing to contemplate is *Not Love*, and is therefore something *not to do* - something he cannot approve of. In these moments, we will sense that this lesson and its consequences have occurred previously. Knowing all we need to know in the moment, he stands quietly by hoping that we will see clearly, remember the earlier lessons and decide accordingly – and if so, feel his approval as he celebrates over us.

Then we will see what the Father is doing and do likewise. Our eyes again on him, we will know his will, what to do - and accomplish it. With compassion. With Love, Joy, Peace, Patience, Kindness, Goodness, Gentleness, Perseverance (Faithfulness) and Self-Control. The Spirit of the Living God leads us in the Self-Control we need when we would rather opt to control situations and outcomes.

1 John 2:3-6

3 And by this we know that we have come to know him, if we keep his commandments. 4 Whoever says "I know him" but does not keep his commandments is a liar, and the truth is not in him, 5 but whoever keeps his word, in him truly the love of God is perfected. By this we may know that we are in him: 6 whoever says he abides in him ought to walk in the same way in which he walked.

1 John 2:28

And now, little children, abide in him, so that when he appears we may have confidence and not shrink from him in shame at his coming.

Adonai made it very simple for us. We complicate it. We sophisticate it. We muddle it up and confuse it so much that we think we can predict outcomes that he wouldn't want, that we would not want, and then lean on our own understanding and take Authority to act for what we *do* want, as we see fit.

But his ways are not our ways. His ways are higher than our ways. His ways are better than our ways. And so he asks us to trust him in all things. For we cannot comprehend the depth of the problems we will cause when we are Caesar. Living according to the opportunities we find in this world to have and to cause and to create and accumulate. Power, Possessions and Security.

Matthew 25:31-46 The Final Judgment

31 "When the Son of Man comes in his glory, and all the angels with him, then he will sit on his glorious throne. 32 Before him will be gathered all the nations, and he will separate people one from another as a shepherd separates the sheep from the goats. 33 And he will place the sheep on his right, but the goats on the left. 34 Then the King will say to those on his right, 'Come, you who are blessed by my Father, inherit the kingdom prepared for you from the foundation of the world. 35 For I was hungry and you gave me food, I was thirsty and you gave me drink, I was a stranger and you welcomed me, 36 I was naked and you clothed me, I was sick and you visited me, I was in prison and you came to me.' 37 Then the righteous will answer him, saying, 'Lord, when did we see you hungry and feed you, or thirsty and give you drink? 38 And when did we see you a stranger and welcome you, or naked and clothe you? 39 And when did we see you sick or in prison and visit you?' 40 And the King will answer them, 'Truly, I say to you, as you did it to one of the least of these my brothers, you did it to me.' 41 "Then he will say to those on his left, 'Depart from me, you cursed, into the eternal fire prepared for the devil and his angels. 42 For I was hungry and you gave me no food, I was thirsty and you gave me no drink, 43 I was a stranger and you did not welcome me, naked and you did not clothe me, sick and in prison and you did not visit me.' 44 Then they also will answer, saying, 'Lord, when did we see you hungry or thirsty or a stranger or naked or sick or in prison, and did not minister to you?' 45 Then he will answer them, saying, 'Truly, I say to you, as you did not do it to one of the least of these, you did not do it to me.' 46 And these will go away into eternal punishment, but the righteous into eternal life."

This is what is at stake for us. For all of us. Goats *become* talmidim of the greatest Rejector. Some will be so Deceived that they will be goats and not even know it. They will be goats who will stand before our righteous God and tell of all the good they did *on their own*. *For* him. But they will be reminded that they did <u>*not*</u> do it <u>*with*</u> him, <u>*by*</u> him, <u>*according*</u> to him. *Together*.

In your passion and zeal *for* the Lord do you work hard to do good things? *For* him? Seeing what needs to be done, do you simply do it? *For* him?

But are these things ours to do? Like Peter and Judas (referenced in the chapter: Eyes That See and Ears That Hear), in our passion and zeal might we be *leaning on our own understanding* (Proverbs 3:5-8)? *Interfering* with his will - because what we have taken on is beyond what is really ours to say or do? What will become of the great

Thinkers, like Marcus Aurelius, who accomplished much during their lifetimes – but never knew God?

Matthew 7:21-23
21 "Not everyone who says to me, 'Lord, Lord,' will enter the kingdom of heaven, but the one who does the will of my Father who is in heaven. 22 On that day many will say to me, 'Lord, Lord, did we not prophesy in your name, and cast out demons in your name, and do many mighty works in your name?' 23 And then will I declare to them, 'I never knew you; depart from me, you workers of lawlessness.'

His yoke is easy and his burden is light (Matthew 11:28-30), how heavy is the weight upon your life these days? Are you thinking that *somebody* has to do it, so why not me? But might some or all of that belong to others? It's not so much about doing *right or wrong* or what is *good and bad* – it's all about *the will of our Father* and *Love and Not Love*. Ask our Father to help you know what is yours to engage and what is not yours to engage. Ask the Spirit to Lead you to only say and do that which is yours. Like Jesus, may we only say and do as our Father tells us, according to the Leading of the Holy Spirit. That our yoke be easy and our burden light – that our Joy may be complete.

Otherwise, having lived lives *leaning on our own understanding*, we will have become goats. And our end will not be as we may suppose: eternity with him, participating with him, ruling with him, together. Rather, we just might find eternal separation *from* him. But whatever it is, that will have been our choice. Perfect gentleman that he is, he always gives us the information we need, allowing us to choose what we will do ourselves. During our *finite period of offering*. For our kingdom, though we may say it is for his.

Revelation 22:10-13
And he said to me, "Do not seal up the words of the prophecy of this book, for the time is near. 11 Let the evildoer still do evil, and the filthy still be filthy, and the righteous still do right, and the holy still be holy." 12 "Behold, I am coming soon, bringing my recompense with me, to repay each one for what he has done. 13 I am the Alpha and the Omega, the first and the last, the beginning and the end."

We cannot comprehend the depth of the problems we cause when we live *leaning on our own understanding*. Meddling with his will. Doing what *we* think is best. Interfering, perhaps with the best of intentions.

Though we may have an idea or opinion, he asks us to share these with him before we act. Made in his image, he very much desires that we would be creative like he is creative. Not robots following his commands, but rather *participants* with him in the administration and operation of his kingdom. *With* him, *through* him, *by* him, *according* to him. *Together as his children*. Contemplate this:

Matthew 18:1-4

1 At that time the disciples came to Jesus, saying, "Who is the greatest in the kingdom of heaven?" 2 And calling to him a child, he put him in the midst of them 3 and said, "Truly, I say to you, unless you turn and become like children, you will never enter the kingdom of heaven. 4 Whoever humbles himself like this child is the greatest in the kingdom of heaven.

O Adonai, thank you for the perspective of us as creative children walking and talking with you as you help us see our way throughout each day. Thank you that we may offer our thoughts & ideas to you as we walk together, and humbly ask for your Teaching, Training and Direction. Thank you that you are available for that unceasingly and that you actually desire that we do so continually. Accomplish your will in us, flowing your blessings through us to others - that our Joy may be complete! As we are taught and trained and led by you, conform us more and more to your image so that our reputation, character and attributes reflect yours. Grow us more and more into willing participants in creative collaboration with you, loving wholly and loving only, that your kingdom come and your will be done on earth as it is in heaven.

Father, the tremendous complexity of the workings of our Enemy in this world are too much for us to figure out. Thank you that - if we will only ask - you are willing to identify for us what is ours to do and what is not ours to do. That your yoke on us be easy and your burden upon us be light. Do your Works in us that we do not enter into the temptation to interfere in things that are not ours, that we do not meddle with your will.

Thank you, Jesus, that like you we may be creative collaborators as the Father does his Works in us and your Holy Spirit leads and guides us. Thank you that we can be sure that, whatever is before us, our clear responsibility is to respond in the attitudes of the Beatitudes and with fruit of the Spirit: Love, Joy, Peace, Patience (a willingness for long-suffering for your purpose), Kindness, Goodness, Perseverance (faithfulness, steadfastness), Gentleness and Self-Control. Give us Wisdom, that we avoid Judgement and Condemnation and do not choose to Manipulate or Coerce to try to gain or regain Control. Though we have all learned these behaviors from the world around us, by the power of your Presence and in your character and attributes, may we always respond as you do with us - freely allowing others to make their own choices.

Refresh us again today, filling us with Living Water and the Bread of Heaven. May we share your Bread of Life and Living Water with others according to your will for us. Lead us to encourage, share, explain, train, inform, coach and describe with your Gentleness, Persevering in your ways, in Unity with your purpose - and give us ears to hear as well! Thank you that you will move in all our hearts and souls and minds again today, drawing us to you and offering to strengthen us. Dwell in us and accomplish your Works, delivering us from evil that we not enter into temptation. May we be fully aware and attentive to your Presence that you produce your fruit through us. Unite your people in more productive service, O God!

In consideration of our ways, his ways and the ways of the world, consider that the original followers of the resurrected Jesus were called followers of The Way. The Way he lived. The Way he loved. The Way he served. The Way he helped people understand *how to live a life pleasing to God*. The Way he trained *talmidim* who *became* like him more and more - not disciples, or students or apprentices who learned *what* he taught and then *applied it* to their own lives as they saw fit. No. Jesus' Way was to point out *how* the world was living according to its *own* way of thinking. Small "g" gods unto themselves, *thinking* their way through to their *own* decisions on *how to live*.

Jesus said many times that he only said and did what the Father gave him to say and do. Further, that we may *become* more and more like him and also do so. That as his sheep we know his *voice* and follow. And that unless we come as a child (seeing, perceiving and listening for The Way as we walk humbly with God) we will not enter into the kingdom of heaven.

As was described in the chapter: Stay Tuned In To The Kingdom Channel, we will all be taught by God if we will more and more enter in to the all-day practice of prayer (continuous conversational worship) with the creator of the universe. Taught by God, we will also have other talmidim with whom we share our lives, such that God may also utilize them for us and us for them - to live lives *pleasing to God* together.

Periodically through history, we see God setting up situations through which we might overcome the ways of the world and return to his. Our current situation is not unlike the time before Jesus' arrival, when the Pharisees and Sadducees were each holding separate positions of power in Corruption and Division. Like the Democrats and Republicans of our day, each claimed a godly mantle, a divine purpose and hid their self-serving intent.

Now, as we listen for his voice with hearts after the Father, walking in the attitudes of Jesus, producing fruit of the Spirit through our language and actions – we have the opportunity of helping those around us to reset themselves similarly. For the children. That none should perish.

****

So be wise. Paraphrasing Jonathan Cahn's posting from May 12, 2026:

"What do they need?" "What will be in THEIR best interest?" James 2:8 says, "Love your neighbor as yourself." It's called the Royal Law because it's God's law that He Himself followed. The gospel is God manifesting the Royal Law. He looked at us with love and said, "If I were them, what would I need?" God was your neighbor in the universe and He loved you with all His life, heart and soul. He gave Himself for you. He put Himself in your shoes.

He loved you as Himself. It's the Royal Law of the King of the universe. Live by it. As He did for you, you do for others. He loved you; you love them. He put Himself in your place; you put yourself in their place. He lowered Himself to raise you up; you lower yourself to raise them up.

Asking Him for His heart of Wisdom, ask of Him, "What would I need if I were them?" Then give "what He says" to them with all your heart, because it will have been balanced by the Mind of Christ, and it will be the will of the Father... because OUR minds alone lack His Wisdom.

Those who live by the Royal Law of the King of the universe will be blessed by the King. And their lives, their souls, their heart, their journey, everything in their life, everything in your life, will become royal.

Chapter Thirty-Five

Before The Birth Of The Christ

Around 150-100 BC God was doing a new thing, but most Christians today do not perceive it. He was preparing the people of a small area of Israel (Bethsaida, Korazin and Capernaum) for the coming Messiah. This area, sometimes called The Triangle, developed a discipleship track that began with elementary school – Beth Sephir. There, they began teaching children to read and write using the Torah, and by the time they were twelve years old, *all* would have memorized most of it.

This was the beginning of a new thing, and it has been confirmed by a broad swath of historians. It had not previously existed within Israel, and was birthed at least a hundred years before Jesus' arrival in Galilee, in preparation, in the area of The Triangle.

After Beth Sephir, somewhere around the age of 12, most boys would go into the family trade and most girls into supporting family life. However, for those who really had a passion for the Word of God, they could instead go on to Beth Midrash. Beth Midrash included study and memorization of most of the rest of the Hebrew Bible (the Tanakh) and provided them opportunity to begin considering a rabbinic lifestyle.

If you completed Beth Midrash and wanted to continue on to become a rabbi, you would observe the various rabbis in the area and ask one of them if you could follow them. If the rabbi agreed, he would give you an opportunity to follow him everywhere he went to talk with him about the great and deep learnings, understandings and interpretations available in the Tanakh. If the rabbi rejected you at some point, you would likely go back and join the family trade.

If your rabbi gained confidence in you as you walked together, you would become a *talmid*, one of his talmidim (plural), and be on your way to becoming a rabbi following several years of training. The role of the rabbi was to "teach the people *how* to fulfill the Torah". That is to say, *how* to live a life pleasing to God. Spending every minute of every day with their rabbi, talmidim would watch and see and hear and learn *how* he helped people understand and fulfill the Torah. Both by his words and by his actions.

But what are talmidim? Talmidim are what we in the USA erroneously call "disciples, students and apprentices":

A talmid is probably different than you think because we do not have any word for it in our English language. Unlike the words disciple or student or apprentice that suggest a learning and doing process, the word talmid is a Hebrew term that describes a becoming process. Talmidim desire to become just like their rabbi. It is more than the practical application of the knowledge gained. It is more than taking actions based upon our understanding of his teachings. A talmid of Rabbi Jesus will have a heart after the Father, be growing to reflect the very character of Jesus and be gaining the mind and attitudes of Christ.

For those a rabbi accepted, the job of a follower was to *become* just like him. It was not just to know what the rabbi knew, but to *be* what the rabbi *was*.

On the Sabbath, all of the rabbis from the insulas of the town (often five or more rabbis with hundreds of people in attendance) would gather in the synagogue to *conversationally* consider the appointed text of that Sabbath day. There would be a reading or two from the Torah and/or Tanakh, and the reader could share a brief testimony regarding the scripture selections for the day. Then the people would listen to the rabbis discuss the text so as to enlighten them with their thoughts on the historical context, likely using related text, each including their interpretations - with respectful consideration of differing perspectives a common element.

With several rabbis present, no one rabbi could steer the people in an unhealthy direction over time. Because of Beth Sephir most people were Torah literate. Because of Beth Midrash, the many talmidim of the rabbis present were Tanakh literate.

Interestingly, it was culturally acceptable for *anyone* present to add to the discussion, request clarification in a related text, provide a testimony or even disagree with something that had been shared. In this way, the collective wisdom of *all* the people was available for consideration *by all the people*. In this way, faith was made more *personal*. In this way, the people learned *how* to fulfill the Torah, *how* to live a life pleasing to God.

In this way, children might hear a testimony from their uncle; or a grandfather their son; and in so doing create the opportunity to discuss it personally together later – expanding upon the learning and adding depth to what was shared.

In *conversational* style, God could send in his *Encouragers*, *Disruptors* or *Correctors* to contribute to the discussions and raise up issues and scripture for community deliberation. It was this setup that made it possible for Jesus (and later the apostle Paul) to speak *in any synagogue on any Sabbath*. This is also one of the reasons that young Jesus was able to speak and amaze so many of those present – in the years *before* he started his three-year ministry.

This, too, helps to explain why Andrew, Peter, James and John immediately dropped their nets and followed him when he called them (Matthew 4:18-22, Luke 5:1-11). All four were raised in the small fishing town of Bethsaida, probably played together, and must have witnessed young Jesus together in synagogue conversations on Sabbaths during the years prior!

Maybe more importantly regarding these four, what does it say about Jesus that *he went to them and called them?!!!* Remember, aspiring talmidim would customarily be required to *ask the rabbi if they may follow him*. What Jesus was saying to them was, "*I believe you can be like me! Come! Follow me, and I will make you fishers of men!*" Near the end of his ministry, he reminded them of this, "You did not choose me, but I chose you." (John 15:16)

He tells modern day believers that *he believes in us, too*, still saying, "Go, make *talmidim* of all nations… "It's not all about teaching *what* we are to *know*, but the *how* we are to *live* to *become like him*. As we adopt the *how*, we will more likely *desire to delve deeper* into the scriptures to learn the supportive *what*.

The lone teacher setup is a heady situation that risks people becoming teacher followers rather than talmidim of Jesus. With several rabbis present, the collective wisdom of the elders would foster a deeper understanding. With several rabbis present, no one rabbi could steer the people in an unhealthy direction over time. With several rabbis and their talmidim present, individuals could more easily find one with whom they could have life-on-life conversations during the week. In conversational style, God could send in his Encouragers, Disruptors or Correctors to contribute to the discussions and raise up issues and scripture for community deliberation. It was this setup that made it possible for Jesus (and later the apostle Paul) to speak in any synagogue on any Sabbath.

****

When Jesus said go and make talmidim of all nations, he did not say go and teach people Beth Sephir and Beth Midrash (the Tanakh) so that they could practically apply the information to their lives, he said to go help people *become* like him! Between the *what to know* and the *how to live*, he spent more time on the *how – how to live a life pleasing to God.*

Following Jesus' resurrection, the bible indicates that there were small talmidic style Sabbath gatherings that met in homes and *went out to serve locally* through the week. This service developed relational connections that could lead to the sharing of the love of God, the fellowship of the believers and invitations to join them. In this way, the ekklesia (or ecclesia) were effective in serving, sharing and inviting for the making of more and more talmidim.

These days our English bible translations use the word "church" where the Greek shows ekklesia. Ancient language historians indicate that this word actually means "called out". This is significant. Jesus set them apart and called them out of the darkness to reflect the light of God to the people of the world.

Today, if you ask someone what the followers of Jesus do, the answer would likely be "Go to church.". Yet if you could ask 1st century followers of Jesus what they did, the answer would likely be "Go <u>out</u> into the community in acts of service, for the development of relationships and opportunities to share.".

Also preaching in community settings as Jesus and Paul did, they piqued the curiosity of people such that the development of additional rabbinic/talmidic type conversational "small groups" could be initiated.

Their goal? To teach them *how to live a life pleasing to God*, that they might become talmidim who make talmidim who make talmidim.

Two thousand years later, we have lost the context of this and many other portions of scripture. Because we are not from that era, we have also lost the images those words would immediately evoke culturally in their listeners. But how did it happen?

The Beginning of our Tradition of Preaching

Imagine with me: As the ekklesia "went out" to the cities of Europe, they found themselves buried in so many individual requests for understanding that they simply could not *conversationally* serve them all life-on-life. Clearly, somewhere along the way we decided it would be good to transition to the build a bigger "church" concept. One that settled for Sabbath preaching alone and took away the opportunity for *anyone* to speak. In so doing, having lost the *conversational* style, God could no longer send in his *Encouragers*, *Disruptors* or *Correctors* to contribute to the discussions and raise up issues and scripture for community deliberation.

Without the focus upon developing *12 or so talmidim first*, as Jesus did, there was not a sufficient number of talmidim around to grow the 70 and the 500. And since it was not possible for *anyone else* to speak, one person could steer the people in an unhealthy direction over time.

Our Build-A-Bigger-Church Culture seemed necessary so as to gather the masses in one place each week to enable times of teaching and communion by the few. Unfortunately, the loss of conversational rabbinic/talmidic life-on-life learning caused the inability to make true talmidim, since the depth of understanding required individually could not be imparted.

As well intentioned "followers" passed along their limited understandings, errors were passed down generationally. Hardly the conversational life-on-life talmidic multiplication that Jesus exhibited, Europe is now littered with huge empty cathedrals… and now *we in the USA* are closing a net of eight churches every day.

Let's return to the Conversational Synagogue Learning Way

If *we* will endeavor to *become* like Jesus, the making of talmidim will require *individual* conversational time in ongoing *life-on-life* discussion. Not forsaking the fellowship, a talmid will also be associated with some sort of *group* of talmidim - continually discussing *how to become more and more like Jesus*. Not only that, but *how to help others understand what it means* to live a life pleasing to God in *their* becoming. This bears repeating:

When Jesus said go and make talmidim of all nations, he did not say go and teach people the Bible, he said to go help them <u>become like him</u>! As with Jesus, the making of talmidim requires individual conversational time in life-on-life discussion.

His yolk is easy and his burden is light. It is much easier to focus on twelve or so than it is to take responsibility for a whole "church" *en masse*. God will bring the increase if we will return to the *conversational Synagogue way*.

Matthew 11:28-30
28 Come to me, all who labor and are heavy laden, and I will give you rest. 29 Take my yoke upon you, and learn from me, for I am gentle and lowly in heart, and you will find rest for your souls. 30 For my yoke is easy, and my burden is light."

The lone teacher setup is a heady situation that risks people becoming teacher followers rather than talmidim of Jesus. With several rabbis present, the collective wisdom of the elders would foster a deeper understanding. With several rabbis present, no one rabbi could steer the people in an unhealthy direction over time. With several rabbis and their talmidim present, individuals could more easily find one with whom they could have life-on-life conversations during the week.

In conversational style, God could send in his Encouragers, Disruptors or Correctors to contribute to the discussions and raise up issues and scripture for community deliberation. It was this setup that made it possible for Jesus (and later the apostle Paul) to speak in any synagogue on any Sabbath.

GO, make talmidim... people who are becoming like me, who GO like I went.

Though Jesus taught thousands from a boat or a mountainside, the teaching that changed the world started *both as a group and individually* with the twelve. I wonder how many of the twelve were eventually involved in ongoing life-on-life conversations with the 70, and how many of the 70 were involved in life-on-life conversations with the 500? I wonder how often it would happen that an inquiring mind could not ask their question of Jesus because he was so surrounded by others trying to do the same. I wonder how often they would then elect to ask their question of one of his talmidim, thereby initiating a life-on-life opportunity for *them*: "Hey, John, you are one of his guys, what does Jesus say, or maybe, what does Jesus think about this…..?"

What I *do* know, is that Jesus was not involved in ongoing life-on-life conversations with all of the 70 or the 500. Dear church leader, just like for you, there is simply not enough time in the day! More importantly, how many cannot get to *you* and eventually give up on asking their questions because there is no one else to ask? Without a high level of visibility and recognition of who your 12 are, how many walk away – and we lose our chance to grow them? If your 12 are frequently speaking in the weekly conversational opportunities, the inquirer will far more easily start with one of *them* if they cannot get to *you*, as in the above example.

Moreover, if you have described to your congregation that your 12 are highly capable of pastoring people through the troubles of life, and that you will be Connecting those that approach you with one of them - you will only have the 12 with whom to focus. Then, like Moses' father-in-law advised (Exodus 18:13-27), any additional load will come almost entirely from those your 12 have first screened, vetted or have previously attempted to support.

****

In Acts 1, just before his ascension, Jesus told his followers to wait in Jerusalem for the promise of the Father - the Holy Spirit. What we see there is that there were 120 talmidim who were waiting. The 70 had already become 120!

Acts 1:15

In those days Peter stood up among the brothers (the company of persons was in all about 120) and said

Clearly, Jesus' way was to make talmidim who would make talmidim. Dear talmid, you may not be a church leader, but do you have one or more that get *that* kind of time with *you*? Do you add another one or more each year as *they* participate with God to develop *more* talmidim themselves? This is where the 70, and then the 500 come from! Are your church leaders facilitating this?

The church leaders I know who *are* have been sending highly impactful service minded talmidim into their communities as yeast, salt and light for decades – and as they serve those in need, they use those opportunities to make more talmidim!

He focused his training upon the 12, setting into motion the 70, the 120, the 500 and the making of talmidim in every nation on earth.

****

The Bible was written to the people of *that* day. It was not written *to* us, it was written *to them* and *for us*. Like the people of Jesus' day who knew the Torah and maybe even the whole Tanakh (the Old Testament), our people need help in grasping the depth and context of the people of the *biblical era* to better live a life pleasing to God today! For though they had been to Beth Sephir and Beth Midrash, the apostles still needed the same kind of help that *our* people do to *become* talmidim.

We admonish people to read their Bibles each day, and we teach them *what* the Bible says each week, but many are having difficulty with understanding the *how*. Like his talmidim, we need to have the *life of the Christ* opened up to us *in context* if we will *comprehend the how* of living the God-led life - with hearts after our Father, eyes that see and ears that hear. Otherwise, without *individual conversational time*, we are causing them to be always seeing, but never perceiving. (Matthew 13:14, Isaiah 6:9, Mark 4:12)

Like the two who encountered Jesus *conversationally* on the road to Emmaus (Luke 24:13-35), their hearts will burn as the scriptures are opened up to them. Jesus availed himself for 40 days after his resurrection to personalize the scriptures for his followers. He connected the scattered references to himself found in the Tanakh, identified the hundreds of prophecies about himself that he fulfilled, and clarified the story (his-story) so that they in turn could help others with *how* to live a life pleasing to God. And us for still others as well.

Like the story of Philip and the Eunuch (Acts 8:26-40), people need to have the scriptures opened up to them *conversationally* if they will *comprehend what they are reading.*

Like the story of Priscilla and Aquila pulling Apollos to the side *conversationally* for the deeper understanding (Acts 18:24-28), how will we support the passionate in passing along the *whole* Bible, context and all? Like Apollos, who eventually went to Achaia and powerfully and *conversationally* refuted the Jews in public, will our passionate people be fully prepared to *go*?

Much of what our present-day leaders do on Sundays *preaches* scripture so as to provide us *the what* head knowledge for *life application*. This is not the *talmidic* approach for *becoming like our Rabbi Jesus*, but rather the individualistic Hellenistic *lecture* approach born in the Constantine era and which became common throughout Europe.

Now, just like Europe, littered with huge empty cathedrals, have we fallen victim to our lack of understanding of how to *scale* in the family of God? According to ChurchLeadership.org, every year more than 4000 churches close their doors compared to just over 1000 new church starts. On average we are losing a net of eight churches each day!

The church in the USA was birthed by the talmidic families of God who escaped Europe in pursuit of freedom. Unfortunately, more and more have adopted the Constantine *preaching* path and process over the past 100 or more years. Looking back, this just seemed to make more sense as our communities grew from small towns and villages of people who knew each other, into cities of the faceless and nameless!

At the city scale, our sermons have lost the conversational synagogue approach of Jesus' day. One of the reasons is because we are overwhelmed at the concept of individually teaching so many via life-

on-life conversations: an impossible burden! Is it not now time to train the 12 he has given us, and them the 70 that he will give them - that we might have a chance with the 500? It was enough for Jesus...

Without ongoing life-on-life conversations individually, how can we expect them to comprehend *how* to live a life pleasing to God as a talmid?

Dear church leader, Jesus was not involved in ongoing life-on-life conversations with all of the 70 or 500. Just like for you, there is simply not enough time in the day! Clearly, Jesus' way was to make talmidim who would make talmidim. Please, ask God to identify for you the first twelve or so that will begin to get that kind of group and individual time with you. Then add to their numbers each year as they then participate with you to develop more and more talmidim. The 70, and then the 500. The church leaders I know who are doing this have been sending highly impactful service-minded talmidim into their communities as yeast, salt and light for decades – and are making more and more talmidim!

I believe that this *Tradition of Lecture*, was passed down to the 3rd and the 4th generation in the USA from roughly a hundred years ago as our small towns and villages of people who knew each other grew into nameless and faceless cities, and that this is the biggest reason that the church has been in decline for so very many decades. While it is an indictment of the ways of our seminaries, Bible colleges, pastors, teachers and parenting down through the generations that our numbers have fallen off so drastically, the *lecture model* was initially *a logical sounding seed Satan sowed in Deception* that we simply did not understand!

En masse, we tend to give people the facts and the logic and fight to persuade them for saving faith and helpful actions. Then, after baptism, continue our fact-filled logical Hellenistic *lecture* approach with weekly self-help Bible teaching and encouragements to serve. As we keep their brains engaged in thinking it all through - *without ongoing life-on-life opportunities in which to ask their questions, and lost in their heads* - many will walk away. Many *have* walked away, and so our families and nation are falling apart.

We would do well to reconsider our tradition of individuals teaching to gatherings by lecture. Rather, let's afford people conversational iron sharpening iron opportunities as Jesus and the apostles did.

****

What if we were to change our approach so as to better facilitate hearts after God with talmidim conversationally? What if we adopted the conversational synagogue method the Father prepared in advance for Jesus in the synagogues of The Triangle? What if all people had the opportunity to be involved in conversational learning in our Sunday services? What if our 12 were sufficiently trained to support the 70 and them the 500?

What if we were to instead *go* into our communities like Jesus *went,* to *pique the curiosity* of the people such that some came to our Sunday gatherings for *conversational* learning? What if the kind of teaching we do now on Sundays (like Jesus did from a boat or mountainside) happened instead in our community centers, our parks, our marketplaces, our homeless encampments and on our street corners?

What if denominationally disparate groups of pastor/teachers advertised a day each month where they would take turns using their current Sunday teaching gifts for several hours together in the local community center? What if *our* target audience was as *Jesus'* target audience was - and was supported there by *each of our congregations'* 12, 70 and 500?

What if the assimilated talmidim used these opportunities to invite people to the weekly or monthly community gatherings on location? What if that led people to come to our Sunday gatherings to conversationally learn *how* to live a life pleasing to God?

What if our marketing simply used the ongoing theme of "Living lives Pleasing To God!"? What if we interspersed two or three of the nearly 100 on-location video teachings of Ray Vander Laan that our people might experience the Bible in its historical context? (ThatTheWorldMayKnow.com)

If you're a megachurch, what if the Sunday gatherings began in the auditorium and then broke out into the smaller rooms where five or six of the 500 could lead *conversational discussion* with the groups in each room? 500 ÷ 6 = 83 potential rooms where this could happen each week.

What if our conversational small group time mid-week was led by *more than one* of the 500 in the Co-Leadership style described in *Leading*?

As is also described in *Leading*, if we will set the ground rules for respectful conversation (as will be briefly referenced in the next chapter) even the most intense Sunday group discussions with the lost and the immature may be kept safe.

Dear church leaders: If you feel God leading you to continue with preaching on Sundays, at least open it up for an hour of questions, discussion and conversational learning afterwards. Those who don't care that much about what they heard can always leave. Those whose interest was piqued will stay. Remember, the goal is that we mature as talmidim – endeavoring to become more and more like Jesus: Learning how to live a life pleasing to God; coming as a child in continual creative conversational worship (prayer) for the accomplishment of the Father's will; hearing his voice and following; sharing how to obey everything he has commanded; seeing, perceiving and being healed.

This is a time commitment we simply must come to value! If we are unable to pique their interest to stay, what does that say about our ability to appropriately share his compelling Good News with others?

What if every Christ follower was a volunteer somewhere? What if they knew how to effectively share the Good News where they serve, work or play? If each one reached just one every year, everyone in the world would have heard their opportunity for a joy filled eternity within 5 years. Now that would be a Great Awakening!

Our people have been going to church for 5, 10, 20, 30, 40 years and more. If we have been making talmidim, most would *be* mature talmidim by now and be out making talmidim who are making talmidim who are making talmidim… and we would not be closing a net of eight churches each day here in the USA. As it says, they should *be* mature talmidim by now…

Hebrews 5:11-6:3

11 About this we have much to say, and it is hard to explain, since you have become dull of hearing. 12 For though by this time you ought to be teachers, you need someone to teach you again the basic principles of the oracles of God. You need milk, not solid food, 13 for everyone who lives on milk is unskilled in the word of righteousness, since he is a child. 14 But solid food is for the mature, for those who have their powers of discernment trained by constant practice to distinguish good from evil. 6:1-3 Therefore let us leave the elementary doctrine of Christ and go on to maturity, not laying again a foundation of repentance from dead works and of faith toward God, 2 and of instruction about washings, the laying on of hands, the resurrection of the dead, and eternal judgment. 3 And this we will do if God permits.

Dear pastor/teacher/elder/deacon: What have you produced? Are you making *mature talmidim*? By this time, after so very many years, *they* ought to be teachers now, too! But perhaps they are simply *your* followers, lacking the confidence to GO out, *with* him and *in* him, making more and more talmidim. Instead, do they return to you each week to hear again and again the promise of eternity? Where is their fruit beyond their offerings, their service in the fellowship and beyond their material contributions to people in need? How many are coming back in with joyful reports of *new* talmidim in the making?

GO, make talmidim... people who are becoming like me,
who GO like I went.

Chapter Thirty-Six

Do This In Remembrance Of Me

Luke 22:17-20
17 And he took a cup, and when he had given thanks he said, "Take this, and divide it among yourselves. 18 For I tell you that from now on I will not drink of the fruit of the vine until the kingdom of God comes." 19 And he took bread, and when he had given thanks, he broke it and gave it to them, saying, "This is my body, which is given for you. Do this in remembrance of me." 20 And likewise the cup after they had eaten, saying, "This cup that is poured out for you is the new covenant in my blood.

1 Corinthians 11:23-25
23 For I received from the Lord what I also delivered to you, that the Lord Jesus on the night when he was betrayed took bread, 24 and when he had given thanks, he broke it, and said, "This is my body, which is for you. Do this in remembrance of me." 25 In the same way also he took the cup, after supper, saying, "This cup is the new covenant in my blood. Do this, as often as you drink it, in remembrance of me."

Do this in remembrance of me.

Most of my life my remembrance during Communion has been of his suffering and death on my behalf. The whipping, the beatings, the crown of thorns, the nails, the mocking, the anguish, hanging there, rejected, in excruciating pain…

Matthew 26:66-68
66 What is your judgment?" They answered, "He deserves death." 67 Then they spit in his face and struck him. And some slapped him, 68 saying, "Prophesy to us, you Christ! Who is it that struck you?"

Matthew 27:26, 28-31, 35,
26 Then he released for them Barabbas, and having scourged Jesus, delivered him to be crucified... 28 And they stripped him and put a scarlet robe on him, 29 and twisting together a crown of thorns, they put it on his head and put a reed in his right hand. And kneeling before

him, they mocked him, saying, "Hail, King of the Jews!" 30 And they spit on him and took the reed and struck him on the head. 31 And when they had mocked him, they stripped him of the robe and put his own clothes on him and led him away to crucify him... 35 And when they had crucified him, they divided his garments among them by casting lots...

...and finally, death. His saving sacrifice.

But, I think, this is not what he wants *most* to be remembered for. Time after time throughout his life he pointed people to our Father in heaven. It doesn't make sense to me that what he wants to do now is point us to himself rather than our Father. No, it seems more likely that what he wants us to remember about him is that he was one *who only said and did what our Father gave him to say and do.*

Throughout his entire life. All the way to the end of it:

He trained the 12, setting into motion the 70, the 500 and the making of talmidim in every nation on earth.

He went to Jerusalem, knowing what would happen there.

He told Judas to get on with it.

He went to Gethsemane and waited for his Accusers in prayerful obedience.

He asked the Father if there might be another way.

He went willingly when they came for him.

He endured and accomplished the purpose for which he was born.

He did *all* his Father's will.

Having taken responsibility for both God and Man as the God-Man, he provided us all a pathway to reconciliation *with* the Father and *into* the Family of God.

We have been told to do the same for others. Paraphrasing his instructions to us he said: "Go, show them *how to live a life pleasing to God*, baptizing them into the life-changing internal Presence of the Father and of the Son and of the Holy Spirit, teaching them to observe all that I have commanded you. It will be for them the pathway to reconciliation with the Father, into the Family of God and therefore *into their abundant joy filled life with us together* - eternally."

Go help people become more and more like me in all the nations...

But how can we help people *become like him*, teaching them to observe all that he commanded, if we aren't really *like him* ourselves?

Unfortunately, so many of us have been focusing upon baptizing and lecturing and have been neglecting the making of talmidim. We have watered down the foundational aspects of who God is and what he desires of us such that our children hardly know him, our families are *becoming* weaker, and the division and degradation of our nation is on the increase.

A Barna Group study in 2007 found that there is very little difference between the lifestyles & behaviors of people who call themselves Christian and those who do not. The evidence from work done by Pew Research and Gallup regarding people in the USA makes it clear that things are getting worse:

- In 2000, 90% believed in God. In 2022 that number was 81%.
- In 2005, 79% were convinced that God exists. In 2017 that number was 64%.
- In 1971, 90% identified as Christian. In 2008: 77%. In 2019: 65%
- Between 2009-2019, the percentage of Christians who say they attend church regularly dropped 7%.
- Half of all Christians say they attend church once or twice each month.
- Half of all Christians say they only attend church a few times per year or less.
- In 1999, 73% were members of a church. In 2019 that number was 47%.
- In 2009, 17% identified as atheist, agnostic or "nothing in particular". In 2019: 26%.

Given that half of all Christians say they only attend church a few times per year or less, another study tried to determine the percentage of believers who take the Great Commission of making disciples seriously. Their results? 7%.

Something must be wrong with our approach. Check the math, our task is not all that daunting. Using the 7% number from above, if *each* year *each* Christ follower will invest themselves in the life of *one person they know* who is not yet a true follower - within 4 years the entire USA will have had the opportunity to secure their eternity.

Each One Reach One Each Year:

- In Year 1: the 7% becomes 14%
- In Year 2: the 14% becomes 28%
- In Year 3: the 28% becomes 56%
- During Year 4: the 56% becomes 100%

Considering the world population, Pew Research states that 31% identify as Christian. Of them, perhaps we could say that 5% take the Great Commission of making disciples seriously. Doing the math again, assuming that every one of the 5% make just one true disciple each year, the entire world will have had the opportunity to secure their eternity within 6 years!

- In Year 1: the 5% becomes 10%
- In Year 2: the 10% becomes 20%
- In Year 3: the 20% becomes 40%
- In Year 4: the 40% becomes 80%
- During Year 5: the 80% becomes 100%

Clearly, our problem is not in our numbers, but likely in that our approaches do not grow disciples who care – with hearts after God.

The Barna group reveals that, on average, children now develop their worldview by age 13 and that 94% of decisions made for Christ happen before the age of 18!

It is an indictment of the ways of our seminaries, Bible colleges, pastors, teachers and parenting down through the generations that these numbers have fallen off so drastically.

What if we were to change our approach so as to better facilitate hearts after the Father, emphasizing our need to use words and actions growing fruit of the Spirit? In the attitudes of the Beatitudes? In the image of God? In the ways of God?

We tend to give people the facts and the logic and fight to persuade them for saving faith and helpful actions. As we keep their brains engaged in thinking it all through, a portion walk away, feeling something amiss.

It is not difficult to learn to live with hearts after the Father walking in the attitudes of Jesus (the Beatitudes). When we do, this posture and humility will prepare us for fruit of the Spirit language and actions always and everywhere.

Would it not be better to first share with them the love of God for us before the foundation of the world? From a heart of Wisdom that leads them into a love relationship with their Creator? Why not help them early on to understand why he allows evil to exist in this world, as well as any other doubts they may have? Otherwise, especially if you do not have 12 around you, many will not ask but go on wondering. Then later, allow that doubt to turn them into a statistic.

With 12, 70 and maybe even 500 available, we will be able to address their doubts, that they might more quickly trust their heart and appreciate The Plan, The Way, The Truth, The Life, The Reason Why - and with a newfound sense of awe want to know more. Then their growing passionate love of God will allow them to do for another what has been done for them. That they live their lives following with hearts after our Father, taught by the Son, and producing fruit of the Spirit by the power of the Holy Spirit. Doing the Father's will, their Joy being made complete.

Individually speaking, please be confident. If Love himself has led you to share with them, then Love himself will have prepared them in advance for you to Love them wholly and love them only.

As talmidim, each of us have the power of the Holy Spirit within us for the making of more talmidim.

Our nation is deeply divided, with many angry "Christians" part of the problem. Romans 1, Colossians 3 and Galatians 5 are but a few of the references that tell us that what we *are* doing is what we are *not* to be doing - and that *those who (continue to) do such things will not inherit the kingdom of God.* (Galatians 5:21)

Many are not loving wholly and loving only but are rather utilizing Landscape of Fear language to accomplish *their* will. For those who might just be willing, are we available to lead them into a greater depth of understanding of *his* ways, a more *intimate* walk with him, for fruit of the Spirit conversations, and in the growth and change described in 2 Corinthians 3:14-18? They will otherwise continue on as blind as the religious of *that* day:

2 Corinthians 3:14-18

14 But their minds were hardened. For to this day, when they read the old covenant, that same veil remains unlifted, because only through Christ is it taken away. 15 Yes, to this day whenever Moses is read a veil lies over their hearts. 16 But when one turns to the Lord, the veil is removed. 17 Now the Lord is the Spirit, and where the Spirit of the Lord is, there is freedom. 18 And we all, with unveiled face, beholding the glory of the Lord, are being transformed into the same image from one degree of glory to another. For this comes from the Lord who is the Spirit.

****

The contents of "*Life*" have been used effectively for years with individuals and in small group studies with people from all walks of life: the impoverished, present & former prison inmates, struggling believers, wayward believers, in marital & premarital counseling, with friends, parents, pastors, teachers and in mentor/counselor training seminars. *"Life"* helps us think about our conversations together with *hearts* after God, the *mind and attitudes* of Christ, *language and actions* that produce *fruit of the Spirit*, and *love* that proves we *care* and are *his*: "A new commandment I give to you, that you love one another: just as I have loved you, you also are to love one another. By this all people will know that you are my disciples, if you have love for one another."

Stating our agreement with him regarding his kingdom and will, we are somehow participating with him to cause that which has not yet been caused, release that which has not yet been released and/or fulfill that which is in the process of being fulfilled. We are collaborators co-operating, him in us spiritually and us in him spiritually, with us in the physical creatively participating with him to bring the spiritual into earthly manifestation. Establishing his kingdom on earth as it is in heaven - in people - his will being done: that all might come to know him, love him and join him, and thereby enter into the Family of God. That none should perish.

We must now, more and more, offer ourselves up as a work in process to the Father, Son and Holy Spirit - *with unveiled face, beholding the glory of the Lord, and be transformed into the same image from one degree of glory to another.* That we make talmidim, doing the will of the Father.

Matthew 6:9-10
9 Pray then like this: "Our Father in heaven, hallowed be your name. 10 YOUR kingdom come, YOUR will be done...

"Do this in remembrance of me."
He only said and did as Our Father told him.
He endured, and accomplished the purpose for which he was born.
He did his Father's will.

On our minds and in our hearts before our meals each day, may we remember Jesus pointing to our Father, speaking of his will and of the Holy Spirit who will flow through us to accomplish it. As we give thanks, may we continue to agree with the Father *as often as we drink it* (1 Corinthians 11:25) that *his will* be done in our life. Because eternity in view, our sacrifice will be over in the blink of an eye – and ours nothing compared to his.

Over two thousand years ago Jesus started conversationally with just twelve. Through him, in him and with him, hundreds of millions, maybe several billion, now know him today. Surely there is someone with whom we might offer to start meeting conversationally each week. Some of us with at least a few. Others with more than a few.

Let us endeavor to offer the talmidic approach,
that we might grow hearts after our Father.

****

I offer you this *Life* book free of charge if you would like to use it conversationally each week - with one other person, a small group of people or an entire church. As many as you need are available free as a pdf file, as well as in book form, at OneKingdomWorldwide.org or CSASNetwork.org (beginning sometime in 2025), that we reverse the statistical trend. That none should perish. Because he left the immature and ineffective Acceptors, as well as his Rejectors, up to us until his return – creatively participating with the Father who is doing his Works in *them*.

If you are concerned, like many are, that your Bible knowledge and understanding are insufficient, please recognize that there is enough scripture quoted throughout this book to suffice. Do not fear those that are perhaps more Bible literate, it may be that God will make you useful to him to touch their hearts and add meaning to their knowledge. Adding matters of the heart to the minds of Thinkers is very badly needed in our Thinker oriented culture. The following quote from 1948, from a book and author famous among Christians, indicates that we still have the same problem we had way back then:

"Sound Bible exposition is an imperative must in the Church of the living God... But exposition may be carried on in such way as to leave the hearers devoid of any true spiritual nourishment whatever... The Bible is not an end in itself, but a means to bring men to an intimate and satisfying knowledge of God, that they enter into Him, that they may delight in His Presence, may taste and know the inner sweetness of the very God Himself in the core and center of their hearts... The continuous and unembarrassed interchangeof love and thought between God and the soul of the redeemed man is the throbbing heart of New Testament religion."

A. W. Tozer, The Pursuit of God
(Christian Publications, Inc., 1948); pp 9-10, 13-14.

If *your* heart is after his, you are ready for whomever he will give you on any given day. As you go through your day, just ask him to give you a nudge for those who *are* yours to engage as well as identify when you *are not* to engage. He will be faithful to train you as you go, little by little, bit by bit, success by success! *Each* one *can* reach *at least* one each year:

"Go and make talmidim..."

Matthew 28:18-20

And Jesus came and said to them, "All authority in heaven and on earth has been given to me. Go therefore and make talmidim of all nations, baptizing them into the name (<u>into the indwelling Presence) of the Father and of the Son and of the Holy Spirit</u>, teaching them to observe all that I have commanded you. And behold, I am with you always, to the end of the age."

Remembering that we are always in your Presence: do your Works in us, Father; lead us on in Unity that we produce your fruit, O Spirit; while we contemplate your teachings and the prayer you taught us, O Jesus. That we be one with you. You in us and us in you, your will being done.

Jesus said, "Pray then like this.", and proceeded to give us what we call The *Lord's* Prayer. But having never sinned, he did not need to say, "Forgive us <u>*our*</u> sins." Rather, I believe he was giving us *Our* Prayer, for *our becoming*.

By the time that he had given them this prayer, he had already spent 3 years teaching them the associated lessons multiple times and in multiple ways. I believe that each section of the prayer therefore served as a reminding reference of the lessons previously learned for whatever future situation they might ever find themselves in. Armed with this brief prayer on their hearts, they would be able to quickly remember and agree with the Father in any moment, in any Life situation, and be able to respond by the power of the Holy Spirit, in fruit of the Spirit, and do the Father's will.

Contemplate the prayer he taught us to pray each morning before you leave your bed, before you rise and begin to prepare for the day that will unfold. Consider the depth of its meaning as he uses each portion to remind us of the lessons we are learning for *our becoming*. Praise and thank him for what he did with you yesterday and for what he will do with you still today. As you do, you will be balancing your mind with your heart after God. As you do, you will *become* better prepared for those you will interact with "today".

Praying in the way Jesus taught us, I have expanded the prayer for myself as follows. In fact, it summarizes the entire content of this book:

Our Father in Heaven, there is nothing better than your Presence and your ways! I don't want to be king anymore. Train me up that, one with you, more and more my behavior be in accordance with your character and attributes, and consistent with your reputation.

Your kingdom come. Lead my life. That your will be done in my life. May it be true for the whole world, your kingdom coming into all our lives and your will being done in all our lives. Across this whole earth, as it is in heaven.

Direct us in doing our part today, that everyone in the world be fed, filled with your Spirit, and be faithfully following you. Thank you for your care and provision of both physical and spiritual food. We greatly desire to participate with you and creatively collaborate with you for the solutions to hunger and poverty in this world. May this be an entire day of communion with you, receiving from you and pouring out what you have given us for the support of others and in support of your purpose in this world, according to your will.

Everything we have is yours, we are indebted to you for our very lives! All that we have has come from you, blessed by you not so much to have, but to be able to also give, and generously! Forgive us our selfishness as we lavish your blessings upon ourselves rather than flow them through as blessings to others. Forgive us for what we have left undone as we do not do what you have been leading us to do! Forgive us as we cross the line and trespass into the lives of others, pressuring people to do what we want, attempting to manipulate and control outcomes - leaning on our own understanding - that our will be done. May we instead learn to offer, share, describe and explain our position without malice, coercion, manipulation or veiled threat. Forgive us our sins, Adonai, in the same way that we forgive those who sin against us, those who are indebted to us, and those who cross the line with us.

Father, we need your help that we not enter into the temptation to act on our own! Open up the scriptures to us that we live lives pleasing to you! We require a better and better understanding of the teachings of Jesus, as you do your Works in us and lead us by the power of your Holy Spirit! Give us the mind and attitudes of Christ, fill us with your Spirit and conform us to your character. That we reflect your love and glory in every interaction! Lead us that we not fail you, but having been prepared and strengthened by the power of your Holy Spirit, we accomplish your will for us.

<u>Deliver us from the evil</u> we would do acting on our own and <u>deliver us from the evil</u> of the Satan and all those deceived by him into the works of darkness. May we not accuse, deliver us from those who would Accuse us. May we not cause division, deliver us from those who would Divide us. May we not judge, deliver us from those who would Judge us. May we not condemn, deliver us from those who would Condemn us. Teach us how to engage. Show us when and where to engage. Your yolk is easy and your burden is light. Show us who & what are ours to engage and who & what are not ours to engage. Unite your people to more productive engagement! May we not speak or act according to our own understanding, but be led by and follow your still small voice - given to us for discernment, for Wisdom, for timing, for strength, <u>for deliverance from evil</u>, for the good that you intend us to do. Fill us with your Spirit, your Helper, your Comforter, your Encourager, your Wonderful Counselor – that we reflect your glory to those who are too much in this world. O Spirit, give us the words to pray and/or words to say, and lead us to actions in accordance with the Father's will.

We agree with you and desire to participate with you for the uniting of your people to more productive service, according to your will. Strengthen us in the attitudes of the Beatitudes, that we Persevere to Patiently speak and act in Goodness, Kindness, Gentleness and Self-Control. In Peace that develops Joy and grows greater Love. For the kingdom and the power and the glory are all yours, Adonai: Father, Son and Holy Spirit. One God, forever and ever.

Give us justice against our Adversaries, O God! May they repent, turn to you and be healed, and follow you all of the days of their lives. Lord of the harvest, send laborers, and lead us to succeed in being ones ourselves! We ask all these things here in your precious Presence,

Adonai, acknowledging Jesus as the Name above all names. Yet not our will be done, but yours!

Amen

Our Father in heaven, hallowed be your name. You are not to blame.

****

As a talmid, I am becoming more and more like Jesus:

- *I only say and do what the Father gives me to say and do.*
- *I see what the Father is doing and behave likewise.*
- *I do nothing of my own accord.*
- *I do as the Father commands, that the world may know I love the Father.*
- *Unless I come as a child, I will never enter the Kingdom of heaven.*
- *My sheep know my voice and they follow.*
- *...for apart from Him I can do nothing.*
- *Blessed am I when I walk in His attitudes.*

Chapter Thirty-Seven

End Religion, Spread Conversational Relationship

Within every denominational and non-denominational division of Christianity, you will find a remnant of pastors who are more about our direct relationship with God than they are to our adherence and allegiance to the tenets of their organizing group. Whether in a mainline denomination, small affiliation or non-denomination, these pastors are conversationally teaching the ways of Jesus as described in the contents of this book. Dedicated to Christ as the Head, they have overcome religion, authority and hierarchy to conversationally grow, mature and expand God's Kingdom - collectively discerning and following as one. These are the fellowships worth attending!

Focusing on growing talmidim individually, in similarly small groups as Jesus did, each are making talmidim who are making talmidim who are making talmidim. As, like Jesus, each only say and do what our Father gives them to say and do, his yoke is easy and his burden light. The joy of the Lord is their strength each day, and as individual grains of salt, God's light causes them to reflect his glory everywhere they go. Ignoring the divisive religious traditions of mankind, God's talmidim are growing loving fellowships that are influencing their communities.

May it be so for you. Go where God sends you: be salt, light and yeast, and have fellowship with others - that you encourage each other along the way.

Be a talmid. Go and make talmidim! Whether God's will is for that to be a few or many, it is enough. As you walk in the attitudes of Jesus, with the mind of Christ, your heart after the Father's, by the leading of the Holy Spirit as the Father in you does his works - though in this world you will have trouble - Peace that surpasses all understanding will be yours. Life is short, the heavenly eternal reunion awaits. Until then, make the most of us, O God, that we do all your will!

Paraphrasing his instructions to us he said: "Go, show them *how to live a life pleasing to God*, baptizing them into the life-changing internal Presence of the Father and of the Son and of the Holy Spirit, teaching them to observe all that I have commanded you. It will be for them the pathway to reconciliation with the Father, into the Family of God and therefore *into their abundant joy filled life with us together* - eternally."

True talmidim will evidence:

- Dominion over the earth, but not over people. (Genesis 1:26-30)
  - Give us a king. (1 Samuel 8:4-22)
  - Jesus said it shall not be so among you. (Mark 10:42-45)
- The Ten Commandments (Exodus 20:3-17)
- Love the Lord your God with all your heart, soul, mind and strength, your neighbor as yourself and one another as I have loved you. (Mark 12:30-31, John 13:34-35)
- "Love" active in service. (John 12:26, Mark 9:35, Mark 10:45, Galatians 5:13, Matthew 20:26-27, 1 Samuel 12:24)
- Hearts after the Father in attitudes consistent with the Beatitudes: Jesus' attitudes. (Matthew 5:2-12)
- Fruit of the Spirit language and actions. (Galatians 5:22-24)
- The Unity, character and attributes of John 17.
- Knowing God's voice and be following *Him.* (John 10:27)
- Creative collaboration and participation in accomplishing the will of the Father. (Genesis 2:19-20, 1 Kings 22:19-23, Mark 6:34-44)
- Only saying and doing what the Father gives them to say and do. (John 5:19, John 12:49-50, John 14:10)
- The elimination of Anger, Judgement, Condemnation, Hierarchy and Manipulate To Control behaviors from their lives. (Romans 1:28-32, Colossians 3:1-17, Galatians 5:13-26, John 17)
- The overcoming of the temptations and desires of the flesh, their sacrifice nothing compared to Jesus' sacrifice on our behalf. (Romans 1:18-32, Colossians 3:1-17, Galatians 5:13-26, Leviticus 18, Ephesians 5:1-21, James 4:1-12, 1 Peter 2:11-12, Ephesians 2:1-7, 1 John 2:3-6)
- That they are *becoming* mature and effective laborers more and more: the 12, the 70 and the 500.

Unfortunately, these core cultural understandings were left behind in Israel as we left for the other cultures of the world. The first European cultures filtered the text of the Bible into their own hierarchical Hellenistic cultural context, and we therefore lost so very much of its meaning. Originally called followers of The Way, that is, followers of Jesus who taught us *The Way to live a life pleasing to God*, we have since become 250 doctrinal divisions, leaning on our own understandings and following them.

Go in my attitudes, talmid. Have conversations that help people understand Me and My ways. That they may come to know Me and My love for them. That they might come to love Me, too, and begin to become more and more like Me – producing fruit of My Spirit.
That none should perish.

To receive additional free copies please contact:
One Kingdom Worldwide
One@OneKingdomWorldwide.org

PDF files of this book may be legally shared.

All of the charts and posters in the Life, Love and Leading books are available for free download at OneKingdomWorldwide.org

Revised March 2026

www.ingramcontent.com/pod-product-compliance
Lightning Source LLC
LaVergne TN
LVHW020707110826
845149LV00012B/2152

* 9 7 9 8 9 9 4 5 8 3 9 1 3 *